To:

Evang. Rev. Rosalie Massie

From:

The Holy Spirit

July 4, 2021

Every Day in His Presence

CHARLES F. STANLEY

COUNTRYMAN
A Division of Thomas Nelson Publishers

THOMAS NELSON
Since 1798

NASHVILLE   MEXICO CITY   RIO DE JANEIRO

Published in Nashville, Tennessee, by Thomas Nelson.

Thomas Nelson titles may be purchased in bulk for educational, business, fundraising, or sales promotional use. For information, please e-mail SpecialMarkets@ThomasNelson.com.

ISBN–13:978-0-7180-1193-2

Printed in China

14 15 16 17 WAI 5

January

THE LIKENESS OF LOVE

*God said, "Let Us make man in Our image, according
to Our likeness." . . . God created man in His own
image, in the image of God He created him.*
GENESIS 1:26–27, EMPHASIS ADDED

Have you ever thought about how profoundly God loves you? You
could spend a long time considering it and never plumb the depths
of how intensely He cares for you. But one thing is sure—pondering
His love will transform your life.

Just think about the fact that the Father made you *in His own image.*
This was a purposeful choice—so important it's repeated four times in
the biblical account. He created you with unimaginable potential and
unquestionable worth—with the ability to experience Him in a deep,
intimate relationship. In fact, He wants to pour His life into you and
work through you in astounding, eternal ways. His desire is that when
people see you, they are reminded of Him (Matthew 5:16).

So no matter how you feel about yourself, embrace the truth:
God loves you, longs to shower His goodness upon you, and calls
you His own (Isaiah 43:1).

*Lord, thank You for loving me. Help me
know You better and understand what it
means to reflect Your likeness, amen.*

**In His presence . . . realize He
formed you with profound love.**

TRULY KNOWN

*My God; I shall seek You earnestly; my soul thirsts for
You. . . . Your lovingkindness is better than life.*

PSALM 63:1, 3

Do you ever wish someone understood, appreciated, respected, and loved you for who you are? This is because you were built for *intimacy*—a close, deeply satisfying relationship that empowers, edifies, and encourages you to the core.

Unfortunately, sin can prevent you from experiencing the communion you were created for. You may even be seeking comfort or significance from sources that cannot satiate your longings—such as possessions, prominence, or addictions.

King David, the author of Psalm 63, understood this. He had everything a person could desire, but concluded that the only One who could genuinely satisfy his soul was God.

The same is true for you. The Father created you in His image so you could interact with Him in a profoundly meaningful way that would fulfill your deepest longings. And it's as He reveals Himself to you that you discover sincere contentment, the reason for your existence, and hope for your future.

*Father, thank You for understanding and
loving me for who I am, amen.*

———— ⊙⊱ ————

**In His presence . . . enjoy
being fully known.**

PUTTING DOWN BAGGAGE

"If the Son makes you free, you shall be free indeed."
JOHN 8:36 NKJV

On a trip to the High Sierra mountain range in California, something hit me: the pack animals that carried our gear had no way of freeing themselves from the burdens on their backs. Unable to reach their heavy loads, they depended on others to remove them.

This is also true of us when we bear the weight of our emotional baggage. We cannot lay it down on our own; nor does it disappear over time. Rather, true freedom is possible only through Jesus. Why? Because we cannot reach our burdens and often don't understand how deep they go. But Jesus does. And He knows the perfect way to heal us completely.

Friend, no person lives free of all problems, hurdles, or pain. However, the Lord will not only protect you from lasting harm but can use difficulties to equip, prepare, and strengthen you for the next stage in your life.

Therefore, ask Jesus to lead you and relieve your burdens. He will set you free to become all God wants You to be.

> *Lord, I cannot reach my emotional burdens, but*
> *You can. Thank You for liberating me from them*
> *and using them to make me whole, amen.*

In His presence . . .
release your burdens.

THE ATTITUDE THAT OVERCOMES

*"In Me you may have peace. In the world you have
tribulation, but take courage; I have overcome the world."*
JOHN 16:33

Are you living in the continual joy and victory of your personal
relationship with Jesus? Are you conscious of His hand in every
detail of your life?

Understand, this question doesn't assume you're free from
challenges. On the contrary, the Father wants you to experience His
comfort and assurance even in the midst of your troubles. You do so
by being conscious of His presence with you and realizing that He's
using your circumstances to deepen your relationship with Him.

This is possible even when you face the worst adversity because
God promises to deliver You in His way and time (Acts 16:16–34).
Whether or not you receive His comfort depends on how deeply
you trust His character and how surrendered you are to His will.

Friend, let go and believe Him. In the midst of trials, voice
your gratitude that God is with you and will provide a way for you.
Surely His joy and victory won't be far behind (Psalm 126:6).

*Lord, sometimes I just don't feel triumphant,
but I am grateful You're with me every step of
the way. Thank You for helping me, amen.*

⚜

**In His presence . . .
overcome your circumstances.**

GENUINE FAITH

"Don't be afraid, for I am with you. Don't be discouraged,
for I am your God. I will strengthen you and help you.
I will hold you up with my victorious right hand."
ISAIAH 41:10 NLT

Many people who think they have faith in God are actually dominated by fears and doubts—overwhelmed by the circumstances of their lives. Are you? What is it that makes you anxious today? Is there something you fear you'll never achieve or receive?

Understand genuine faith means realizing God *wants* to provide His very best for you and will not let you miss it as you walk with Him (Hebrews 11:6). True, sometimes what He perceives as best for you is different from what you do. But take heart, the One who created you ultimately knows what will truly satisfy your soul—even better than you do.

So let go of whatever you fear you will never have or accomplish. He is faithful to provide. And if God does not give you what your heart presently desires, it is because He has something far better planned for you.

Lord, I trust You will provide Your very best for
me. You are my delight. Thank You for fulfilling
the deepest desires of my heart, amen.

❦

In His presence . . .
He reveals life at its very best.

WHICH DIRECTION?

The LORD directs the steps of the godly. He
delights in every detail of their lives.
PSALM 37:23 NLT

Why won't God show me what to do? you may wonder. And perhaps it doesn't *feel* like He is giving you direction today. But take heart—the Father is actively working in your situation and guiding you even when you don't perceive Him.

Friend, God hears you. He understands the cries of your heart and the confusion you feel when you don't know what direction to take. And it would be completely out of character for Him to hide His plans for you when you seek Him (Jeremiah 29:11–13).

The truth is, the Father would move heaven and earth to show you His will and help you walk in it. Yet the Lord also understands what it will take to teach you genuine, abiding faith; so He is careful not to reveal all to you at once.

Therefore, rest assured that even at this moment the Father is teaching you to trust Him. And He will give you just enough light on the path to walk with Him one step at a time.

Lord, I trust You. This is difficult, but I will
walk in faith—step by step—and believe
You are fully trustworthy, amen.

❧

In His presence . . .
receive trustworthy guidance.

FAITH THAT HE IS

Without faith it is impossible to please God, because
anyone who comes to him must believe that he exists
and that he rewards those who earnestly seek him.

HEBREWS 11:6 NIV

What is it you hope for? What desire is stirring in your heart? When God spoke to you about it, did you believe Him?

True faith is not just assurance in a certain outcome; rather, it's absolute confidence in God's unfailing character and ability, regardless of your circumstances. When He speaks to your heart, He means what He says and will accomplish what He promises (Isaiah 55:10–11). Therefore, real faith trusts that the living God will fulfill His word.

But I've been waiting so long, you may lament. Yes, and the Father may have you wait even longer (Isaiah 64:4). However, the important questions to focus on here are: Do you believe God exists and will help you? And do you believe He has your best interests in mind?

You don't have to keep pleading for God to do what He's promised. He will. Rather, rely on His faultless ability and character. And trust He will *always* keep His word.

> *God, I do believe You will help me. Thank*
> *You for having my best interest in mind*
> *and leading me successfully, amen.*

⊶⊷

In His presence . . . true faith becomes reality.

AN ASTOUNDING PRIVILEGE

The LORD has established His throne in the
heavens, and His sovereignty rules over all.

PSALM 103:19

Have you considered what an astounding gift it is to be able to know the living God? To be able to approach Him at any time with whatever issue presses on your heart?

No matter what you encounter today, He already knows all about it and has the best plan for leading you successfully through it. He knows you better than you know yourself—your past, present, and future; the thoughts you think; the motives of your heart; the places where you need to heal, and the ways you must grow.

With His sovereign, omnipotent hand, He can handle any obstacle or difficulty you face. With His unfathomable knowledge, He guides you with perfect wisdom. And because of His unfailing, unconditional love, He makes sure everything that touches your life will ultimately be used for your good (Romans 8:28).

Is your heart set on knowing Him? I hope it is, because there's absolutely nothing better or more encouraging than walking with Him and experiencing His awesome presence.

God, truly You are sovereign and greatly to be
praised. Teach me who You are and show me
how to appreciate You more every day, amen.

❦

In His presence . . . experience the King of kings.

EFFECTIVE THINKING

We take captive every thought to make it obedient to Christ.
2 CORINTHIANS 10:5 NIV

The devastating whispers may come. The enemy may tell you you're a failure, your case is hopeless, the petition you most hope for will never be answered, and God doesn't want anything to do with you. Your enemy knows the messages that will most dishearten you, and he is very effective at striking you where it hurts the most.

But right now remember, *he is a liar* (John 8:44). Do not give in to him. Those demoralizing whispers are absolutely not true, so you must immediately reject them and replace them with the truth of God's Word.

And what is true for you as a believer? That Jesus takes responsibility for your success as you walk with Him (Proverbs 16:3). That with your Savior, there is *always* hope (John 16:33). That not only does God hear your prayers, but He is faithful to answer you (Matthew 7:7–11). And that the Father loves you so much, He will never let go of you (John 10:11, 27–28).

*Lord, please root out the enemy's lies and replace them
with Your Word. Remove his strongholds so I may
walk in Your freedom and glorify Your name, amen.*

--- ⚜ ---

**In His presence . . . embrace the
liberating truth of being His child.**

A Deep Relationship

"The Spirit of the LORD is upon Me, because He
anointed Me to preach the gospel to the poor. He has
sent Me to proclaim release to the captives."
LUKE 4:18

There may be aspects of yourself—your choices, history, or circumstances—that are difficult to face. In fact, they may be so painful that you just want to block them out. You'd rather no one know about them—especially not God.

But understand, the Father is not surprised or repulsed by your profound wounds, fears, and failings. He knows all about them, and His response is to pursue you and heal you fully. This is why He sent Jesus to save you (Romans 5:8).

This is also why He invites you into an *intimate* relationship with Him—communion with Him that goes far deeper than what you see, touch, and feel. He desires for you to encounter His presence in the depths of your personhood where true freedom and healing take place. So don't be afraid to be honest with Him, because that's the path to genuine peace and strength.

Father, I'm so grateful that when You see my failings,
Your compassionate desire is to heal me. Thank
You for helping me walk in Your freedom, amen.

In His presence . . . you are
accepted, liberated, and empowered.

UNYIELDED TERRITORY

"Love the LORD your God with all your heart, with
all your soul, and with all your strength."
DEUTERONOMY 6:5 NKJV

There will always be an indescribable longing in you as long as you keep areas of your life from God. You were created to know Him with your entire being. This is why as long as there are aspects of your personhood you withhold from Him, the indefinable yearning will persist (Romans 8:20–21).

"But I love God," you may say. Of course you do. But consider: Are there any sins, issues, relationships, grudges, dreams, or thoughts you still haven't surrendered to Him? Is there something He is reminding you of that hasn't been relinquished?

"That couldn't possibly be what is causing my emptiness and pain," you may reply. But if the Holy Spirit has brought it to mind, it's most likely the reason you continue to struggle.

Friend, let it go. Whether it seems minor or constitutes the foundation of all your hopes—give it freely to the Father. He is faithful and just to help you and give you what is truly best for you (Psalm 84:11).

Father, please reveal any areas of my life that
are unyielded so I may relinquish them to You.
Thank You for setting me free, amen.

In His presence . . . submit yourself to Him fully.

DECISIONS, DECISIONS

In all your ways acknowledge Him, and
He will make your paths straight.
PROVERBS 3:6

Have you ever considered why you make decisions the way you do? Whether you "go with your gut" or engage in a rigorous analysis of your choices, what is the defining factor for how you determine the path to take?

When you truly begin to examine your decision-making process, you may be surprised to find what really drives you. Perhaps you avoid negative consequences at any cost, or maybe you are motivated by what others think. It could be that you live for the moment—seeking whatever makes you feel better. Or maybe you are simply interested in protecting yourself from pain.

Whatever your determining factor, if God is not the compass for your choices, then your decision-making skills are faulty. Only He knows the paths you should take and can provide options you may not even know are available.

So if you have a decision to make today, seek His direction. Lean on His wisdom because He will never, ever lead you astray.

Lord, thank You for guiding me in my decisions. I know
Your wisdom is perfect, and whatever You lead me
to do, You will also equip me to accomplish, amen.

In His presence . . . trust Him to lead you.

EVERYTHING FOR GOOD

God causes all things to work together for good to those who
love God, to those who are called according to His purpose.

ROMANS 8:28

Is there a difficulty in your life that continues to persist no matter what you do? You may not understand it at the moment, and that's okay. It is not necessary that you comprehend your circumstances or why they affect you as they do. Instead, what's important is that you honor the Lord in them.

The key to maintaining your hope as you experience adversity is found in this one foundational truth: *God is absolutely sovereign* (Psalm 103:19). And because He is Lord over all creation, you can know for certain that He will work through *everything* that touches your life for your benefit. That's right—*everything*. Nothing gets through to you if it won't somehow refine or edify you eventually.

Therefore, the wisest course of action whenever trials arise is to ask, "Father, what would You have me learn?" Listen to Him. Trust Him. Obey Him. And endure with confidence, knowing that eventually you'll see how He's worked through every detail to bless you.

Father, thank You that something good is coming from
this adversity. Teach me, Lord; I'm ready to learn, amen.

—————————— ❀ ——————————

In His presence . . . trust there's a
good purpose for what you're facing.

MOVING FORWARD

*Whatever things were gain to me, those things
I have counted as loss for the sake of Christ.*
PHILIPPIANS 3:7

There is a cost to knowing God. Yes, Jesus paid the ultimate price on the cross so you could enjoy an eternal relationship with Him (Romans 5). That's not a penalty you ever have to worry about again (Ephesians 2:8–9). But as you progress in your relationship with God, you'll find there are certain attitudes and actions that hinder you from really knowing Him—and you have to give them up.

Perhaps you're at such a crossroad today. God has shown you what's preventing your progress, but you fear the sacrifice you must make. This is where many people get stuck—they refuse to change. Sadly, they never experience Christ's surpassing joy and power either.

Friend, please realize that the behavior God is asking you to release is speeding you along the path to destruction (Proverbs 16:25), while with Him is the path of life (Psalm 16:11). Don't stay trapped in your old, destructive ways. Make the choice to move forward with the Father. I promise, He's absolutely worth it.

*Lord, I truly desire the fullness of an intimate
relationship with You. Please help me be
brave and move forward, amen.*

———————— ⚜ ————————

**In His presence . . . experience
the joy of spiritual growth.**

The Daily Choice

He who believes in Him will not be disappointed.
1 Peter 2:6

Are you able to say, "Not my will, but Yours be done" today? Can you cast yourself wholeheartedly unto God's loving care, knowing that what He wants and has for you is better than what you could ever seek or find for yourself? It's a difficult lesson, to be sure. And yet it is what the Father is always striving to teach you—complete and unhindered dependence on Him and confidence in His love, wisdom, and power.

That is why you are facing what you are today. Once more, God is presenting you with a choice of faith: Will you trust Him or will you seek your own way? Will you accept what He sends as an instrument of discipleship to train you? Will you say, no matter what happens, "Lord, instruct me; I trust You even in this"?

I hope you will. There is absolutely nothing better you can do than abandon yourself to His will, provision, and protection. That is the path through adversity to abundant, fulfilling, joyous life.

Lord, I know You will never lead me astray but will
help me exceedingly, abundantly, above all I ask or
imagine. Thank You for leading me so faithfully, amen.

꧁꧂

In His presence . . .
choose His will over your own.

INTO THE UNKNOWN

"I will lead the blind by a way they do not know,
in paths they do not know I will guide them."
ISAIAH 42:16

At times, God will beckon you to step out into the unknown. Perhaps this is what you face today—the choices and situations ahead are new, unusual, and you're not quite sure how to handle them. This is the essence of the call of faith. The Father bids you to do the unfamiliar or to go in a direction that is untried.

Just remember, if the way were known to you—if you could handle it in your strength and wisdom—this would not be a step of faith for you. It would carry no potential for revealing the Father's character, love, power, and wisdom in your life.

So whatever God is challenging you to do, remember He will employ the full power of heaven to ensure you are able to triumph in it. Your responsibility is simply to seek, trust, and obey Him as He directs you.

Lord, lead me; I will follow! I will go wherever You
send me. You see the path ahead and will not fail or
forsake me. Keep me in the center of Your will, amen.

In His presence . . . step into
the unknown with confidence.

BEYOND REASONABLE

*"As the heavens are higher than the earth, so
are My ways higher than your ways."*
ISAIAH 55:9

Be prepared—at times, the Lord's instructions may not make sense to you. In fact, it's a principle you must embrace if you wish to know the Father: *God doesn't require you to understand His will, just obey it, even if it seems unreasonable.*

Think about it. Why would the Lord ask Abraham to leave his home without telling him where he was going (Genesis 12:1–2)? Or why would God promise Abraham a son at age seventy-five, and then wait *twenty-five years* to fulfill His word? Humanly, it doesn't make sense.

But that's the point. You are not supposed to *understand* the Father—His desire is that you would *honor Him as God*—as the sovereign One who transcends all earthly limitations. Because when You do, He does the miraculous on your behalf and your faith grows strong.

Reason will always interfere with faith. As long as you're looking for everything to make sense, you're not fully depending on omnipotent God. Friend, give up your earthbound notions and allow Him to show you who He really is.

*Lord, I accept that Your wisdom is beyond my
own. Help me honor You with my life, amen.*

———————————— ⚬⊱ ————————————

**In His presence . . . accept that
He is the ultimate reality.**

WHO YOU REALLY ARE

*I praise you because I am fearfully and wonderfully
made; your works are wonderful.*
PSALM 139:14 NIV

You may be tempted to define yourself according to what other
people say about you—your looks, occupation, education, or even
your wealth. But such measures of your worth are faulty, temporary, and ultimately unproductive. And perhaps you've noticed that
it's the negative experiences that influence how you view yourself
far more profoundly than the positive ones do.

This is because in our human wisdom we don't have an accurate idea about what gives a person value. If we did, the Son of God
wouldn't have been crucified. We would have honored Him, knowing one day "EVERY KNEE WILL BOW . . . and . . . every tongue will
confess that Jesus Christ is Lord" (Philippians 2:10–11).

No, friend, the only One truly capable of judging your worth
is the One who created you and paid the price to call you His own.
In Jesus, you're eternally loved (Jeremiah 31:3), accepted (Romans
15:7), adequate (2 Corinthians 3:5), and victorious (1 Corinthians
15:57). Trust what He says about you and embrace your true identity.

*Lord, teach me to see my worth through Your eyes.
Thank You for creating, loving, redeeming, and
planning a wonderful future for me, amen.*

———————— ❧ ————————

In His presence . . . discover your true worth.

WHICH IS TRUE?

Revive me, O LORD, according to Your lovingkindness.
The sum of Your word is truth, and every one of
Your righteous ordinances is everlasting.
PSALM 119:159–160

You read it yesterday, but it is worth repeating. In Jesus, you're eternally loved (Jeremiah 31:3), accepted (Romans 15:7), adequate (2 Corinthians 3:5), and victorious (1 Corinthians 15:57).

At times, however, everything within you may fight against believing this. Difficult circumstances, painful memories, or the harsh words of others may make you feel fearful, unworthy, inadequate, and absolutely helpless to endure the problems you're facing.

But remember, "The heart is deceitful above all things" (Jeremiah 17:9 NKJV). Scripture will *always* be far more trustworthy than your own judgment. The enemy, remnants of your sin nature, or your limited perspective may taint what you perceive to be true. But God's Word has stood the test of time, and you can always rely on what He says.

Therefore, confess it to yourself often: in Jesus, you are loved, accepted, adequate, and victorious. Allow His truth to permeate your heart and find your worth in Him.

Jesus, transform my heart
completely with Your truth, amen.

In His presence . . . embrace
His everlasting truth.

STOP DOING

The LORD longs to be gracious to you, and therefore
He waits on high to have compassion on you. . . .
How blessed are all those who long for Him.
ISAIAH 30:18

Are you consumed with a desire to *do* something? Are you trying to earn God's grace or convince Him to bless you with some heart's desire? If you find yourself thinking, *Father, what do You want from me? I just don't know what to* do*!* you are most likely trying to *deserve* His good gifts rather than simply trusting Him to give them to you freely.

Friend, stop wrestling with God. The more you struggle, the more you show you're relying on your own strength rather than His. This stems from a lack of faith and He will not bless it (Isaiah 30:15). Yes, when He directs you to take a step or repent from sin, obey Him immediately. But stop trying to earn His love and the good gifts He's planned for you.

The Father *wants* to bless you even more than you want to be blessed. So stop striving and set your heart on Him. Surely He will lead you to life at its very best.

Father, thank You for being gracious to me.
I will set my heart to trust You, amen.

In His presence . . . trust Him.

SPEND THE TIME

My soul, wait in silence for God only, for my hope is from Him.
PSALM 62:5

Do you set aside time to contemplate the Lord, listen to Him, and allow Him to transform your spirit? You should. Because when you do, you get to know His character and ways—you discover His will for your life. This doesn't happen in an instant—it takes regular, dedicated communion with Him.

At times, He will even send adversity to motivate you to linger in His presence. This is because He knows if you're distressed about an issue, you'll be willing to abide with Him longer, seeking His strength and wisdom. And it's amazing how He will minister to your troubled heart—giving you unfathomable life, joy, peace, and direction—when you take the time just to sit in His presence.

Friend, the important thing is that you meditate on God and His Word daily. You were created for fellowship with Him. And when you focus on the Father, you'll be transformed from within and equipped to face the challenges that await you.

Lord, as my Source and Creator, I will make
time for You. Transform me so I may carry out
Your wonderful plans for my life, amen.

In His presence . . . renew your heart
and mind by meditating on Him.

RELEASING OFFENSES

If you see a Christian brother or sister sinning
in a way that does not lead to death, you should
pray, and God will give that person life.
1 JOHN 5:16 NLT

When you see a brother or sister in Christ disob[...]
can be disheartening. What should you do with t[...]
illusionment that flood your heart?

First, never allow another person to distract you i[...]
relationship with God. Instead, cling to the promise that i[...]
never fail you, even when others do.

Second, pray for the person in the hope that he will turn back
to Christ. If the individual has done anything to wound you, forgive him and refuse to harbor bitterness.

Third, draw comfort from the Holy Spirit. When you are grieved
by issues that displease God, remember that He is your greatest
source of encouragement and the One who will redeem the situation.

Friend, pray for the person who disappointed you and release
him to the Lord. Your Savior can handle the situation—so don't
allow it to become a stumbling block in your heart.

Lord, I pray that _____ will acknowledge their
offense and turn back to You. Help me forgive them
and draw comfort from Your Holy Spirit, amen.

⟡

In His presence . . . trust Him to restore the believer.

ARE YOU LISTENING?

*"Oh that My people would listen to Me.... With
honey from the rock I would satisfy you."*
PSALM 81:13, 16

Even now God is drawing you near to Him. He wants you to know
Him intimately—to experience His profound love and presence deep
within your inmost soul. He has truth to reveal to you—lessons His
Holy Spirit will teach you only when you take time to quietly focus
on Him.

You may wish to pray to the Father because of all the issues
that press on your heart, and that's fine. But realize that the wisest
thing you could ever do is sit silently before Him with His Word
open in front of you. Because it's during those times of communion
that He allows you to catch a glimpse of His absolutely astounding
character and wisdom.

Don't miss out on the overwhelming blessing of knowing God
as you simply abide in His presence. There is no deeper joy, no
greater energizer, no more worthy use of your time than experiencing Him. Sit quietly and enjoy. He loves to be known.

*Lord, I love You and long to know You.
Please speak to my spirit and reveal Yourself
to me through Your Word, amen.*

In His presence . . . experience the living God.

YOUR CHOICE

"Everyone who hears these words of Mine and acts on them, may be compared to a wise man who built his house on the rock. . . . The winds blew and slammed against that house; and yet it did not fall."

MATTHEW 7:24–25

The situations you face today can either build you up or tear you down. The good news is—you have a choice in the matter. Either you can invite God to work through your circumstances to develop your faith and character, or you can permit the problems to control you. The key is in *who you allow to interpret what happens to you.*

If you look at your challenges in light of your own abilities, you will likely feel disheartened, irritated, or overwhelmed because your only choice is to fight with the tools at your disposal.

However, a much wiser course of action is to go to God's Word for wisdom and do as He says. No matter what you face, the Father can certainly handle it. And if you look to Him to direct your path, He will use the adversity to edify you and teach you more about His wonderful ways.

Lord, help me seek Your wisdom in every situation. When You lead, my life is built on a solid foundation, amen.

❀

In His presence . . . is true security.

STRONG, STEADFAST, IMMOVABLE

*We who have fled to him for refuge can have great
confidence as we hold to the hope that lies before us. This
hope is a strong and trustworthy anchor for our souls.*
HEBREWS 6:18–19 NLT

Some days you may feel as if God is distant and find it difficult to sense His presence. This can be especially true if your circumstances are changing at a rapid pace.

Yet Hebrews 13:8 promises, "Jesus Christ is the same yesterday and today and forever." Your Savior has not moved; His love for you is powerful, unshakable, and eternal (Jeremiah 31:3)—an anchor for your soul no matter what happens.

Still, whenever you sense your relationship with God growing cold, it's wise to examine your heart. Have you been distracted from seeking Him? Are you more concerned with the details of your life than your relationship with Him? Have you compromised any biblical principles?

Like a boat in turbulent waters, it's easy to drift from Him if you're not anchored to the truth of His Word. So return to Him by opening Scripture and listening for His voice. Then, no matter what happens, you'll certainly be strong, steadfast, and immovable.

*Father, don't let me drift. Draw me close and reveal the
nearness of Your presence through Your Word, amen.*

———————————— ⚜ ————————————

In His presence . . . stay anchored and strong.

KNOW HIM

The LORD . . . is the faithful God who keeps his covenant
for a thousand generations and lavishes his unfailing
love on those who love him and obey his commands.

DEUTERONOMY 7:9 NLT

How do you view God? What do you suppose He's like? Whether you realize it or not, the characteristics you ascribe to the Lord will shape how you respond to Him.

For example, if you see Him as your loving, compassionate, wise, and wonderful heavenly Father who provides for you perfectly, you'll want to confide in Him and will trust His leadership. But if instead you view Him as a distant, strict, legalistic, and self-serving Commander, you may feel it's your duty to report to Him, but your relationship to Him won't be motivated by love.

Therefore, seek to truly know God through His Word and ask Him to show You who He really is. You will find that the One who formed you is more wonderful than you can possibly imagine and completely worthy of all your time, service, honor, glory, adoration, and praise.

Lord God, I want to see You as You really are. Reveal
Yourself to me and clear away the misconceptions I
have of You. Help me love You more every day, amen.

In His presence . . . discover who He really is.

FULL FAITH RESPONSE

If any of you lacks wisdom, let him ask of God. . . .
But let him ask in faith, with no doubting.
JAMES 1:5–6 NKJV

Are you hoping for God to work in a mighty way through your life? As a believer, it would be understandable if you did. After all, you know the Father has great plans for you (Jeremiah 29:11); it's only natural that you'd ask Him to lead you and bless your future. The question, however, is how you receive His instruction when you seek Him.

Scripture is clear that when you seek God and He answers you, it's of utmost importance that you believe Him (Mark 11:23–24) and act in accordance with how He responds to you (Jeremiah 7:23). If you react to His instruction with unbelief, not really expecting the Father to come through, you're simply demonstrating to Him that you're not ready for His full blessing.

So how do you keep your faith strong until the Lord acts on your behalf? Fix your focus on Him—His character, ability, and love—rather than on your circumstances. And as you keep your eyes on God, He will do immeasurably more than you can imagine.

Lord, strengthen my faith so I can follow
wherever You lead without doubting, amen.

——————————— ⚜ ———————————

In His presence . . . respond in full faith.

ENCOURAGEMENT FROM THE PAST

*Everything that was written in the past was written to teach
us, so that through the endurance taught in the Scriptures
and the encouragement they provide we might have hope.*

ROMANS 15:4 NIV

One of the most painful, destructive ways the enemy will attack is by suggesting you're alone in your struggles. But understand, that's a lie. God has given you the testimonies of His faithful servants so you'll know He "will not fail you or forsake you" (Deuteronomy 31:6). They experienced times that tried their faith just as you do. And because they endured and trusted God, you can too.

So what is it you struggle with today? Do you need faith to receive a promise like Abraham (Romans 4)? Deliverance from the pit to the palace like Joseph (Genesis 37–50)? A path through a difficult obstacle like Moses (Exodus 14)? Strength to overcome adversaries like Joshua (Joshua 6)? Forgiveness like David (Psalm 51)? Or provision like the disciples (John 6:1–14)?

Look to your predecessors in the faith and be encouraged. God didn't fail them. Rest assured that He won't disappoint you either.

*Lord, thank You that I'm not alone in the trials
I face. You've intervened for people throughout
history, and I know You'll help me, amen.*

**In His presence . . . draw
encouragement from Scripture.**

THE SENSE OF HIS PLAN

I remain confident of this: I will see the goodness of the LORD.
PSALM 27:13 NIV

Is there anything in your life that just doesn't make sense? You've tried to figure it out, but the questions persist. Why would God allow such difficulties to plague you?

You're not alone. The greatest earthly ruler of Israel, David, most likely felt this way at times. After God called him to be king, David spent years running from King Saul, who actively sought to kill him. David must have wondered why the Lord was taking so long to place him on the throne.

It might have been confusing and disheartening to David, but God knew exactly what He was doing. During that time, He was meticulously preparing David to honor Him in everything—strengthening David's faith for the battles he would face as king.

Likewise, the Father may be using adversity to prepare you for an important assignment. So don't fret, fear, or rely on your own understanding about your situation. It will make sense eventually (Romans 8:28). Trust God regardless of how your circumstances appear and He will lead you perfectly (Proverbs 3:5–6).

Lord, thank You for training me to experience Your
wonderful plans for my life. I will trust You, amen.

In His presence . . . be assured His plan is good.

OBEDIENCE AND DIRECTION

Blessed be the name of God forever. . . . He gives wisdom
to the wise and . . . reveals deep and secret things.
DANIEL 2:20–22 NKJV

Are you willing to do whatever God tells you to do? Are you pre-pared to trust Him—even when His direction doesn't make sense? Be assured, if you do, He will reveal astounding truths to you.

The Lord certainly did for Daniel. Cruel Babylonian king Nebuchadnezzar demanded that his counselors interpret a dream he'd had, but he then refused to disclose the contents of it. He threat-ened that if they couldn't give him understanding into his vision, he'd have them all killed (Daniel 2). Their situation seemed hopeless.

Yet the godly Hebrew named Daniel told Nebuchadnezzar, "There is a God in heaven who reveals mysteries" (v. 28). Daniel described the dream and revealed its meaning faultlessly—all to God's glory.

Do you need wisdom for a no-win situation like Daniel did? Then take the step of faith, obeying however God directs and trust-ing Him even when you don't understand how He's moving. You'll be astounded at what He reveals when you put complete trust in Him.

Lord, You know my dilemma. Disclose what
I need to know and lead me successfully
through this difficulty, amen.

— ❈ —

In His presence . . . obey His
direction with confidence.

YOUR INDWELLING RESOURCE

May the God of hope fill you with all joy and peace in believing,
so that you will abound in hope by the power of the Holy Spirit.

ROMANS 15:13

Whatever you must decide or achieve today may seem absolutely overwhelming. You may wonder, *How in the world will I get through this?* And yet God's still, small voice is assuring you, *I am your adequacy and strength* (2 Corinthians 3:5). *I will show you the way you should go* (Psalm 32:8). *I will accomplish all that concerns you* (Psalm 138:8). *Trust Me, I will help you* (Proverbs 3:5–6).

How will God help you succeed in all you have to do today? He gave you the most important Resource you will ever need when you accepted Jesus as your Savior. It was at that time that the Spirit of God came to indwell you—to teach, prepare, enable, equip, energize, and empower you for challenges just like the one you face today. He wants to guide you and give you strength. Look for His activity in your life, listen to Him, and obey His promptings.

Lord, I know You have no problem handling all
I must do today. Please make me sensitive to
Your Spirit. I trust You to lead me, amen.

In His presence . . . you have
victory over every challenge.

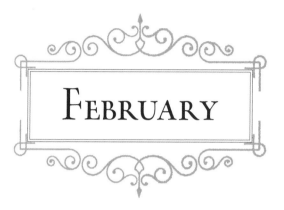

FEBRUARY

LISTEN OPENLY

"Today if you hear His voice, do not harden your hearts."
HEBREWS 3:7–8

To listen to God *openly* means to be willing to hear whatever He has to say. Whether He wants to correct or comfort you, convict or assure you, it's important you focus on Him wholeheartedly.

Doing this isn't always easy. You may be looking for encouragement from God when instead He has a word of admonishment for you. But be warned—if you are unwilling to hear what He has to say, your heart will harden toward His Spirit and your need for discipline will most likely increase.

Therefore, as you listen to the Father—humbly dependent upon His Holy Spirit—don't be surprised when He brings to mind areas of your life that need to change. Do not pick and choose what you want to hear. Listen to and obey Him—He is revealing these issues for your benefit and healing. If you refuse to hear His warnings, it could lead to your ruin.

Friend, the Savior always speaks for your good. Therefore, accept whatever He says—both the positive and the negative—trusting that He has a positive goal in mind.

Lord, open my ears that I might hear both
Your comfort and correction, amen.

⚜

In His presence . . . listen to all that He has to say.

THE PROCESS OF FORGIVENESS

As far as the east is from the west, so far has
He removed our transgressions from us.

PSALM 103:12

An unforgiving spirit is a malignancy in a person's soul that spreads like cancer. Yet the Father offers a sure healing process for the heart that is consumed with bitterness:

Repentance: Assume responsibility for your unforgiving spirit and ask God to pardon you for your resentment. You must also forgive the person who offended you.

Release: Forgo any expectation you have of restitution, even if you feel the person owes you something.

Recognition: Acknowledge that the person's wrongdoing toward you was not just hurtful or offensive, but that the behavior ultimately grieved God. The Lord is the One who will judge the offense and you can trust Him to vindicate you.

Remembrance: Recall how often God forgives you.

Friend, you cannot truly experience the joy of God's forgiveness until you follow His model and pardon those who've wronged you. Do not allow the cancer of bitterness to continue in your heart. Life is much sweeter when the heart is tender and not tainted.

Lord, thank You for Your gift of forgiveness.
Help me always to extend it to others, amen.

In His presence . . . seek to have a
tender, forgiving heart.

WHEN

When I am afraid, I will put my trust in You. In God, whose word I praise, in God I have put my trust; I shall not be afraid.

PSALM 56:3–4, EMPHASIS ADDED

Perhaps you've noticed that in Psalm 56:3, David doesn't say, "*If I am afraid.*" He says, "*When.*" Times of fearfulness *will come* into your life. Anxieties will arise—not only because this is a fallen world, but also because, in order to teach you faith, the Father must bring you to the end of yourself so you will choose to trust Him. This is a necessary lesson and an indispensible part of maturing you as a believer.

So today, consider: Is your heart in despair? Are questions, painful thoughts, or fears flooding your mind? Is there an overwhelming situation that you cannot handle?

Do as David did and come back to the truth of your Father's perfect provision and unfailing care for your every need. God has not abandoned you and He never will (Deuteronomy 31:6, 8). Trust Him to help you.

Lord, when I am afraid, I will trust You and have faith in Your provision and protection. Thank You for loving me and drawing me closer to You, amen.

───────────── ༄ ─────────────

In His presence . . . abandon yourself to His loving, trustworthy care.

GROWING PAINS

*The creation was subjected to frustration . . . in hope that the
creation itself will be liberated from its bondage to decay and
brought into the freedom and glory of the children of God.*

ROMANS 8:20–21 NIV

Sometimes as you spend time in God's presence and grow closer
to Him, painful memories or feelings may surface. This is because
Jesus wants to make you a healthy, whole person. To work toward
that goal and heal you, He must touch the wounded areas of your
life, rooting out the lies and strongholds you've been living in
bondage to.

This is why you may suddenly become sensitive to certain
personality types, stressors, or memories you thought you had conquered. He exposes them to you, illuminates the fact that they are
impeding your progress, and shows you how to move past them.

It is difficult, but if you'll trust the Lord Jesus in it, you'll experience the fullness of freedom and purpose that He created you to
enjoy. Therefore, don't be afraid. Invite Him in and allow Him to
make you whole.

*Lord Jesus, I trust You to heal the wounded areas of my
life as my Great Physician. Reveal the lies in my life,
and teach me the truth that makes me free, amen.*

In His presence . . . be made free.

NOT ALONE

I am continually with You; You have taken hold
of my right hand. With Your counsel You will
guide me, and afterward receive me to glory.
PSALM 73:23–24

There may be times in your life when you just cannot share your burdens with others. Maybe that is because it would worry your loved ones; would cause you shame; or would violate legal, security, or strategic restrictions to divulge the information that presses on your heart. Whatever the reason, you feel isolated in your struggle.

At such times, it is important for you to remember that you're never truly alone once Jesus is your Savior. You are sealed in Him with His Holy Spirit who indwells you as a guarantee of your redemption (Ephesians 4:30). And the most wonderful thing about God is that He knows even more about your situation than you do. His is the only counsel you really need.

Don't isolate yourself from the Father. Sit in His wonderful presence and allow Him to reveal Himself and His profound solution for every need you have. Surely He is the wisest and most trustworthy Companion you will ever have.

Lord God, thank You for never leaving or forsaking
me. Guide me along Your perfect path, amen.

———————————— ✵ ————————————

In His presence . . . develop
an intimate relationship.

BLESSED WITH SUFFICIENCY

All praise to God, the Father of our Lord Jesus Christ,
who has blessed us with every spiritual blessing in the
heavenly realms because we are united with Christ.
EPHESIANS 1:3 NLT

God is more than sufficient for you today. Your heavenly Father has inexhaustible resources—all of which are at His disposal to help you in the way that will best build your faith and relationship with Him. And He has promised to give you every spiritual blessing because you have faith in Jesus.

The problem is not the Father's ability to bestow what you need, but your ability to receive it when fear or the desire for control governs you. You must deny those strongholds and accept Him as Sovereign God.

So ask yourself: Are you willing to trust God today? Will you watch for His activity? Will you take His Word as true—that He's blessed you with every spiritual blessing? Will you obey Him?

Because when you have what you need spiritually, all else falls into place. Therefore, trust Him to sustain you. He is more than sufficient.

Lord, You are God. Thank You for being sufficient for
my every need—spiritually, physically, and materially.
I trust You to help me with all I face, amen.

—— ❧ ——

In His presence . . . know you are blessed.

JUST WHAT YOU NEED

*"Certainly I will be with you, and this shall be
the sign to you that it is I who have sent you . . .
you shall worship God at this mountain."*

EXODUS 3:12

God reveals Himself to you in specific ways that are important for your journey. For example, when the Lord spoke through the burning bush, He was powerfully demonstrating that Moses would not be destroyed before Pharaoh and that His supernatural presence and provision would be with Israel in the wilderness (Exodus 3). Did God divulge the whole plan to Moses? No. But He disclosed enough that Moses could trust His character, step out in faith, and obey Him.

Likewise, God reveals Himself to you in the manner you need, through prayer, Scripture, and the circumstances that touch your life. In fact, the situation you face at this moment is the perfect training ground for you. And if you'll make a conscious decision to listen for His counsel, you'll be absolutely amazed at what He reveals to you through it.

Your Protector, Provider, Great Physician, Prince of Peace, Redeemer, and King wants to make Himself known to you. Let Him. And step forward in faith.

*Lord, thank You for being exactly what I need and
revealing what is important for me to know, amen.*

───────────────── ❖ ─────────────────

In His presence . . . receive what you need.

THE GREAT GARDENER

"Every branch that bears fruit, . . . He prunes it so
that it may bear more fruit. . . . Abide in Me, and I
in you. As the branch cannot bear fruit of itself."

JOHN 15:2, 4

If you were to list all your afflictions, burdens, and challenges, it might seem overwhelming. You know that the Father has allowed it all for a good reason. But you may be frustrated with yourself for not being able to accomplish more or muster the energy for the next step.

Do not despair. The difficulties are not evidence of His displeasure, but of the wonderful potential He sees in you. Your Savior, Protector, and Provider is also your Great Gardener, and He knows exactly how to help you flourish. He trims areas that drain your energy, removes decaying parts, and harvests the fruit so more may grow. It's all for good, even if it's painful for a season.

So how do you take the next step today? By abiding in Him and allowing His ability, energy, inspiration, and power to flow through you in His way and time. He is the Vine; you are the branch. Let Him do the sustaining.

Lord, I trust You as my Great Gardener.
Thank You for helping me grow. Help
me bear good fruit for You, amen.

❊

In His presence . . . abide.

HIS IMAGE

Just as we have borne the image of the earthy, we
will also bear the image of the heavenly.

1 CORINTHIANS 15:49

God does for you what you cannot do for yourself—even some things you do not know to ask for. In fact, He will put you in situations specifically to reveal His goodness to you and work His character in you because He knows it's what you need most.

You see, the Father's goal for your life is far better than merely making you prosperous, popular, or healthy—though those gifts may follow. Rather, His objective is to conform you to His likeness—teaching you how to enjoy genuine, profound, eternal life and reflect His glory (Romans 8:29).

You may not realize how deeply your soul cries out to be like Jesus, but it does. And because He's your Creator, He knows what would truly satisfy you and give you purpose.

So don't degrade or devalue yourself because of the situation you see before you. Just realize you are being conformed to the image of the Most High God. And He is doing in you what you cannot do for yourself so that others can see Him through you (2 Corinthians 4:7).

Lord Jesus, thank You for meeting my
profound need to be like You, amen.

In His presence . . . reflect His glory.

NO ACCIDENTS

After you have suffered for a little while, the God of all grace, who called you to His eternal glory in Christ, will Himself perfect, confirm, strengthen and establish you.

1 PETER 5:10

God will use everything. Whatever you are facing right now, you can be sure there is a higher purpose in it. David may not have known that fighting a bear and a lion would prepare him to face Goliath. As he scattered the predators of his flock with his slingshot, he may not have realized how the Lord Almighty was honing and perfecting his aim. But neither of those incidents was happenstance. God was working.

Likewise, it is no accident that you are experiencing what you are today. You may not sense God's instructive, purifying, and refining work in your life, but the Father is certainly working through it to restore, establish, and strengthen you.

God doesn't make mistakes, and He doesn't do anything without a purpose. This challenge you face will most certainly work for your good. So take comfort that His hand is in this, and thank Him for being your help, hope, and salvation.

Father, thank You for being with me in this situation and working through it to perfect, confirm, strengthen, and establish me. Truly, You are good, amen.

❧

**In His presence . . . discover
the purpose for your trial.**

LITTLE BY LITTLE

*"Little by little I will drive them out from
before you, until you have increased."*
EXODUS 23:30 NKJV

When your problems persist, it can be disheartening. Today it may seem like the healing of old wounds is taking forever or that you just can't seem to get past certain challenges.

But take heart. When God prepared the nation of Israel to conquer the promised land, He made it clear that there would be many enemies and that it would take some time to drive them all out. This was for a purpose—so that the people would depend upon Him daily, learn to trust Him, and grow.

The time it takes for you to overcome the difficulties is all part of God's plan to make sure you have complete and unshakable victory. It may seem as if the progress is slow, but be assured, the Lord is doing a thorough job. And the lessons you learn as a result will be with you forever—to His praise and glory.

*Lord, thank You for teaching me so thoroughly. Father,
I trust Your timing and the way You are training
me. Thank You for loving me so much, amen.*

———————— ❧ ————————

**In His presence . . . discover complete
victory and unshakable growth.**

ABSOLUTELY NOTHING

I am convinced that nothing can ever separate us from God's love. Neither death nor life, neither angels nor demons, neither our fears for today nor our worries about tomorrow—not even the powers of hell can separate us from God's love.

ROMANS 8:38 NLT

There may be something on your mind—a sin, a bad decision, someone's rejection, or a particular trial—that makes you feel as if the Father does not or could not love you. However, once you believe in Jesus as your Lord and Savior, *nothing* can separate you from His love. Not people. Not circumstances. Not angels, nor demons, nor the enemy's entire army. Absolutely nothing.

Psalm 34:18 is clear, "The LORD is near to the brokenhearted and saves those who are crushed in spirit." So when you feel at your most unworthy or defeated is when the Father is closest, tenderly bidding you to return to Him.

The most dangerous move you can make is to resist His love. So seek His face. Confess your failings. Ask Him to teach you. Thank Him for inviting you back. Then praise His holy name and love Him in return.

Lord, thank You for accepting me. I am so grateful for Your wonderful, unconditional, unchanging love. Help me hear Your voice, amen.

In His presence . . . enjoy His love.

DEPENDENCE AND SURRENDER

He reached down from heaven and rescued
me; he drew me out of deep waters.
2 SAMUEL 22:17 NLT

Do you feel anxious? Do you long for God to speak to you about something pressing and specific? At times, He will bring you to the point of desperation so you'll rely on Him and be open to what He says.

You see, dependence on the Father and surrender to His will go hand in hand. You must be convinced that He has the best plan, and usually that means coming to the realization that there's nothing you can do to improve your situation.

Until then, you're like a person who is drowning—struggling and flailing for air against the inundating waters and inadvertently fighting the One who is trying to rescue you. It is not until your strength is gone and you give up that He can lead you to safety.

So stop working against Him. Lean on God's power, wisdom, and love. And yield to your Rescuer's plan. Allow your desperation to lead you to dependence on Him, for that is the path to your sure deliverance.

Lord, I do feel like I am desperately drowning at
times. Thank You for rescuing me. I will depend
on You and surrender to Your plan, amen.

❖

In His presence . . . allow Him to rescue you.

FOR THE LOVE OF GOD

We love Him because He first loved us.
1 JOHN 4:19 NKJV

At times you may be tempted to focus on the relationships that fall short of your expectations and wishes. It is understandable that the people who cause you pain often receive the lion's share of your attention. You want to figure out what went awry.

But realize that human love will never really fulfill your needs. And God allows you to experience how short it falls so you'll recognize how much you need His perfect, unconditional love.

People may seem to provide the care, validation, and acceptance you desire, but only the Lord can truly fill you with the love that never ceases. So if you feel a longing for someone or emptiness inside, don't focus on the person who is being unloving. Rather, take it as an indication you have not received God's love as fully as you can. The Father's love is sufficient to sustain you, no matter what you face. Allow Him to drive out your fears and bring you peace.

Father, thank You for loving me. You know who is on
my heart today and the pain I feel toward that person.
But I look to You and know You will sustain me, amen.

In His presence . . . seek His love first.

A SECURE RELATIONSHIP

Perfect love casts out fear.

1 JOHN 4:18

Friend, do you have any doubts that God really loves you? If you're uncertain about how He sees you, it would explain some of the anxieties you feel. You see, whenever you fear someone is going to hurt you, you hide your true self from them. You don't develop the intimate relationship that inspires trust and safety. Sadly, when you do so with the Savior, you close yourself off from experiencing the wonderful security, joy, and fulfillment He offers.

But be assured, your heavenly Father wants to put all your uncertainties to rest so that you can enjoy His freedom. In Jesus, your eternal life is absolutely secure. He promises, "No one will snatch [you] out of My hand" (John 10:28). Likewise, He guarantees that nothing in all creation can separate you from His unconditional love (Romans 8:38–39).

Friend, God wants you to have a healthy relationship with Him and enjoy the wonderful blessings He has for you. So seek His face and ask Him to reveal His love. Surely doing so will drive out your fears.

Lord, reveal Your perfect, unconditional love to me.
Draw me close, drive out my fear, and make our
relationship deep, strong, and unshakable, amen.

In His presence . . . find security in His love.

WAIT FOR HIM

From days of old they have not heard or perceived
by ear, nor has the eye seen a God besides You, who
acts in behalf of the one who waits for Him.

ISAIAH 64:4

One of the most difficult aspects of waiting is battling the thoughts that arise. The imagination can create terrible scenarios of disaster and defeat. Your mind can also conceive of every reason for why God *shouldn't* bless you.

This is why Psalm 37:4 instructs, "Delight yourself in the LORD; and He will give you the desires of your heart." Because when you concentrate on the object of your longing, you may chase the wrong option or pursue it in a destructive manner. When your attention is on yourself, you can become disheartened at your inability to attain what you're yearning for.

But when you focus on the Father, you not only get to know Him better, He also makes you into who you need to be to receive the blessing and keeps you on the path to obtaining it. Therefore, turn your thoughts to Him. Surely He is achieving more for you than you can ask or imagine (Ephesians 3:20).

Lord, thank You for working on my behalf
during this waiting time. Please help
me keep my focus on You, amen.

❧

In His presence . . . delight in Him.

WHAT TO DO?

From where shall my help come? My help comes
from the LORD, who made heaven and earth.
PSALM 121:1–2

Each day there will be issues the Lord has gifted you to manage and those that you have no idea how to handle. The challenges that are beyond your control are usually the ones that will dominate your thoughts. You mull your circumstances backward and forward, wondering what to do. In conclusion, you may find yourself saying, "I just don't know."

The Father allows these difficulties so you will rely upon Him. Remember, God's goal is to develop your endurance and faith, and He does so by creating situations whereby you have no choice but to turn to Him (Romans 8:24).

When this happens, don't rush ahead or invent solutions. First begin by setting your mind on God. Second, do all He has given you the wisdom to accomplish. Third, leave the rest in His hands and expect Him to reveal the path as you go. You may not know what to do, but He always does. Trust Him.

Lord, I trust You. When I don't know what
to do, remind me to fix my eyes on You.
And keep me sensitive to Your Spirit so I can
remain in the center of Your will, amen.

❧

In His presence . . . let Him lead.

TO FEAR OR KNOW?

Truly know me and understand that I am the
LORD who demonstrates unfailing love.
JEREMIAH 9:24 NLT

God *wants* you to know Him and His will. This may not seem true, especially if you are seeking Him for a specific answer to prayer. It can feel as if He is silent, distant, and even uninterested in your problems. But nothing could be further from the truth. He cares for you deeply. In fact, He may have allowed these difficulties in your life for the express purpose of drawing you to Him.

The question is: Is there anything that frightens you about really knowing God? Perhaps you fear He will find you unworthy or that He'll call you to a difficult field of service. Maybe you're worried there are behaviors or goals He will ask you to give up. It's even possible you're afraid that you'll seek Him and find nothing there.

Friend, God exists, He loves you unconditionally, and He has a wonderful plan for your life that will delight you. Do not be afraid. Today, open His Word and sit silently in His presence. He wants you to know Him. Allow Him to reveal Himself to you.

Lord, I really want to know You and experience Your
presence. Please reveal Yourself to me, Father, amen.

❧

In His presence . . . know God.

DELAYS

Wait for the LORD; be strong and let your heart
take courage; yes, wait for the LORD.
PSALM 27:14

It is exceedingly difficult to see what you desire and not be able to reach for it. Perhaps the Lord has even given you a promise about what you hope for, but is preventing you from pursuing it for the moment.

David faced such delays. God promised David would become king of Israel (1 Samuel 16). But David waited *more than two decades* and endured many trials before he took the throne (2 Samuel 5), though it was just within his grasp (1 Samuel 24, 26). Yet even David recognized this was for the development of his character (Psalm 119:71).

This is why David could confidently counsel, "Wait for the LORD." He knew that no matter how long it took, God would faithfully fulfill His promise.

Friend, the Father hasn't forgotten you or denied your request. But He won't allow this opportunity to pass without working faith into your soul. Every moment of delay is a chance to express your trust in His unfailing character and for Him to develop yours. So be strong. Trust Him. And wait for the Lord.

Lord, I trust You. Help me wait on You
with patience and faith, amen.

In His presence . . . wait expectantly.

WORSHIP HIM

Come, let us worship and bow down, let us kneel
before the LORD our Maker. For He is our God.
PSALM 95:6–7

At this moment, you may be tempted to focus on the stresses and challenges that await you today. But instead of turning your attention to them, think about the Lord God who is able to help you conquer no matter what you face (Romans 8:37).

Worship the Father. Honor Him for who He is. Meditate on His attributes. Praise Him for your salvation and all the ways He has helped you in the past. Thank Him for even greater provision, protection, and evidence of His love in the future.

Open His Word and read about all the ways He faithfully delivered His people throughout history. Express your gratefulness that He is as present and powerful in your life as He was with the saints of old. Because when you worship the Almighty and truly think about who He is, your troubles will not seem so overwhelming.

Surely nothing can stand against you when you walk with Him. Therefore, put your hope in God.

Father, I praise and worship You, the God of all
creation—mighty in power, perfect in wisdom,
and abounding in unfailing love, amen.

In His presence . . . express your adoration.

HIS WORD TO YOU

All Scripture is inspired by God and is useful to teach us what is
true and to make us realize what is wrong in our lives. . . . God
uses it to prepare and equip his people to do every good work.
2 TIMOTHY 3:16–17 NLT

There are questions that keep surfacing in your heart—inquiries you wish God would answer. And though the Lord may respond to you in prayer and through other people, often He does so as you read and think about His Word.

Scripture is powerful. The Holy Spirit works through it to transform your life. He brings verses to mind when you need comfort, renews your hope through its wonderful promises, gives you direction through its principles, and convicts you of sin. And through the pages of the Bible, He also answers the deepest questions of your heart.

So if you feel desperate to hear God's voice, open the Word and drink in His life-giving wisdom. Even right now, He is drawing you through those very questions in your heart. Therefore, open Scripture and listen for Him. He will certainly speak to you through it.

Lord Jesus, thank You for speaking to me
through the Bible. Help me always hear
and obey Your direction, amen.

In His presence . . . let His
Word speak to your heart.

THE CHALLENGE TO OBEY

I trust in You, O LORD.

PSALM 31:14

For your growth, God may challenge you to obey Him in an area that is particularly difficult. In fact, He may strike at the very foundation of your worldly security so you'll rely on Him.

Such was the case of the widow of Zarephath. After a terrible drought, all she had left to feed her son was a handful of flour and a little oil. It was just enough for one more small meal. Yet God challenged her to give it to His prophet Elijah (1 Kings 17:1–16).

It would've been understandable if she'd been afraid to give up her last bit of nourishment—especially after so much suffering. But she obeyed. And because of her faith, the Lord supernaturally fed her and her son for the remainder of the famine.

Likewise, the Father may ask you to give up something important. Do not fear, but trust Him and let it go. Anything you hold too tightly you will lose, but what you entrust to Him will surely return a hundredfold. So do as He says and allow Him to prove that He truly is your great and faithful Provider.

Lord, I will obey You, even when what You ask
is difficult. I know Your way is best, amen.

In His presence . . . commit to obedience.

YOUR EVER-PRESENT HELP

*God is our refuge and strength, always
ready to help in times of trouble.*
PSALM 46:1 NLT

Of course God *can* and *will* help you. You don't have to worry about that. Your responsibility is to cling to the Father with all your heart, mind, soul, and strength regardless of what happens. Ultimately, He will provide what is absolutely best for you as you seek Him. But it is immensely important that you remain rightly related to Him, so that even when you do not understand why He is allowing certain challenges to touch your life, you are still connected to His love, wisdom, and strength. Having His unlimited power to support you will be a constant comfort to you.

When you have a steady, intimate relationship with God, you *always* have hope. However, when you turn to your own resources, of course you become vulnerable to despair—when you fall short, your situation falls apart.

Thankfully, the Lord never fails. He can easily handle whatever problems arise. So keep focused on Him. Certainly He can and will help you today and every day.

*Lord God, thank You for always being my ever-
present help. You never fail, Father, and I thank You
for this opportunity to trust You more, amen.*

⸕

**In His presence . . . count on
His provision and strength.**

THE DIFFICULTY OF TRUST

Those who know Your name will put their trust in You,
for You, O LORD, have not forsaken those who seek You.

PSALM 9:10

What the Father is asking of you is not supposed to be easy. If trusting God were easy, everyone would do it. In some ways, maintaining your faith in Him is the most difficult challenge you'll encounter because it means turning away from every natural instinct in you.

You must deny your fleshly need to control your circumstances, to rule your life, and to see evidences of your heart's desire coming to fruition. This is absolutely essential if you are to truly know and serve Him. But God is a patient and gentle Teacher, and He will give you the grace to place your full confidence in Him.

Friend, God's help to you may not always unfold the way you imagine it will, but you can always trust that He will bless you when you faithfully obey Him. So focus on Him and His activity—not on your circumstances. And be assured, you *can* trust Him. All He wants is the opportunity to prove it to you.

Father, I want to trust You more. Increase my faith
and make me sensitive to Your loving presence, amen.

In His presence . . . let go and trust Him.

COMPETING PURPOSES

We can make our plans, but the LORD determines our steps.
PROVERBS 16:9 NLT

It can be exceedingly frustrating when nothing goes your way. You know what you must accomplish during the day, but from the moment you wake up, you can tell that you will have innumerable obstacles to overcome if you're going to succeed in your goals.

This is not by chance but to train you. You must come to the place where you understand that your life is in God's hands and He directs your path (Proverbs 3:5–6).

You may have your plans for today, but the Lord has His own. Your main tension and frustration will come when you work against Him and fail to trust His good purposes.

Friend, don't fight Him—He always wins. Rather, allow the Father to lead you step-by-step and leave what you don't accomplish in His hands. This may make you feel vulnerable, but trust Him anyway—loving others who need you and peacefully accepting the challenges that come. He will help you and position you perfectly to succeed.

> *Lord, I don't want to fight You—I want to submit to Your will. Help me obey You and sense Your presence throughout the day. I trust You with my life, Father, amen.*

In His presence . . . accept His purposes for your day.

ASSURED SUCCESS

"Not by might nor by power, but by My Spirit," says the LORD.
ZECHARIAH 4:6

You are not alone in your fear that you will fall short. Everyone you meet worries about this as well. Others may hide it, but every person wrestles with the anxiety that they will somehow fail, be rejected, or be deemed unworthy of possessing their heart's dearest desires.

The difference in you is the Holy Spirit who indwells you. Others may rely on their abilities, charms, or strengths. But you have a divine Helper who ensures you are accepted, important, and competent for the tasks He gives you to do (Philippians 2:13).

Likewise, you know that everything in your life comes from the Father's hand. If God closes someone's heart to you or denies you access to a particular opportunity, it's not because you've failed but because it's not His will. The denial is merely evidence of His protection and plan.

Friend, count on God not only to open the right doors for you but also to enable you to succeed in all He gives you to do. He will certainly not fail you.

Lord, I know You will lead me in the right path.
You are my ability, strength, wisdom, hope,
and success. I praise Your name, amen.

❧

In His presence . . . accept His plan.

DON'T GIVE UP

Do not throw away your confidence, which has a great reward.
For you have need of endurance, so that when you have
done the will of God, you may receive what was promised.
HEBREWS 10:35–36

Don't give up. Do not give in to hopelessness or imagine there is nothing left for you. Your situation may be frustrating because you cannot see any relief for the pain you feel and the setbacks you've endured. But you will make a terrible mistake if you quit because you think your circumstances will never change or get better.

God can intervene at any moment in ways that would absolutely astound you. He has not left you, nor is He perplexed by the challenges you face. These have all come so that He can show Himself mighty on your behalf. But you cannot give up on obeying Him and doing what is right because if you do, you will miss His wonderful provision.

So wait for Him and allow Him to be your strength (Psalm 27:13–14). Soon you will see His deliverance and reward if you will faithfully endure (Galatians 6:9).

Lord, I am weary, but I will trust in You and
obey. I know You will come through. I thank
You for teaching me greater faith, amen.

⚜

In His presence . . . find the strength to persevere.

PREVAILING PEACE

You will keep in perfect peace all who trust in you, all whose thoughts are fixed on you! Trust in the LORD always, for the LORD GOD is the eternal Rock.
ISAIAH 26:3–4 NLT

Your unbelief tears you apart. It may feel natural and reasonable because you see no evidence of relief for your situation. But the thoughts that arise because of your doubts will wear you out, discourage you, cause you to act rashly, and limit you from perceiving God's perfect work on your behalf (Isaiah 64:6).

Yes, your situation may appear disheartening. But you must remember your help comes from the unseen—from the Lord your God who accomplishes all that concerns you (Psalm 138:8).

So when the questions flood in, turn your mind to Him—because that is where your battle is won (2 Corinthians 10:5). Speak faith in Him. Praise Him for His unfailing and mighty attributes. Give thanks that He will lead you to triumph. And not only will He conquer your fears, but He will give you the Spirit of power, love, and discipline that will keep you in perfect peace (2 Timothy 1:7).

Lord God, I will trust You! Help me fix my thoughts on You so I can enjoy Your steadfast, prevailing peace, amen.

❀

In His presence . . . discover His perfect peace.

MARCH

MORE THAN YOU

*We were under great pressure, far beyond our ability
to endure, so that we despaired of life itself. . . . But this
happened that we might not rely on ourselves but on God.*

2 CORINTHIANS 1:8–9 NIV

There are circumstances that come along that require more than you are humanly able to give. No matter how hard you try, they continue overwhelming you. In fact, the more you work to overcome your difficulties, the more they seem to defeat you.

This is an indication that the Lord is stretching you— readying you to accept His power and wisdom for all you face. You see, He never meant for you to live the Christian life on your own. He meant it to be more than you can imagine.

So do you fear that you won't stretch far enough or be able to do all that you've been called upon to accomplish? Does honoring God with all the challenges you face feel impossible?

Good. You are ready to accept the help He is so willing to provide for you. Entrust yourself fully to the Father and discover how much He can do in and through you.

*Jesus, I cast my cares upon You, knowing You
are faithful to help me. Thank You for this
opportunity to experience Your provision, amen.*

❈

In His presence . . . see beyond yourself.

YOU ARE FORGIVEN

Everyone has sinned. . . . Yet God, with undeserved kindness,
declares that we are righteous. He did this through Christ
Jesus when he freed us from the penalty for our sins.
ROMANS 3:23–24 NLT

Do you ever quake in fear after reading the sins listed in God's Word? Are there transgressions that make you feel as if the Father could never accept you? After all, the apostle Paul warns, "Those who practice such things will not inherit the kingdom of God" (Galatians 5:21). Is it possible that you've offended Him in a way that He would reject you forever?

Friend, Romans 3:23 is clear—every person has *some* aspect of sin in his or her life. That's why we need Jesus in the first place. We cannot enter the kingdom of God without Him!

But when you accept Jesus as your Savior, you are washed in His blood and sin's stain is removed. You have a restored, permanent, personal relationship with the Father.

Friend, your sin does not surprise God. He has forgiven you in Christ. You no longer have any reason to fear.

Jesus, through Your death and resurrection You've
washed my soul, removed the stain of sin, and brought
indescribable joy to my heart! Thank You! Amen.

--- ❧ ---

In His presence . . . accept
God's gift of forgiveness.

APPEALING TO THE FLESH

*When the woman saw that the tree was . . . desirable
to make one wise, she took of its fruit and ate.*
GENESIS 3:6 NKJV

Did you know that Satan is very aware of the desires of your flesh? He convinced Eve to eat from the Tree of Knowledge by appealing to her longing for wisdom. And as he did with her, the enemy will stir up your fleshly desires in order to lure you into destroying yourself.

You see, once the enemy gets you to sin, you will feel shame in the presence of God and avoid Him—much like Adam and Eve did in the garden. You will hide from the Lord and cease to listen to Him. Ultimately, the enemy works to make you feel completely estranged from the Father so he can render you useless to God's kingdom.

But, friend, you're not alienated from the Father—the powerful blood of Jesus has reconciled you to Him forever! The Lord always wants you with Him. So don't give the enemy a foothold by gratifying the desires of your flesh. Seek God's direction and be confident He always has your best interest in mind.

*Father, thank You for loving me and truly
satisfying the desires of my heart, amen.*

**In His presence . . . you're always
welcome, loved, and forgiven.**

UNCOMMON SENSE

*The fear of the LORD is the beginning of wisdom, and
the knowledge of the Holy One is understanding.*

PROVERBS 9:10

Common sense will not suffice in your situation. So no matter how tempted you are to draw a conclusion about your circumstances before seeking God, don't do it. Without the Lord's point of view, you can only make a faulty assessment of what's happening to you.

A good example of this was when the king of Aram sent his massive army to capture the prophet Elisha (2 Kings 6:8–19). Filled with fear because of the horses and chariots arrayed against them, Elisha's servant Gehazi asked, "Master! What shall we do?" Elisha responded by calmly praying that God would open Gehazi's eyes. Immediately, Gehazi perceived the spiritual reality—the Lord's heavenly battalions were standing ready to defend Elisha. The victory was already won.

Likewise, there are influences in your situation that you cannot see—spiritual forces that almighty God has set in motion on your behalf.

So don't rely on your natural eyes or pass judgment on your situation. You'll draw the wrong conclusion. Rather, look to Him for understanding and allow Him to lead you to triumph.

*Lord, truly You are God! Thank You for working
on my behalf and leading me to victory, amen.*

❈

In His presence . . . trust He's working.

No

This I declare about the LORD: he alone is my
refuge, my place of safety; he is my God, and I trust
him. For he will rescue you from every trap.
PSALM 91:2–3 NLT

It's difficult to hear the word *no*. You plead for God to answer a request, but it is denied. Especially if the appeal is for something godly or positive, you may feel confused, dejected, and even question the Lord's purposes in refusing you.

But understand, when your will clashes with God's, you instantly come to a point of decision. Will you demand your way or will you accept His? Will you take the throne of your life; or will you acknowledge that your Lord and Savior is absolutely sovereign, caring, and wise, and He would never hurt you?

Be assured, the Father's no is both compassionate and good. Because of His holy character and unfailing love, He always strives to give you the absolute best direction for your life. You may not understand the reason for His no at the moment, but eventually you will. And surely you will give Him thanks for saving you from a mistake.

Jesus, You are my authority, and no matter how
difficult it is, I accept Your "no." I trust You to
lead me in the best way possible, amen.

❧

In His presence . . . accept His unfailing protection.

LEAVE IT TO HIM

Commit your way to the LORD, trust also in
Him, and He shall bring it to pass.
PSALM 37:5 NKJV

When a difficult decision arises, the natural response is to examine the consequences you can anticipate. You weigh how challenging the choice will prove, your ability to manage it, and whether it is worth the trouble.

This is all fine until the Lord directs you to step out in absolute faith. When He does, you can expect that the obstacles will appear greater than you can handle and that defeat is sure unless He intervenes. That is the very nature of faith—you must trust Him rather than yourself or your resources.

Is such a decision before you today? Do you sense the Father calling you to take a difficult path? Remember that God has the very best plan for you and there are astounding rewards you cannot possibly anticipate when you submit to Him.

So don't miss His best because of what you can or cannot see concerning your choice. Rather, obey God, leave the consequences to Him, and expect Him to work powerfully on your behalf.

Lord, I will obey You. I trust Your plan for my life,
and I know You will never lead me astray, amen.

❦

In His presence . . . trust Him to lead you.

A CALL TO REPENTANCE

*The sorrow that is according to the will of God produces
a repentance without regret, leading to salvation.*

2 CORINTHIANS 7:10

There are three words that describe the process of repentance: *recognition, agreement,* and *commitment.*

Recognition comes as we study Scripture and learn what God identifies as sin. Until we acknowledge that our actions are wrong, we won't see any real need to confess them to Him.

Next, we must *agree* with the Lord's assessment of our behavior. Without agreement, our confession would be more about the consequences of our sin rather than genuine remorse over violating His holy standard.

Finally, *commitment* is also necessary. We must dedicate ourselves to turning away from sin by choosing to walk obediently—in the manner God commands—knowing He will empower us to do so.

Remember, Christ promises that when He sets you free, you'll be free indeed (John 8:36). This means when you belong to Jesus, you can change permanently—you can be completely liberated from the bondage that enslaves you. Therefore, repent fully so you can experience the abundant life He created you for.

*Lord, I recognize my sin, agree with what Your Word
says about it, and commit my life to You, amen.*

❀

In His presence . . . repent and be cleansed.

FOR YOUR GROWTH

I have directed you in the way of wisdom;
I have led you in upright paths.
PROVERBS 4:11

Are you experiencing the fullness of the Christian life? There is so much more to having a relationship with God than simply having your sins forgiven. In order to grow, you must be willing for the Father to speak to your heart and direct you through faith-stretching situations.

Friend, you can count on the fact that whatever the Lord allows in your life is for the purpose of increasing your intimacy with Him. So when you face trials or must make decisions that require strength and wisdom far beyond your own, it's because He wants you to seek Him through His Word and in prayer. Likewise, He asks you to pay attention to the promptings of His Holy Spirit and be confident He'll work through your obedience to Him in an awesome way.

Friend, no one loves you like God does. So trust Him to lead you to the abundant Christian life by acknowledging Him in everything, even when faith-stretching situations arise. He will surely bless you abundantly as you seek and serve Him obediently.

Lord, thank You for leading me into the
abundant Christian life. Help me always
trust Your will and Your ways, amen.

In His presence . . . learn from
faith-stretching situations.

ABOUT YOU

Thanks be to God, who always leads us in triumph
in Christ, and manifests through us the sweet
aroma of the knowledge of Him in every place.
2 CORINTHIANS 2:14

Are you critical of yourself, constantly evaluating how you fall short? Do you see the blessings others receive and believe you're just not good enough to have them too? You do unimaginable damage to yourself with such negativity, talking yourself into a spirit of defeat that God never intended for you to endure.

"You don't understand," you may say, "I've been rejected. I've failed. I feel worthless." Perhaps you've done wrong or have been hurt by others. But the fact remains, how you perceive yourself isn't how God sees you. He's made you into a new creation (2 Corinthians 5:17).

Friend, Jesus loves you so much, He died for you. His indwelling Spirit provides everything necessary for you to be triumphant. And Christ gave you the great honor of commissioning you to be His representative to the perishing.

Stop putting yourself down. Instead, search His Word and discover how deeply gifted, cherished, and blessed you truly are.

Lord, thank You for loving me. Help
me see myself as You do, amen.

─────────── ⚜ ───────────

In His presence . . . find your true
worth and significance.

READIED DEFENSES

We use God's mighty weapons, not worldly
weapons, to knock down the strongholds of human
reasoning and to destroy false arguments.
2 CORINTHIANS 10:4 NLT

What is it that makes you stumble in your faith? Are you particularly prone to discouragement or greed? Do you struggle with lust or gossip? If you wait until you're in the midst of a temptation to fight it, you will fail. However, you can win the battle against your flesh by readying your defenses before the fight begins.

How do you do so? First, identify the thoughts that trigger you to sin. Often you'll find that your difficulties begin with deep-seated anxieties. For example, greed can result when you fear that you will not have enough or will be deemed unworthy. So observe what makes you feel vulnerable and elicits your reaction.

Second, do as Jesus did when He was tempted—use Scripture as a shield. Ask God to reveal the verses that best combat the thoughts that make you stumble.

Commit your thoughts to Him and ready your defenses. It may take time, but the Savior is more than able to lead you to victory over temptation.

Lord, please reveal the thoughts that trigger this
sin and the Scripture I need to fight it, amen.

In His presence . . . triumph over temptation.

PURPOSE IN ADVERSITY

Don't be surprised at the fiery trials you are going through,
as if something strange were happening to you. Instead, be
very glad—for these trials make you partners with Christ
in his suffering, so that you will have the wonderful joy
of seeing his glory when it is revealed to all the world.

1 PETER 4:12–13 NLT

Some days the burdens may seem so heavy and the weariness so profound that you may wonder if God has forsaken you. Why would He allow you to experience such deep adversity?

Yet do not despair. He has a clear purpose for your suffering: so you will know the Savior better and reflect His character.

Friend, God is forming His very likeness in you so that the wonderful fruit of His Spirit—love, joy, peace, patience, kindness, goodness, faithfulness, gentleness, and self-control (Galatians 5:22–23)—will shine through you to His glory.

The good news is, your Savior Jesus knows exactly how you feel (Hebrews 2:17). And because He understands, He comfortingly and faithfully guides you through your time of brokenness. So trust Him to teach you and give you His joy.

Lord, thank You for forming Your character in me. I will
trust You in this trial and give You all the praise, amen.

In His presence . . . find joy in times of pain.

TRULY GOD

When all the people saw it, they fell on their faces;
and they said, "The LORD, He is God!"
1 KINGS 18:39

Either you truly believe the Lord is God or you don't. That is the choice before you today. Either you'll trust the Father has brought you to the end of your options, strength, and ability for His glory; or you'll give in to the notion that you're alone without hope.

The prophet Elijah knew he could always count on the Father. And in order to demonstrate that there is only one true God, he challenged 850 prophets of the false deities Baal and Asherah to send fire from heaven to consume an offering. Whomever responded—whether their idols or the Lord—would prove to be sovereign.

With no other resource than wholehearted confidence in the Father's ability, Elijah stood courageously against the multitude of enemies (1 Kings 18).

And the Lord powerfully honored his faith.

God didn't let Elijah down, and He won't fail you either. Circumstances may be aligned against you that you feel powerless to overcome, but it's all to display His glory. So trust Him and be assured—He *will* respond and prove He is truly God.

Lord, You are God! I trust You to
answer my prayers, amen.

❦

In His presence . . . acknowledge He is sovereign.

AN OPEN HEART

You desire truth in the innermost being, and in the
hidden part You will make me know wisdom.
PSALM 51:6

Are you debating whether or not to talk to God about a certain concern? Are there burdens weighing you down because you're afraid to give them over to Him? Do they seem unworthy of His attention or cause you shame? Do you think to yourself, *I should be praising Him, not complaining?*

Friend, transparency is absolutely necessary for growing closer to Jesus. The Father wants you to feel confident enough in His unfailing love to be completely honest before Him with whatever is in your heart. He is devoted to you and cares about what concerns you. You can always feel free to speak with Him honestly about the matters that weigh on your heart.

The Father already knows every thought and emotion you have, but you express your trust in Him when you can openly confess your sins, anxieties, desires, doubts, and frustrations. So share all the details that concern you with God, and allow Him to minister to the deepest part of your soul.

Father, I want to be completely honest with You.
Surface my doubts, frustrations, and fears and help
me experience Your healing presence, amen.

In His presence . . . be completely open-hearted.

Your Heavenly Father

*We have all had human fathers who disciplined
us. . . . But God disciplines us for our good, in
order that we may share in his holiness.*
HEBREWS 12:9–10 NIV

You have a Father who loves, protects, and provides for you. Regardless of how your earthly dad treated you, your heavenly Father never fails you and He would never reject you. This is because through Jesus' sacrifice on the cross, you've been permanently adopted into God's household and have been given the Holy Spirit as a guarantee of His love forever (Ephesians 1:13–14).

Truly understanding how wonderful this is may require a shift in your thinking and the removal of strongholds in your life. So your wise and merciful heavenly Father allows you to experience circumstances that reveal His faultless character to you, demonstrate the depth of His love, and help you trust Him more.

So today, embrace that He is your Father. In whatever you face, look to Him to teach you and be assured you remain in the center of His perfect provision and love no matter what happens.

*Father, thank You for adopting me into
Your family. Help me learn all it means
to be Your beloved child, amen.*

❈

In His presence . . . accept Him as your Father.

Rest in Him

*"Only in returning to me and resting in me will you be
saved. In quietness and confidence is your strength."*
Isaiah 30:15 NLT

You need God. That is the frustration that's been surfacing repeatedly in your heart—your deep, unacknowledged yearning for His presence and provision. The problem is you continue to fight Him, trying to handle the problems you encounter on your own. And when the details of life don't go the way you expect, your faith fails.

Friend, you don't have to be "good enough" or handle things perfectly to succeed in these trials or please God. On the contrary, the struggle you feel is that you refuse to rest in His wonderful care.

But understand, the Father loves you just the way you are and wants you to rely upon Him. You cannot do anything to make Him love you more, and no failure will make Him care for you less. His devotion to you is complete, perfect, and unconditional.

So return to Him. Agree with His wisdom and obey what He commands. Allow Him to be your unfailing strength. Because He will undoubtedly make a wonderful way for you when you rest in Him.

*Lord, I need You. Please teach me how to let
go and rest in Your loving care, amen.*

In His presence . . . rest with confidence.

EACH STEP

He renews my strength. He guides me along
right paths, bringing honor to his name.
PSALM 23:3 NLT

The light on the path before you may be limited, but this is for a purpose. The Lord will lead you step by step. His desire is for you to depend on Him inch by inch and centimeter by centimeter as you progress in His purposes.

This may feel disheartening because others expect you to have answers, and the pressure to have the path charted clearly continues to mount. But do not be fearful or dismayed. It is the Lord Himself who has engineered these circumstances for your success and His glory—"so that your faith would not rest on the wisdom of men, but on the power of God" (1 Corinthians 2:5).

So depend on Him. Surrender to Him fully. And obey immediately when He reveals the next step. He will give you strength for every move you must make and bring you to a better destination than you could have hoped for or imagined (Ephesians 3:20).

Father, thank You for renewing my strength and
guiding me each step of the way. I praise You
for teaching me to trust You more, amen.

In His presence . . . submit to His leadership.

FORGET THE WHAT-IFS

*"Be strong and very courageous; be careful to do according
to all the law . . . do not turn from it to the right or to the
left, so that you may have success wherever you go."*
JOSHUA 1:7

You don't have to be anyone other than who God created you to be.
You don't have to fear you're inadequate. The Lord is with you and
knows exactly how to help you.

This was certainly true for Joshua. When Moses died, Joshua
understood that he would be responsible for leading the people of
Israel into the promised land, where untold enemies and challenges
awaited them. But what if the people didn't trust him as they had
Moses? What if he couldn't handle the difficulties? What if Joshua
couldn't hear God as Moses did? What if he failed?

The "what-ifs" could have completely paralyzed Joshua with
fear. Instead he overcame by heeding the Lord's instruction and
focusing on His provision.

You can too. God made you unique and placed you in these
circumstances for a purpose. It's His responsibility to lead you to victory. So forget the what-ifs. Obey Him and He will give you success.

*Lord, I'll focus on You. Thank You for teaching
me and leading me to triumph, amen.*

In His presence . . . leave the uncertainties to Him.

EXAMINE YOUR BELIEFS

*Remember the word to Your servant, in which You
have made me hope. This is my comfort in my
affliction, that Your word has revived me.*

PSALM 119:49–50

Are you continually living in defeat? Do even small challenges
throw you off balance? It may be time to examine what you believe.

Your beliefs form a filter through which you evaluate what you
experience. So if trials cause you to question God's character and
plan, it may be because of the doctrines you live by.

For example, if you think you can lose your salvation, it'll be difficult to trust the Father. You'll never really know if you're pleasing to
Him. But if you accept that your eternal life is absolutely secure—as
Scripture testifies—you'll feel more confident because you'll realize
nothing can separate you from His love (Romans 8:38–39).

This is why it's crucial to know what you believe and base your
convictions on God's Word alone. Doing so will prevent you from
being misled or intimidated.

Therefore, saturate your mind with Scripture and allow the
Lord to surface any beliefs that don't align with His Word. Certainly,
as you learn the truth, it will strengthen you and set you free.

*Lord, align my beliefs to Scripture. In
You I will hope forever, amen.*

In His presence . . . believe Him completely.

WORD OF LIFE

Forever, O LORD, Your word is settled in heaven. . . . I will
never forget Your precepts, for by them You have given me life.
PSALM 119:89, 93 NKJV

People's words can have a profound effect on your life. They can build you up or wound you deeply. In fact, you may be thinking of what someone said even now—considering their remarks and wondering what you did to deserve them.

However, let this truth sink deep into your heart. No matter what anyone says—whether good or bad—it's never as important or accurate as what God's Word says about you. Only Scripture testifies to God's character throughout history and how He—the One True Judge of the living and the dead—sees you.

Through the pages of God's Word, you know the Father better, understand your salvation, strengthen your faith, find your identity as His child and heir, discover the principles for a successful life, and learn how to lead others to the Savior.

This is why there's nothing more important than meditating on Scripture. Therefore, give more importance to His Word than anyone else's. And allow the Lord to breathe life into you through it.

Lord, Your Word is life. Plant it deep within my
heart so Your life can flourish in me, amen.

In His presence . . . embrace His Word.

LET HIM LEAD

A person's steps are directed by the LORD. How
then can anyone understand their own way?
PROVERBS 20:24 NIV

The Father wants you to come to the place where all that truly matters to you is His will and you're no longer fearful about the unknown. Rather, you trust Him so deeply and remain in such close fellowship with Him that you're confident He won't allow you to stray from His special path for your life.

There's no doubt that God has great plans for you, but the questions before you are: Can you let go of control and allow the Father to work through you? Are you willing to accept whatever comes from His hand each day in faith?

Don't miss God's blessings because you're fearful about giving up control. You may think, *If I let go, everything will fall apart.* But this is evidence of your limited understanding. It's possible that everything is going to pieces because you refuse to loosen your grasp.

Friend, the Father promises to strengthen and uphold you (Isaiah 41:10). So believe Him. Seek His will. Let go of your fear. And allow Him to instruct you step by step.

Lord, please help me let go. I want to rest
in You and trust You more, amen.

⚜

In His presence . . . relinquish control.

LISTENING CAREFULLY

The word of God is alive and active. . . . It judges
the thoughts and attitudes of the heart.
HEBREWS 4:12 NIV

Everything you hear should be sifted through the Word of God before you take it to heart. Allow me to repeat that for emphasis: Before you accept *anything* into your life, you should ensure that it aligns with Scripture. If it doesn't, reject it outright.

Why? Because the Word of God is your defensive weapon—protecting you, revealing your innermost intentions and motivations, and guarding you from the lies of the enemy. Scripture reveals the reality of who you are as a child of the living God and enables you to discern the truth from error. With it, you are able to defend yourself against anything that would oppose God's will being accomplished in your life (2 Corinthians 10:5).

So consider: What decision are you grappling with today? What confirmation do you need? Open your Bible and be diligent, persistent, careful, and discerning in finding your answers. Find your answer in Scripture, because His Word will not steer you wrong.

Father, please answer my questions
with Your Word and eliminate anything
that contradicts Your truth, amen.

In His presence . . . find understanding
for every situation through His Word.

BE STILL

"Cease striving and know that I am God."
PSALM 46:10

The most profound need of your soul is to be still in the presence of God. Stop wrestling with your troubles or worrying about circumstances—the Lord Almighty is greater than all of them. So calm your soul and focus on His astounding wisdom, ability, and timing.

Think of His faithfulness to the saints of old—many who struggled with the same trials and fears that you do. They overcame by trusting God, and He rewarded their faith in miraculous ways. Remember also Exodus 14:14: Trapped between the Egyptian army and the Red Sea, doom seemed inevitable for Israel. But the instruction was clear, "The LORD will fight for you; you need only to be still" (NIV).

The same is true for you. The Father wants to surround you with His peace and demonstrate His power, but He will only do so as you rest in His care and release your troubles to His omnipotent hand.

So let down your guard and stop striving. Let the full meaning impact you to the core: He is *God*. He loves you. He will help you. You have no reason to fear.

Lord, You are God. You are all I need.
I set my heart on You, amen.

❈

In His presence . . . be still and focus on Him.

STABILIZING FAITH

"Do not be afraid! Don't be discouraged . . .
for the battle is not yours, but God's."

2 CHRONICLES 20:15 NLT

When pressures assail from every side, maintaining your faith can feel like a battle. One or two of the problems you face are overwhelming enough. But as circumstances deteriorate, you may feel even more unbalanced—swinging from absolute trust in the Lord to deep, despairing doubt whenever new troubles appear.

Perhaps this is how King Jehoshaphat felt as he learned of the impending onslaught by the Moabites, Ammonites, and Meunites. Even one of these armies would have been too much—defending Judah against this three-fold invasion was absolutely unfeasible.

So Jehoshaphat did the one thing that's always wise—he sought God. And the Lord showed Jehoshaphat that the battle wouldn't be won by weapons or strategies, but by praise (2 Chronicles 20).

Likewise, the issues bombarding you aren't contingent upon your resources, but upon your focus. These aren't your battles to fight. This is your moment to look to God, trust, and obey. So stabilize your faith by praising Him whenever you feel doubt creeping in. Then watch with joy the amazing way He delivers you.

Lord, thank You for handling this overwhelming battle
for me. You are good, powerful, wise, and able! Amen.

❧

In His presence . . . adore Him.

GREATER PURPOSES

The LORD will work out his plans for my life.
PSALM 138:8 NLT

At times, life doesn't seem fair. You see others enjoying the gifts you long for and wonder why God doesn't bless you too—especially as trials and pressures mount. You question, "Father, don't You love me? Why won't You help me?"

The pain may be profound—the uncertainty, rejection, loss, and even disrespect may tear you apart. But understand, the Lord uses challenges in your life for your benefit and His greater purposes.

This was true for all the biblical saints. Abraham spent decades painfully watching unbelievers have children when he couldn't, but eventually his offspring became a great nation that endures to this day. Joseph was sold into slavery and thrown unjustly in jail, but God eventually made him second to Pharaoh. Paul was beaten and imprisoned for his faithful testimony to Christ, yet his words have encouraged millions of believers throughout history.

So don't lose heart or be afraid. Your loving Father is using these circumstances to strengthen your faith, equipping you for higher service. Just keep trusting Him and expect great blessings to come from this adversity.

Lord, this situation appears unfair, but I trust Your will for my life. Thank You for training me, amen.

In His presence . . . trust His greater purposes.

INVESTING TIME

*Teach us to number our days, that we may
present to You a heart of wisdom.*
PSALM 90:12

Time is a precious resource, and there often doesn't seem to be enough of it. But the truth is, how you invest the minutes and hours you've been given demonstrates what's most important to you.

For instance, consider: Are you distracted by needless pursuits—diversions that have no eternal value—when the Lord is calling you to His higher purposes? Are you choosing entertainment over knowing God through His Word and prayer? Do you spend hours pondering your fears rather than thanking Him for all He's done and resting in Him? Do you spend more time complaining about others than ministering to them?

The time you have is indeed limited. So the Lord calls you to surrender yourself to His wisdom—to invest your time in pursuits that are eternally worthwhile such as seeking Him and blessing others. So ask Him, "Lord, how can I spend my life in a manner that pleases You?" He will show you how to employ your time wisely if you'll listen to Him and respond to Him in obedience.

*Lord, teach me to spend my days in a manner
that honors You. Thank You for making
my minutes count for eternity, amen.*

In His presence . . . give Him your time.

YOUR DEFENDER

"No weapon that is formed against you will prosper;
and every tongue that accuses you in judgment you will
condemn. This is the heritage of the servants of the LORD,
and their vindication is from Me," declares the LORD.

ISAIAH 54:17

It may seem that the forces and circumstances aligned against you are overwhelming today. Perhaps there are powerful people who are attempting to undermine you or there are others who are spreading ugly rumors about you that aren't true. It could even be that you've taken a stand for Christ and are being persecuted because of it. At such times take heart—your life is in God's hands. He is your Defender. Nothing can touch you that He doesn't first allow for your benefit.

Friend, keep your heart clean before God and remember His promise, "They will fight against you, but they will not overcome you, for I am with you to deliver you" (Jeremiah 1:19). Your hope, your defense, your vindication, and your future are all in the hands of the Lord God Almighty. The people and challenges aligned against you cannot overpower Him. Trust Him. No matter what comes, He will bring good from it.

Lord, I will trust You. You have my next steps planned
and no one can thwart Your eternal purposes, amen.

❦

In His presence . . . find security for the future.

OVERWHELMINGLY OVERCOME

Despite all these things, overwhelming victory
is ours through Christ, who loved us.
ROMANS 8:37 NLT

Sometimes what you need most is simply the assurance that everything is going to be okay. Your spirit longs for the guarantee that you will make it through this challenge—that all is well and God is still active on your behalf.

But, friend, be assured—not only will you endure this trial, you will emerge from it as *more than a conqueror* (Romans 8:37). In other words, not only will you survive this difficulty, but when it is done, it will lift you to new heights in your life and relationship with God (Habakkuk 3:17–19).

For example, Joseph did not just "make it through" his prison years—they were the training ground the Lord used to make him the second most powerful man in the world. Had he not gone to prison, he would never have made it to the palace (Genesis 39–50).

Therefore, live above your circumstances and enjoy great confidence because Jesus gives you everything you need to live the abundant life. He assures you of victory. All is definitely well.

Lord, thank You for making me more than a conqueror.
I praise You for leading me to eternal victory, amen.

———————————— ⚜ ————————————

In His presence . . . overwhelmingly
overcome all difficulties.

MAKING PROGRESS

Don't just listen to God's word. You must do what it says.
JAMES 1:22 NLT

Do you ever feel you should be developing faster in your relationship with God? If so, you may be tempted to work harder and serve more—but that's not how spiritual growth actually occurs. Yes, you obey the Father when He calls; but it should be out of love, not to earn His favor.

So how is it that some believers mature so much more rapidly in their walk with Jesus than others? The answer is in *application*—spiritual progress occurs when you actively put the truth you learn to practice.

Remember, the One who saved you is able to teach you to follow Him. Jesus knows exactly what you need to grow. So He constantly reveals His principles to you from His Word, in prayer, via adversity, and through other believers. You know when it happens—a particular Scripture, sermon, or admonition touches your heart profoundly. But here is the key: don't just remember it; rather, ask the Father how to incorporate it permanently into your life. Indubitably, He is more than happy to honor your request.

> *Lord, I want to grow closer to You and*
> *mature in my faith. Teach me to apply*
> *Your Word. I'm ready to learn, amen.*

❦

In His presence . . . apply the truth.

COMFORT FROM GETHSEMANE

It was necessary for him to be made in every respect
like us, his brothers and sisters, so that he could be
our merciful and faithful High Priest before God.

HEBREWS 2:17 NLT

Jesus knows exactly how you feel—even at this very moment. The struggles you face are not foreign to Him in the least. Actually, they are very personal. Rejection, betrayal, loss, grief, physical pain— He's experienced them all. And when you face them, He feels compassion for you (Matthew 9:36).

Indeed, Gethsemane proves your Savior understands what it's like to be in so much agony that all you can do is weep and pray. Remember, He knew what anguish awaited Him on the cross. And as He wrestled with the task before Him, He went not once or twice but three times to the Father for comfort, strength, and wisdom.

Jesus understands how deep your feelings go and exactly what you need to survive the trials you face. In fact, He suffered just so He could fully comprehend your pain. So hold on to the fact that He's with you, cares about you, and can minister to your hurting heart. And go to Him as often as you need.

Jesus, how kind and loving You are! Thank You for
understanding me and comforting my heart, amen.

❧

In His presence . . . accept His comfort.

As from Him

"You would have no authority over Me, unless
it had been given you from above."
JOHN 19:11

Think of the sacrifices asked of you as coming from the hand of your Savior—from the One who gave His life for you on the cross—rather than others. After all, absolutely nothing can touch your life without His permission. He has allowed these circumstances for your discipleship. He is teaching you to trust Him.

Jesus made this clear as He stood before Pilate. As the Roman governor of Judea, Pilate believed he played a key role in Jesus' fate (John 19:10). But Jesus proclaimed the truth—authority had been given to Pilate by God for the plan of salvation to be accomplished. Pilate really had no say; he merely played a small role in the fulfillment of God's promises.

Likewise, others may seem to be responsible for your difficulties, but the Father has allowed this situation for His purposes. So trust Him, even when the sacrifices seem unfair or painful. Jesus gave His life for you; do this for Him. You'll be amazed at how He responds on your behalf.

Lord, help me accept this as coming from Your hand
and not grow bitter. I want to obey You, amen.

———————— ❦ ————————

In His presence . . . accept
challenges as coming from Him.

The Love of the Cross

God demonstrates His own love toward us, in that
while we were yet sinners, Christ died for us.

ROMANS 5:8

Whenever you struggle with whether or not God truly loves and accepts you, realize it is time to go back to the cross. Spend time thinking about how profound the Savior's love is for you that He would endure such terrible suffering—how deep, forgiving, sacrificial, and unconditional His divine and unfailing care.

Though the Lord rightfully could have judged the sinfulness He saw on earth and destroyed all humankind, He didn't. Instead, He graciously decided to pay the eternity-shaking price for the sins of every person—whether we acknowledged His provision or not.

Jesus did this voluntarily (John 10:17–18). Nothing you did earned this gift of salvation, and there's nothing you can do to lose it (Ephesians 2:8–9).

So if you're struggling because you've sinned and wonder if you've gone too far for God to love you anymore, take heart. You cannot stop Him from caring for you. He loved you at your worst. Now honor Him with your very best.

Jesus, thank You for giving me an unfailing reminder
of Your love through the cross. Thank You for forgiving
my sin. You are truly merciful and good, amen.

In His presence . . . thank Him for the cross.

APRIL

CLING TO THE PROMISE

"Blessed are they who did not see, and yet believed."
JOHN 20:29

In the midst of great trials, it's normal to feel isolated, dejected, and helpless. But remember, *you're not alone*. Though it may seem as if all hope is gone, it's crucial you trust that your powerful Deliverer will be with you always (Deuteronomy 31:8).

There's no better example of this than the disciples after the Crucifixion. Though Jesus had warned them of what was about to happen, they didn't fully comprehend it. So when they saw their beloved Rabbi on the cross, they gave in to despair.

Just three days later He rose from the dead and not only restored their faith, He increased it a hundredfold. But how different their time between the Crucifixion and Resurrection would have been if they'd simply clung to the Savior's promises.

The same is true for you. There will be difficulties when God does not provide you answers but comforts you with, "Trust what I've said." Do not give in to the darkness of the moment, but cling to His Word. Soon enough you'll see your hopes rise from the grave as well.

Lord, thank You for never leaving or
forsaking me. I trust You to turn my moment
of mourning to songs of joy, amen.

In His presence . . . believe He will be victorious.

How Great His Love

God . . . because of His great love with which He loved
us, even when we were dead in our transgressions,
made us alive together with Christ.

EPHESIANS 2:4–5

The Lord Jesus—God incarnate—*chose* to endure the cross for you. Think about that truth. Crucifixion was the most horrible way a person could die—humiliating, horrifically painful, and reserved for the worst offenders. But realize, it wasn't only earthly anguish Jesus experienced on the cross—He also felt the unbearable spiritual agony of bearing the sins of the world. For the first time in eternity, He understood the profound hopelessness of being separated from the Father.

Why would Jesus make such a sacrifice? Because that's how deeply He loves you. He preferred to suffer an excruciating death among the worst criminals rather than be separated from you.

So the next time you feel unworthy or unlovable, remember what your Savior endured to save you and keep you safe for all eternity. He laid down His life willingly for you. And even now He holds nothing back so you can know Him. Surely that is reason for you to praise His name.

Jesus, I am humbled at all You've sacrificed
for me. Truly, You are worthy of my love,
obedience, and praise, amen.

❖

In His presence . . . appreciate His sacrificial love.

ACCEPTED

If we are faithless, He remains faithful,
for He cannot deny Himself.
2 TIMOTHY 2:13

Allow this truth to set you free: you don't have to be perfect to experience the Father's love and provision.

Do you constantly worry about how your next mistake might make God react toward you? Friend, this is an exhausting way to live. While it's essential you honor Him through obedience, He doesn't love you any less when you mess up.

What grieves the Father about sin is that it separates you from Him. You feel the shame of falling short of His holy standard and hide from Him as a consequence.

But what God wants is deep, uninterrupted, abiding fellowship with you, which is why He provided so perfectly for you on the cross. Now He readily invites you—no matter what you've done—to confess your sins to Him. Because when you do, you're promised He will forgive you and cleanse you from all unrighteousness (1 John 1:9).

Why is He so ready to pardon when you fail? Because of His unconditional love for you. He wants you back. He wants you close. Don't allow your imperfections to keep you separated from Him.

Lord, I'm so grateful for Your love and acceptance. I
confess my sins. Thank You for forgiving me, amen.

—————— ✻ ——————

In His presence . . . know you're loved.

Truth from the Resurrection

*Our Lord Jesus Christ . . . has caused us to be born
again to a living hope through the resurrection.*

1 PETER 1:3

In the midst of painful circumstances, do you find it challenging to trust that your situation can be better or that good can come from it? It's understandable. After all, even the disciples who walked with Jesus were completely devastated after the Crucifixion. They couldn't see past their earthly circumstances to remember His promises.

But you don't have to get caught up in an attitude of defeat. Understanding the truth of the resurrection, you can see past your situation to your extraordinary Redeemer. What does His triumph over the grave teach you?

First, when you think all is lost is when Your Savior reveals His awesome power.

Second, God *always* succeeds in carrying out His plans for you—nothing is too big to stop Him.

Third, nothing—not even death—can separate you from His love.

So when you find it difficult to endure, overcome your doubts by applying these three principles. These triumphant truths from the resurrection can give you true and lasting victory—today and every day.

*Jesus, You've overcome sin and death—truly You
are worthy of my trust and praise! Amen.*

❀

In His presence . . . find victory.

RESURRECTION POWER

God has fulfilled this promise . . . in that He raised up Jesus.
ACTS 13:33

The empty tomb is a beautiful reminder to you that all that God has promised you is true. Nothing—not even the grave—can prevent Him from keeping His word to you (Isaiah 55:11).

Friend, Jesus has risen from the dead! Sin—the most violent force that keeps you shackled—has been defeated. Death—the most painful foe you could ever face—has lost its grip on you. Your most brutal, insurmountable enemies were conquered, and the very power of the resurrection is yours forever as a child of the living God (Ephesians 1:18–21).

So today, consider: What stands in the way of God fulfilling His promise to you? Are there obstacles greater than sin and death that block your path? What problems do you face that require more power than was available at the resurrection?

You know the answer—the challenges before you are no match for the Lord. So trust Him and be assured that He will faithfully do all He has said.

*Jesus, thank You for making Your astounding power
available to me. No challenge I face is a match for
You—and I am so grateful You are my Savior, amen.*

———————————— ✺ ————————————

In His presence . . . experience resurrection power.

To Succeed, Believe

"Don't be faithless any longer. Believe!"
JOHN 20:27 NLT

Thomas was missing when Jesus first appeared to the disciples, and he was also the one to voice the greatest doubts about the resurrection. He declared that he wouldn't believe Christ had risen from the grave unless he touched Jesus' hands and side (John 20:25). You can imagine the shock and embarrassment he felt when Jesus appeared.

Yet what happened to Thomas can be instructive for you today—especially if God's made you a promise that you've waited a long time to see fulfilled. What you believe about Him will ensure either your success or your failure.

You may, like Thomas, demand the Lord show you signs, but when you do so, you only prove the weakness and immaturity of your faith.

But Jesus said, "Blessed are they who did not see, and yet believed" (John 20:29). If you'll unwaveringly trust Him to do as He says, you will receive a great blessing. You'll not only see your dearest prayers answered, but you'll glorify Him, and your faith will grow.

So don't embarrass yourself by doubting Him. Trust that He is able, and that one day your faith will be turned to sight.

Lord, I do believe! Please help my unbelief and keep my trust in You strong and steadfast, amen.

In His presence . . . succeed by believing Him.

HOLY DECISIONS

Who is the man who fears the Lord? He will
instruct him in the way he should choose.
PSALM 25:12

Life is one continuous decision-making process from childhood through the golden years. Thankfully, God is willing to give us clear guidance about every choice we make—regardless if it's major or minor. However, when He speaks, He expects us to respect Him—doing as He instructs.

In fact, His Word tells us, "The fear of the Lord is the beginning of wisdom" (Psalm 111:10 NIV). In other words, if you're going to be wise, you must honor His direction, serving Him instead of yourself. And you do so because of your steadfast confidence in His sovereignty and character.

So consider—are you in the midst of a difficult situation today? Friend, understanding that the Savior is perfect in His knowledge, all-sufficient in His strength, and unconditionally loving toward you is key to submitting to Him for your future. So reevaluate your situation in light of His trustworthy character and obey however He directs you to proceed. Because you'll be sure to make excellent decisions when you do.

Lord, I submit to Your unfailing wisdom.
Lead me in the way I should go, amen.

In His presence . . . be reverent, yielding, and confident.

OUT OF THE PIG PEN

"This son of mine was . . . lost and is
found." So they began to celebrate.
LUKE 15:24 NIV

Imagine the prodigal son looking at the pigs he was feeding. As he dropped pods into their sty, his stomach growled, and he realized they were eating better than he was. He was actually envying the hogs! Life couldn't get much worse. The only alternative this young man could imagine was to return to his father in humiliation. You can imagine his joy as he returned home and found his father had not only forgiven him, but greeted him with open arms.

Likewise, no matter how far you are from God, His arms are open to you as well. You have not slipped too far away from Him—you can't (2 Timothy 2:13). His grace is always available to lift you out of the pit of sin and defeat, back to victorious living.

So do not envy the pigs or give in to despair. Run back to the Father. He desires to restore you by His grace and fill you with all of His goodness.

Lord, show me the ways I've strayed and bring
me back to the safety of Your love. Thank
You for always accepting me, amen.

In His presence . . . be restored by His grace.

The Best Defense

My eyes are always on the Lord, for he rescues me.
PSALM 25:15 NLT

What are sound biblical principles you can practice as you face the difficulties of your life?

First, recall past victories. Recounting times when the Lord has come to your aid will fortify you for your present challenge.

Second, examine your motivation. What is really driving you in this trial—your goals or your devotion to the Lord?

Third, reject discouragement. Well-meaning people can sometimes quench your faith. Listen to and obey the Father, who will never fail nor forsake you.

Fourth, recognize the real purpose for the battle. Nothing touches your life unless it first passes through the Lord's protective hand. This means there's a benefit for you in this challenge if you'll set your heart to learn from Him.

Finally, rely upon God's power for victory. Trust the Lord so much that the victory already is decided in your mind. You know your all-powerful, all-wise, perfectly loving Father would never let you down.

Friend, trust in the Lord, obey Him, and count on Him to deliver you. He is your best defense no matter what you face.

Lord, I trust You in the challenges of life,
for You are always triumphant, amen.

In His presence . . . stand strong.

GUARANTEED

Delight yourself in the LORD; and He will
give you the desires of your heart.
PSALM 37:4

A promise is only as good as the character of the one making it. So when it comes to your loving, heavenly Father, there should be absolutely no question about whether or not He will do as He says. You can count on the fact He will (Joshua 21:45).

But God calls you to delight in Him because nothing will satisfy your soul like being close to Him in intimate fellowship. As you draw near to Him, He not only provides the wisdom you need at every turn, but He also directs you in how to accomplish His plan for your life—including receiving the promise you yearn for.

Be assured—the Father will not fail you. The desire of your heart may take a different form than you expected and may appear in a way you never imagined, but God will keep His word. And the Lord Himself will be your joy. So take heart, seek Him faithfully, and remind yourself often, "Not one word has failed of all His good promise" (1 Kings 8:56).

Lord, I delight in You. Help me remain focused
on You as my joy and my life, trusting fully
that You'll keep Your promises, amen.

❧

In His presence . . . trust His promise.

FOCUS ON HIS CHARACTER

Don't worry about anything; instead, pray about everything.
Tell God what you need, and thank him for all he has done.
PHILIPPIANS 4:6 NLT

Friend, today you may be tempted to do as you will and not wait for God's answer to your prayers. But realize, you will not calm your anxiety by doing what you want. You will only find peace by obeying the Father and trusting His character.

No, the Lord may not act as quickly as you wish. But remember, He is all-powerful, all-knowing, and unfailingly merciful. If He has not responded to you yet, it is certainly for a good purpose.

You must embrace the fact that having a solid foundation of faith in His trustworthy character is essential if you desire to experience His unshakable security and peace. If you are unclear about who Jesus is, then your faith will fail you when you need it most.

So when anxiety takes hold and you feel driven by fear to act—stop. Open the Word. Seek God's face and meditate on His steadfast, unshakable, faithful character. And soon the peace that transcends understanding will comfort and strengthen your heart and mind.

Lord, You are good and You lead me faithfully. I will
trust You. Thank You for calming my soul, amen.

In His presence . . . focus on Him.

REFUSE TO DOUBT

Though the fig tree does not bud and there are no grapes on the vines, . . . yet I will rejoice in the LORD, I will be joyful in God my Savior. The Sovereign LORD is my strength, . . . he enables me to tread on the heights.

HABAKKUK 3:17–19 NIV

Nothing can shake your faith as when your situation takes an unexpected turn for the worst. Suddenly, the foundation of what you trust is shattered. As you grasp for earthly forms of security and relief, they crumble. The pressure compounds.

God has not allowed these circumstances to destroy your faith but to build it. However, at this moment you must *decide* to believe that the Father is worthy of your trust. He desires the best for you. It may not seem so at the moment as you face incredible pressures, but He does.

Therefore, refuse to doubt. Like David confronting Goliath or Moses standing before the Red Sea, refuse to accept defeat. Know that God is waiting to reveal His mighty provision to you. And rejoice in the fact that He will never fail you.

Lord, I will not doubt You. You are leading me to victory and I am so grateful for Your love, amen.

❦

In His presence . . . believe He will sustain you.

FIND ENCOURAGEMENT AND REST

Seek the LORD and His strength; seek His face evermore!
PSALM 105:4 NKJV

Do you need encouragement today even though you received it yesterday? Are you continuously looking to God's Word for strength? Do not be discouraged if you are often finding yourself in need of His inspiration and reassurance. You don't have to question this driving desire for the loving presence of your heavenly Father. You're looking in the right place. God *wants* you to seek Him.

Go to Jesus with your problems. Others may grow weary addressing the issues that concern you, but your Savior never will. He will encourage you every moment of the day when you look to Him.

However—and this is extremely important—obey Him immediately when He directs you to take a step of faith. Whether He asks you to confess a sin, turn away from some activity, seek Him in a specific manner, or reject a pattern of thinking, do so immediately. He wants to heal you of the issues that discourage you and give you true rest for your soul.

Lord Jesus, thank You for encouraging me.
You faithfully provide rest for my soul,
and I praise Your holy name, amen.

━━━━━━━━━━ ❧ ━━━━━━━━━━

In His presence . . . rest in His care.

CREATED FOR A PURPOSE

We are His workmanship, created in Christ
Jesus for good works, which God prepared
beforehand so that we would walk in them.

EPHESIANS 2:10

Never forget that the Father knows your life from beginning to end and has a plan for all He created you to accomplish. Understanding this will help you avoid rushing into the unknown when you should be waiting for His guidance.

In your desire to see the Lord work in your life, you may often wish that He would reveal more about the path ahead or that He would speed you along to the destination more quickly. This is not uncommon; in fact, it is the inner struggle of every believer He uses powerfully.

But remember that God knows the big picture and what is best for you. He will not allow your passions and gifts to go to waste. He understands the level of faith you need in order to succeed and sees the best path for forming His character in you.

So endure and wait for Him to open the doors of opportunity. He knows what He created you to do. Trust Him to accomplish what concerns you.

Lord, thank You for giving my life purpose. I wait
for You to reveal the path for my life, amen.

In His presence . . . receive your purpose.

HOPE IN GOD

Put your hope in the LORD. Travel steadily
along his path. He will honor you.
PSALM 37:34 NLT

If only today would be the day. The thought crosses your mind as it often does. How many times have you started the morning with the same hope? As time passes, it may be challenging to maintain confidence. Yet you comfort yourself with the promise, "With God all things are possible" (Matthew 19:26).

Waiting is undoubtedly difficult, but it's also necessary. Through delays you discover your failings and are trained to trust the Father.

Yet understand this: If what you want draws you away from the Lord or you would forsake Him if He refused to give it to you, there is a problem. Your desire has become your god.

So today, examine your heart. Would you still love the Father if He said no to your dearest request? Is He still on the throne of your heart? Make sure. Ask Him to remove any idols and help you acknowledge Him as God. And trust that what He has for you is immeasurably above what you could hope for or imagine.

Lord, You are my God. There is nothing I desire
above You. Remove the idols from my life and
help me wait for Your very best, amen.

In His presence . . . put your hope in Him.

EXALT HIM

*Paul and Silas were praying and singing hymns
to God. . . . Suddenly, there was a massive
earthquake. . . . All the doors immediately flew open.*
ACTS 16:25–26 NLT

Today, regardless of what is happening, focus on God, who is your Help and Defender. There is nothing more freeing than praising Him and expressing your trust in His power, wisdom, and love.

Consider Paul and Silas, who were unjustly arrested, beaten, and incarcerated in a Philippian jail (Acts 16:16–34). Instead of dwelling on their pain, they focused on the Lord and sang praises to His holy name. And because of their unfailing trust in Him, God released them from prison and many trusted Jesus as their Savior.

There is power in praise. When you exalt the Father, you recognize His love, respect His sovereignty, and prepare the way for His provision.

So today, even if circumstances seem insurmountable, make the choice to rejoice in the Lord. Cry out to the One who is capable of turning your sorrow into joy. And praise Him—not only for what He is planning for your future, but also for what you can learn from your present situation.

*Lord, You are God! You are worthy of all honor, glory,
power, and praise. Thank You for Your love, amen.*

ॐ

In His presence . . . exalt Him.

USEFUL

*We ourselves are like fragile clay jars containing
this great treasure. This makes it clear that our
great power is from God, not from ourselves.*

2 CORINTHIANS 4:7 NLT

Yes, friend, God can work through you. It is not only those with extraordinary gifts or talents that the Lord chooses to be His representatives. On the contrary, He uses people who will humbly rely on His power to achieve His goals. The more dependent you are on Him, the more His glory can shine through you.

Of course, the temptation is to look at your faults and failings and deem yourself unworthy of the Father's service. If you believe that He cannot use you because of your past, your lack of resources or education, or even your appearance, then please realize you are focusing on the wrong thing. Scripture is clear: your "adequacy is from God" (2 Corinthians 3:5).

The Lord can work through you to accomplish His wonderful purposes, and all He requires is for you to trade your weakness for His strength and obey Him. So place your faith in Christ and rejoice at all He does in and through you.

*Father, thank You for creating me for
good works and working through me. May
my life bring You praise, amen.*

❧

In His presence . . . receive the strength to serve Him.

SOWING AND REAPING

He who sows sparingly will also reap sparingly, and he
who sows bountifully will also reap bountifully.
2 CORINTHIANS 9:6

You will have many choices today. But as you make decisions, please remember that you'll reap what you sow: you will harvest that which you've planted in the past, and the choices you make today will influence what you reap in the future.

With this principle in mind, consider: What would you like to accomplish with your life? Are you seeking to fulfill the purpose for which God created you? If so, then what type of seeds are you planting? Are you sowing behaviors that will deepen your relationship with the Father such as prayer, Bible study, and fellowship with other believers? Are you being generous with the gifts and talents He's given you? Are you sowing love, joy, peace, patience, kindness, goodness, faithfulness, gentleness, and self-control in your relationships with others?

Be conscious of the choices you make every day—each one is a seed that you are planting for your future. Invest bountifully in honoring and obeying God and you will surely be glad when harvesttime comes.

Lord, help me invest my life bountifully in ways that
honor You. To You be all the honor and glory, amen.

In His presence . . . sow that which honors Him.

AN ETERNAL FOCUS

*"Do not work for the food which perishes, but for the food which
endures to eternal life, which the Son of Man will give to you."*

JOHN 6:27

If you are continually experiencing frustration, one reason may be
your point of view. You see, although it's natural for you to focus
on the problems directly before you, God's interest is in developing
you for His eternal purposes. And when your immediate interests
and His everlasting goals collide, you may experience frustration.

For example, you may plead for the Father to move quickly
in solving your problems, but His priority is developing godly
character in you. If your troubles serve His aim, they will endure
regardless of how uncomfortable they make you.

This is why it is exceedingly important for you to pursue God's
point of view—serving His worthy, timeless objectives rather than your
temporary aspirations. Because when you focus on the eternal, you
begin to understand how the Father is working all things for your good.

So today, what is causing you frustration? Look for God's everlasting purposes in those circumstances. Because when you do,
you'll find the peace and strength to persevere no matter what
challenges assail you.

*Lord, I accept Your everlasting purposes. Please
help me learn these lessons quickly, amen.*

⚜

In His presence . . . think eternally.

DAILY HELP

Blessed be the LORD, who daily bears our burden.
PSALM 68:19

Are you trying to carry all of your burdens by yourself? If so, it's no wonder you're weary. The Father never meant for you to carry everything all alone. Rather, He's given you more than you can bear so you'll allow Him to sustain you. So don't be surprised that you cannot help yourself. God makes Himself known to you by rescuing you from trouble.

However, your desire to manage everything may reveal a deeper problem. Perhaps you do not fully trust that the Lord is enough to meet your needs. Although you trust Him for salvation, you may think He is either too busy or unwilling to bear your day-to-day needs.

But think this through carefully: How can the One who paid so dearly for your salvation deny you when it comes to the trials that affect you daily? He cannot. In fact, not only does He know exactly what you need, but He desires to satisfy your soul to the depths of your being. So relinquish your problems to the Father. He can certainly handle anything that comes your way.

Lord, thank You for being my Great Burden-Bearer.
You are so good to me and I praise Your name, amen.

❧

In His presence . . . accept His help and provision.

BELIEVE GOD

Take courage! For I believe God. It will be just as he said.

ACTS 27:25 NLT

Sometimes you may feel as if you're walking in loving oneness with Jesus that'll never end. But then there are seasons He appears so distant, you wonder what's blocking your fellowship with Him.

Yes, some of the seeming detachment may be due to unconfessed sin, but that's not always the case. Remember, His goal is to build your faith, and that may mean removing any visible evidence of help as you continue to trust Him.

This was certainly true for Paul. Transported as a prisoner to Rome—where he knew he'd die for testifying about Jesus—Paul's ship was torn asunder by a violent storm. The crew went without food or relief from the tempest many days, but Paul didn't question why God allowed the suffering. Instead, he refused to give up hope. Paul knew the Lord was working all circumstances for good, no matter how desperate the situation appeared.

How about you? Even when you don't sense His presence and all circumstances seem adverse, can you continue to testify, "I believe God"? Will you allow Him to grow your faith through the storm?

Father, I will take courage, for I believe You. I trust
it will be just as You've promised me, amen.

———————————— ❧ ————————————

In His presence . . . believe Him.

ALREADY ACCOMPLISHED

*This promise is from God himself, who makes the
dead live again and speaks of future events with as
much certainty as though they were already past.*

ROMANS 4:17 TLB

In your limited sight, the fulfillment of God's promises may appear distant. You cannot see the future or how the Lord is working, so it's understandable to focus on the challenges ahead. However, your loving Father calls you to look to Him rather than your circumstances and to believe, "If He has promised me, then it's already done."

This is the faith that Abraham demonstrated. Although God promised him a son, the decades passed without fulfillment. No one would have blamed Abraham for being disheartened. After all, could a one-hundred-year-old man and a ninety-year-old woman really conceive a child?

But Abraham continued to believe, understanding that to his timeless God, Isaac already existed, as did the generations after him.

Friend, when God challenges you to trust Him, look beyond the natural, knowing what He's promised has already been accomplished. Then you can trust Him to work, even when He's undetected, and praise Him for His provision.

*Lord, thank You that the blessings of Your plans
have already been accomplished, amen.*

In His presence . . . trust the promise is fulfilled.

TURN IT FOR GOOD

If you reject discipline, you only harm yourself; but if
you listen to correction, you grow in understanding.
PROVERBS 15:32 NLT

It's amazing how another person's unloving attitude or critical words can pierce your heart. It hurts to be censured, and you may be tempted to retaliate against the offender. Though there will be times when criticism directed at you is untrue or misguided, God's Word is clear—don't allow anger or bitterness to take root (Hebrews 12:15). Do not respond negatively to the discipline. Rather, listen to the correction, and you'll mature in your understanding of yourself and others.

This exercise may be uncomfortable, but seek God's wisdom anyway. Pray, "Search me, O God, and know my heart . . . see if there be any hurtful way in me" (Psalm 139:23–24). He will reveal if there is anything true in what was said to you.

If there is, allow God to correct your behavior. If not, forgive your accuser and seek to understand him or her better. The Father can give you invaluable insight into the human heart through the experience if you'll simply trust Him and set your heart to learn from Him.

Lord, I trust You. Help me forgive and love
others more through this experience, amen.

In His presence . . . find good in negative situations.

POWERFUL AND EFFECTIVE

The prayer of a righteous person is powerful and effective.
JAMES 5:16 NIV

Oh, the mighty power within your reach today—for change, healing, vindication, liberation, endurance, and eternal transformation. Your astounding, all-powerful God waits to respond to your requests with His unlimited supernatural resources.

However, you may be thinking, *I pray, but I sense no such power. Am I doing something wrong?* If so, consider: Have you truly connected with your loving heavenly Father in deep fellowship with Him? Do you recognize who He is—the King of kings of all creation? Or do you merely take Him your list of requests without thought to His desires?

Likewise, do you truly believe He will help you? Do you have such confidence in His character and abilities that all your doubts are stifled? Finally, have you sought oneness with His heart—seeking His will in all things?

Friend, you can be a person of powerful and effective prayer. Don't give up or be blinded by feelings of defeat or doubt. Rather, be faithful to God in intercession, fight your battles on your knees, and trust Him. He hears—and He certainly answers.

God, I desire deep fellowship with You. Help
me understand the power of prayer, amen.

᪥

In His presence . . . pray believing.

YOUR INTERCESSOR

*He is able also to save forever those who draw
near to God through Him, since He always
lives to make intercession for them.*

HEBREWS 7:25

When you bear a great burden, you may feel isolated because it appears no one truly understands what you're experiencing. But take heart, Jesus knows and is praying for you. In fact, even before your struggle begins, He's interceding on your behalf.

Such was the case for Peter. As the Crucifixion neared, Jesus discerned Peter would face especially rigorous sifting by the enemy. So the Savior told His disciple, "I have prayed for you, that your faith may not fail; and you, when once you have turned again, strengthen your brothers" (Luke 22:32). In other words, "The time ahead will be tough, but I'm with you. And when you've made it through, support others who are hurting."

The same is true for you. You *will* survive this. So don't give up or stop trusting Him. Just focus on the wisdom and power of Jesus' prayers for you and know He's sustaining you every step of the way. Then when it's over, you'll have a ministry of encouragement to others who need to experience His love.

*Jesus, thank You for praying for me. I know I can
make it through anything with You, amen.*

꧑꧒

In His presence . . . trust His prayers.

RADIANT

Those who look to him for help will be radiant with
joy; no shadow of shame will darken their faces.
PSALM 34:5 NLT

It is said that many of the loveliest saints do not know their own beauty. The Holy Spirit works through them so effortlessly, they don't even realize His fruit has been made manifest in their lives. But those around them do.

So consider: Do you ever receive compliments that take you by surprise? Do people see things in you that you just don't perceive in yourself? Perhaps someone has recently called attention to the joy of your countenance or the love you so freely express. Or maybe it is your faithfulness and self-control others admire about you.

If so, give credit to God and thank Him—He is demonstrating His wonderful presence in and through you. You may not notice any difference in yourself. In fact, you may be even more aware of your faults and failings. But be encouraged, the glory of the Lord is shining through you. And every time you meet your heavenly Father, you reflect His likeness even more.

Lord Jesus, thank You for shining through me and
making me radiant with Your likeness. I pray others
will know You as Savior and love You more, amen.

༺ঔৡ༻

In His presence . . . reflect His glory.

BETTER THAN YOU IMAGINE

No mind has imagined what God has
prepared for those who love him.

1 CORINTHIANS 2:9 NLT

Are you tempted to dream about the desire of your heart, to imagine what it would be like to enjoy it fully? If so, you may be setting yourself up for a fall.

Why? Because what you think about determines how you live. And when you envision certain situations, expectations form in your mind. Your cravings grow stronger; your thoughts become lustful. Eventually you lean on your understanding of circumstances rather than trusting God for His blessings—and when that happens, sin and despair are sure to follow. As James 1:15 (NIV) testifies, "After desire has conceived, it gives birth to sin."

The good news is your imagination is no match for the Lord's. No matter what wonderful things you can conceive, His provision for you is even better (Ephesians 3:20).

So when you're tempted to dream about the desire of your heart, stop sin in its tracks by focusing on the Father's faithfulness, creativity, power, and wisdom. And thank Him, knowing that what He's creating for you is beyond what you can imagine.

Lord, please forgive my sin and teach me
to focus my mind on You, amen.

————————— ✺ —————————

In His presence . . . trust His plans.

PREPARATION FOR BLESSING

The LORD God is a sun and shield; the LORD
gives grace and glory; no good thing does He
withhold from those who walk uprightly.

PSALM 84:11

As you wait for God to fulfill His promises to you, the thought may enter your mind: *I'm not good enough for the Lord to bless—that's why this is taking so long. He finds me unworthy.*

Friend, nothing could be further from the truth. The fact the Father is making you wait means He sees precious qualities in you that must be developed so you can fully enjoy the blessing. He wants you to be a success. That means He must be your shield—protecting you from the wrong options. He must also be your glory—conforming you to His character, teaching you His wisdom, and preparing you for His power to shine through you.

No, friend, do not despair. He wouldn't withhold any blessing that is truly good for you. But you are so deeply loved that He wants you to receive the full beauty and impact of His gift. So trust Him in this waiting time and get ready to be profoundly blessed.

Lord, thank You for loving me. You are so wise and kind
in the way You bless me—so I will wait for You, amen.

In His presence . . . wait in hope.

FIGHTING TEMPTATION

Who will free me from . . . sin and death? Thank
God! The answer is in Jesus Christ.
ROMANS 7:24–25 NLT

Do you feel powerless against your sinful desires? Do you want to obey God but find yourself failing repeatedly? Perhaps you've realized willpower simply isn't enough to overcome your sinful drives. And it's true. If you want to fight temptation, you must do so as Jesus did—with His Word.

You see, sin begins with your thoughts—though they may appear innocent, they trigger a desire to meet your needs rather than allowing God to do so. You want to feel loved and respected, so lust springs up. Accepted—so you gossip and malign those who act unkindly toward you. Secure—so you chase money, relationships, and power. Clean—so you drown your shame with addictive behaviors that only add to your pain. But none of that works.

No, to stop sin, you must replace your thoughts and tactics with His truth.

Friend, you're a new creation in Christ—fully loved, accepted, secure, and clean. And Scripture is your best defense against temptation. So allow His truth to set you free and give you victory over sin.

Lord, thank You for cleansing me of sin and giving me
victory over temptation through Your Word, amen.

In His presence . . . find victory over temptation.

SEEK HIS UNDERSTANDING

*Trust in the LORD with all your heart and do
not lean on your own understanding.*

PROVERBS 3:5

You may wish to examine your situation—turn it over in your mind repeatedly and analyze it until you can figure out what's happening. In doing so, you try to control it—maintaining a false sense of security that can be painfully undermined when circumstances don't proceed the way you expect.

Don't fall for that trap. God's command is clear: *trust Him and don't rely on your understanding.* You don't have the full picture— only He does. Rather, when everything appears to contradict what the Father has promised you, remember that your view of the situation is limited and that your obedience to Him is more crucial than ever. Though everything within you may fight against it, remain pure, submissive, loving, faithful, self-controlled, forgiving, and above all, exhibit faith in His faultless character.

Don't allow your faulty perspective to drive you. Rather, "Humble [yourself] under the mighty hand of God, that He may exalt you at the proper time" (1 Peter 5:6). Seek Him and, soon enough, you'll see all the glorious work He's done on your behalf (Isaiah 64:4).

*Lord, my life is in Your hands. You're sovereign!
Thank You for directing my path perfectly, amen.*

In His presence . . . humbly trust His leadership.

MAY

WHAT YOU'RE ASKING

*"How much more will your heavenly Father
give good gifts to those who ask him."*
MATTHEW 7:11 NLT

Perhaps you've wondered, *How can I be sure I'm asking God for the right thing? How do I know my request is in line with His will?* Such thoughts may be causing you undue anxiety.

First, realize the Holy Spirit indwells you "to will and to work for His good pleasure" (Philippians 2:13). Not only does He help you pray, but He will show you *what* to pray to remain on His path for your life (Romans 8:26–27).

Second, God *wants* you to know His will. In fact, He's even more motivated to accomplish it than you are. So when you're seeking Him faithfully, you don't ever have to worry you'll miss it (Psalm 25:12).

Friend, if you're asking for something that would ultimately hurt you, your heavenly Father will change your heart. It may take time, but He wants the absolute best for you. So don't worry about whether you're asking the right thing. Rather, be sensitive to His guidance and trust Him to lead you to His good and perfect gifts.

*Father, I trust You to lead me in Your perfect
will. Thank You for loving, protecting,
and providing for me, amen.*

❧

In His presence . . . pray without fear.

KNOWING GOD

Set your heart and your soul to seek the LORD your God.
1 CHRONICLES 22:19

Never underestimate how significant you are to God—or how important He wants to be to you. You were created to know Him—to fellowship with Him and represent Him to others.

Sadly, when you only know facts about the Lord rather than truly experiencing Him, you may not fully grasp how deeply He loves you or the wonderful plans He has for your life. You'll also sense an abiding void in your life that nothing can fill.

So consider, are you seeking information about the Father or are you really getting to know Him? Are you pursuing God to receive a blessing or is your interest intimate fellowship with your Creator?

The Father wants you to understand far more about Him than just what He can do for you—He wants you to experience His eternal, all-sufficient, loving presence. He wants to satisfy the deepest parts of your being and heal the wounded places of your heart. So surrender yourself to Him with a complete and intimate trust. Be vulnerable with Him, hold nothing back, and discover the One your soul truly desires.

Lord, I want to know You. Draw me into Your
loving presence and reveal Yourself to me, amen.

In His presence . . . know Him.

A Fresh Outlook

With You is the fountain of life; in Your light we see light.
PSALM 36:9

When you meditate upon the Lord, you'll see life from a different perspective. The issues that worry you lose their grip; the burdens that weaken you, God will turn to strength. Your viewpoint of relationships, tasks, problems, your enemies, and even your own personhood changes because you learn to see them all with the Father's wisdom.

Of course, when you first approach the throne of grace, your frustration levels may be high. But the pressures will dissipate as you sit still before God, who accomplishes all things for you. After all, you'll come face-to-face with the One who is fully able to help you with whatever concerns you. Why should you be afraid? There's nothing that can defeat your God, who protects, provides for, and delivers you from all harm.

Friend, true biblical meditation will transform your spirit, emotions, and even your physical body. So today, spend time focusing your attention on God. Surely He will provide a fresh outlook for your life and peaceful rest for your soul, despite the difficulties of the day.

Father, remind me always to seek You
for every burden so that I may have Your
perspective and rest in Your care, amen.

In His presence . . . seek His
perspective on all that concerns you.

OBEY GOD

"Obey me, and I will be your God, and you will be my people. Do everything as I say, and all will be well!"

JEREMIAH 7:23 NLT

Today, no matter what you face, *obey God and leave the consequences to Him*. Perhaps there's a decision that immediately springs to mind. Regardless of how difficult or seemingly impossible the path the Lord calls you to, do as He says.

If there's a conflict, be a wise and humble peacemaker (2 Timothy 2:24–26). If anxieties arise, trust the Father (Isaiah 41:10). If someone wrongs you, be forgiving (Ephesians 4:32) and trust God for vindication (Isaiah 54:17). If others are hurting, be comforting (2 Corinthians 1:3–4). If a person you encounter is burdened with sin, proclaim the gospel (John 3:16).

If you need guidance, pray (Psalm 32:8). If temptations assail you, flee (1 Corinthians 10:13). And in every task you are given, "Do your work heartily, as for the Lord rather than for men" (Colossians 3:23).

Friend, you simply cannot go wrong when you obey God. So trust Him even if it is difficult. And be assured that He will certainly bless your faithfulness.

Lord, I will obey You. Show me what to do and give me the courage and wisdom to carry out Your will, amen.

❊

In His presence . . . submit to His wisdom.

ALWAYS WITH YOU

"Be sure of this: I am with you always,
even to the end of the age."
MATTHEW 28:20 NLT

Are you aware of God's presence with you—even right now? This is a reality that, at times, cannot be sensed with your emotions. In fact, if you're hurting or facing a great deal of stress, the Father may seem distant indeed. But if you're a believer, He has given His Holy Spirit to indwell you—so He is *always* with you (Ephesians 1:13–14). It's an absolute fact: *you can never be out of His presence.*

Allow this to give you confidence today. The all-powerful God, your wise Creator and loving Lord, doesn't leave you to fight battles or figure things out by yourself. His perfect strength, unlimited knowledge, and unfailing love sustain you always—even when you don't perceive His presence.

So look for God's intervention, ask what He is teaching you, be sensitive to His promptings, and acknowledge His blessings. Keep watch for His activity in your life. Because when you see how dynamically He is working on your behalf, you'll be amazed at how profoundly amazing His love and provision for you really are.

Lord, make me sensitive to Your presence.
Thank You for opening my spiritual eyes
to Your love and activity, amen.

In His presence . . . acknowledge His provision.

WAIT IN HOPE

We wait in hope for the LORD; he is our help and our shield.
PSALM 33:20 NIV

It can feel as if things will never change. Your challenges persist—perhaps over an extended period of time—and it seems all your prayers are met with closed doors. Like David, you cry out, "How long, O LORD? Will You forget me forever?" (Psalm 13:1).

But take heart. Your dark moments will last only as long as is necessary for God to accomplish His good purposes. And your heavenly Father is well aware of your limits.

You *can* endure. You *will* overcome this. How? By turning to the Savior often—in prayer and through His Word. Whenever you feel weak, go to His throne of grace and find the strength you need—even if it's every two minutes. He will sustain you. He *wants* to teach you His ways, build His character in you, and grow your faith. Just rely on Him.

Friend, don't give up—this pain will end. You *will* prevail over this difficulty and your circumstances *will* change. Look to God to uphold you as He works out His good purposes.

Lord, I will hope in You. Thank You for
sustaining me and teaching me Your
ways during this dark time, amen.

❧

In His presence . . . wait
expectantly for His deliverance.

ANCHORED

*"My word . . . will not return . . . without
succeeding in the matter for which I sent it."*
ISAIAH 55:11

Anchor yourself to God's Word. No matter what storms arise, His truth always stands firm and prevails. Every form of earthly security may disappoint you, but Scripture will not. It *cannot*. Backed by the awesome power of almighty God, His promises are fully accomplished and absolutely victorious (1 Kings 8:56).

However, here is the true challenge: believing Scripture when all else seems contrary. This is what Peter faced as he walked on the wind-battered sea to Jesus (Matthew 14:25–33). Though Jesus called him, he was distracted by the storm and began to sink under the raging waves. But genuine faith takes God's Word as even more reliable than whatever else may appear—no matter how real it seems.

Likewise, as you cling to God's promises during the storms, eventually you'll come to a crisis of faith; either you'll accept what He says and put it to practice, or you'll sink back into your state of helplessness. Keep your eyes on the Savior and your heart anchored to Scripture. His Word doesn't fail, and neither will you when you trust Him.

*Jesus, help me cling to Your Word during the
storm, believing You above all else, amen.*

———————————— ✺ ————————————

In His presence . . . trust His Word.

Deal with It

"When He, the Spirit of truth, comes,
He will guide you into all truth."
JOHN 16:13

Whenever you pray about a certain topic, do particular emotions or failings come to mind? If so, the Holy Spirit may be bringing them to the surface so you'll deal with them.

For example, if you try to pray for a person, but begin tearing the individual apart in your mind instead, it's likely the Father is revealing your envy or unforgiveness. Take your feelings of anger or jealousy to the Lord.

Or perhaps as you intercede for another, lustful thoughts unexpectedly assail you. God is not tempting you—He is revealing the sin hidden in your heart so you can repent.

It may even be that as you're praying about a challenge, the Father repeatedly reminds you of an incident from your childhood. It's not a mistake—He is revealing truth to you. Don't ignore it; rather, ask Him what it means.

The Lord desires to heal you to the core of your being—even in the places you've forgotten exist. So listen to Him and deal with whatever He surfaces, confident He is leading you to freedom.

Lord, I repent of these hidden sins. Thank You for
surfacing these issues and liberating me of them, amen.

In His presence . . . allow Him to set you free.

BE AVAILABLE

*"He who believes in Me, the works that I do, he will
do also; and greater works than these he will do."*

JOHN 14:12

When you feel useless, remember, God has an important purpose for your life. Of course, you may be tempted to focus on the reasons the Lord would overlook you—such as failings and feelings of inadequacy. But this simply shows you're looking in the wrong direction—at yourself rather than the Lord (2 Corinthians 4:7).

Friend, you have the Spirit of the living God actively working through you. You're a living testimony of His amazing power, wisdom, and salvation—whether you feel it or not. And the truth is, *everyone* you meet needs the love and hope Jesus offers. You can be a blessing just by listening and reminding them of the Savior's perfect grace and provision.

So the question isn't, *Can* God use you? It's, *Will you* allow Him to care for others through you? Will you show people the awesome, unconditional, sacrificial love of Jesus? Your part is simple—just be available for Him to do His great works through you. He will certainly do the rest.

*Lord, use me to draw others to You. Help
me proclaim Your salvation and inspire
others to love You more, amen.*

❧

**In His presence . . . allow Him to
love others through you.**

WORTHY OF YOUR PRAISE

I call upon the Lord, who is worthy to be praised.
PSALM 18:3

There may certainly be times when you find it challenging to praise God. Conflicts and burdens can weigh so heavily on your heart that worry and despair consume you.

But even during times of adversity, your Savior is worthy of your adoration. Jesus has not only given you eternal life (John 3:16) and conquered every challenge you face (John 16:33), but He loves you with an everlasting love (Jeremiah 31:3) and would never abandon you (Hebrews 13:5).

This is the very reason you must set aside time to know Him. Because when you meditate on His Word, you discover who He really is—wonderful, holy, omnipotent, wise, and merciful God. And the better you know your loving Lord, the more you'll want to exalt Him for who He is and all He's done for you.

So what's preventing you from praising God? Do your circumstances seem overwhelming? Then take a moment to be still before Him. Think about Jesus—His unconditional love, His unfailing friendship, and His wonderful plans for your life. Focus on Him. Soon enough, the praise will certainly flow.

Jesus, You are certainly worthy of my praise and
adoration! To You be all the glory and honor! Amen.

⊷⊶

In His presence . . . praise His name.

WINNING THE WAR

Our struggle is not against flesh and blood, but against . . . the spiritual forces of wickedness.

EPHESIANS 6:12

Do you ever feel like you're engaged in a war? Perhaps situations explode without cause, prompting division, strife, and undue stress. Simple tasks become complicated. Miscommunication abounds. Temptations and frustrations increase. And all the while, you're bombarded with terrible thoughts of defeat and worthlessness.

Friend, you're in a spiritual battle, and your enemy is trying to undermine your faith and impede your progress. Satan cannot destroy your soul, but he can demolish your effectiveness. And he does so by building strongholds in your life that influence your thoughts and actions—ultimately enslaving you to sin. Thus he renders you ineffective for the kingdom of God. Don't fall for his trap.

Instead, defeat the enemy by declaring your trust in God. Allow the Lord to identify strongholds and deliver you from them. Remember who you are in Christ. The Lord is greater than any weapon the enemy can bring against you. So commit yourself to God wholeheartedly and let Him defend you.

Father, open my eyes to the enemy's strongholds and tactics. Thank You for Your protection and deliverance, amen.

❧

In His presence . . . is ultimate victory.

FORGIVE

Forgive anyone who offends you. Remember, the
Lord forgave you, so you must forgive others.

COLOSSIANS 3:13 NLT

Who is it that you need to forgive? Even now, the Holy Spirit brings the person to mind because He wants to liberate you from bitterness. He may even remind you of individuals you thought you'd already pardoned and prompt you to examine your heart. Listen to Him—He knows when more healing is necessary.

Likewise, you may be tempted to stop reading because confronting unresolved anger is painful. But realize, unforgiveness can damage your health, thwart your peace, hinder your joy, and harm your relationships. Bitterness prevents you from living the abundant life God created you to enjoy. And as long as you refuse to forgive the offender, you allow him or her to control you.

Friend, don't allow resentment to imprison you. Release your anger to the Lord and trust Him to heal you. The Father knows what's happened and He judges the situation with wisdom and righteousness. So let go of the pain, forgive, and trust Him to vindicate you. Then allow Him to heal your heart as only He can.

Lord, please help me forgive. Heal me
of this bitterness and show me how
to live in Your freedom, amen.

In His presence . . . forgive those who've hurt you.

BE PATIENT

*Let us hold unswervingly to the hope we
profess, for he who promised is faithful.*
HEBREWS 10:23 NIV

Do not run ahead of God's purposes. Be patient. Expect Him to show you His path and provision.

If you've waited a long time to see the desire of your heart come to fruition, this may be exceedingly difficult. It was for Abraham and Sarah. And after hoping for a child for so many years, Sarah's faith failed and she decided to take matters into her own hands. She offered her maidservant Hagar to Abraham as a surrogate.

But it was a colossal misstep that had unimaginably destructive consequences. You can see in the Middle East how descendants of Hagar's son Ishmael and Sarah's son Isaac continue to fight to this day (Genesis 16–17, 21).

Do not make the same mistake. Don't run ahead of the Lord's timing. Patience is a fruit of the Holy Spirit, restraining you and allowing you to persevere until the Father fulfills His good purposes for you. He will help you endure if you turn to Him. Yes, it is difficult, but absolutely worthwhile. So wait for Him and enjoy the fullness of His blessing.

*Lord, it's so difficult to wait. Strengthen me with
Your Spirit and keep me focused on You, amen.*

In His presence . . . trust His timing.

First Focus

*"Seek first His kingdom and His righteousness,
and all these things will be added to you."*
MATTHEW 6:33

What is it that you desire first and foremost? Is God the focus of your life or have other people and dreams taken His place in your heart?

Friend, nothing can satisfy you as He can. So if you're struggling with feelings of doubt, anger, jealousy, fear, despair, or bitterness, it may be that you've allowed a goal or relationship to become an idol in your life. In fact, Isaiah 26:3 (NKJV) promises, "You will keep him in perfect peace, whose mind is stayed on You, because he trusts in You." So when you lack God's peace, it is evidence your focus is misplaced.

Therefore, in your prayer time, ask God to reveal anything that is preventing you from experiencing His love. Be willing to let go of whatever is taking His place in your life and ask Him to stir up your desire for Him. Because when you seek God first, the blessings will come. And not only will He reveal Himself to you, but He also will use you as a blessing to others.

*Lord, reveal whatever has taken Your
place in my life. Take Your throne in my
heart and be my first focus, amen.*

In His presence . . . acknowledge Him as your life.

SUCCESS

The world and its desires pass away, but
whoever does the will of God lives forever.
1 JOHN 2:17 NIV

Today, remember that God's definition of success may be different from the standards you measure yourself by. From early on, you might have been taught that power, wealth, fame, position, beauty, or knowledge determines your worth. However, such a belief is destructive—inspiring pride about the things you've accomplished and despair over setbacks and disappointments. That's no way to live.

The Father, however, does not appraise you according to these faulty, temporary standards. To Him, you're important, lovable, and valuable even before you're born. This means success is not about proving yourself, but about honoring Him and becoming all He created you to be.

So instead of chasing after what is fleeting and unsatisfying for your worth, seek God's eternal purposes for your life through an intimate relationship with Him. See challenges as coming from His hand and glorify Him in them. And remember, setbacks here on earth are merely platforms for His praise (2 Corinthians 12:9–10). So trust Him and be assured—those who do His will always succeed.

Jesus, help me do Your will in all things so
I may glorify Your holy name, amen.

In His presence . . . remember He defines true success.

DEMONSTRATIONS OF POWER

*Don't be afraid. Just stand still and
watch the LORD rescue you.*
EXODUS 14:13 NLT

Are you experiencing situations that you're absolutely powerless to manage on your own? Perhaps you're facing vocational, physical, relational, or financial challenges that make you feel completely helpless and you wonder, *God, why have You allowed this?*

No doubt the children of Israel felt the same way as they stood defenseless between the advancing Egyptian army and the impassable Red Sea. Yet the Lord had not abandoned them. He was teaching them a lesson they would need repeatedly as they followed Him—that their weaknesses were simply the place to display His profound power. And as they stood watching, God divided the mighty waters of the sea and allowed them to pass on dry ground.

Friend, you do not have to feel afraid or helpless. The Lord is with you—He opens the way before you with His wise, omnipotent hand. He has allowed these circumstances for the purpose of demonstrating you can count on Him completely. So do not fear. Obey His direction and trust Him to deliver you.

*Lord, I'm overwhelmed by these challenges, but I
will trust You. Thank You for showing me Your
power and making a way for me, amen.*

❧

In His presence . . . praise Him for His mighty power.

FREEDOM THROUGH HIS LOVE

Stand fast therefore in the liberty by which Christ has made us free, and do not be entangled again with a yoke of bondage.

GALATIANS 5:1 NKJV

God loves you unconditionally. He doesn't care for you less when you fail or more when you accomplish great things for Him. His devotion to you is based on His unfailing character—not anything you can say or do (Romans 5:8).

Take this to heart regardless of how your situation turns out today. If circumstances go awry, you may wonder if God is punishing you. But remember that Jesus paid the full penalty for your sins—past, present, and future—by His death (Romans 6:23). The Father will discipline you to liberate you from your bondage to sin (Hebrews 12:5–11), but He will never condemn you (Romans 8:1).

Friend, you don't have to earn God's love or try harder. You're precious in His sight, covered by the priceless blood of Jesus, and indwelt by His Holy Spirit. Don't hide your heart or fear you're not good enough for Him to care for you. Accept His love, obey Him, and allow Him to keep you in His wonderful freedom.

Jesus, thank You for accepting me fully. Help me love You with my life in return, amen.

❧

In His presence . . . trust His love.

The Desired Haven

He stilled the storm to a whisper. . . . They were glad when
it grew calm, and he guided them to their desired haven.

Psalm 107:29–30 NIV

The desires and goals God has put in your heart may appear exceedingly far away. But your heavenly Father has the wisdom and power necessary to get you to your destination. He understands the best, most effective way to take you—the path that prepares you perfectly for what is ahead. No, it may not be the way you would have chosen for yourself, but be assured—there is no more wonderful or impactful plan for your life than the one He has created for you.

Some people fail to follow God because they're afraid of the storms of adversity that arise. But those difficulties are necessary for the Father to reach the deepest places of your soul and grow to your full potential. He does so not to hurt you, but to mature you. Not to limit you, but to show you what's possible and to ready you for His astounding purposes.

So cling to Him and trust His navigation. And be absolutely assured—He will get you to your desired haven.

Lord, You are my faithful Commander—always
leading me perfectly. Help me trust You more, amen.

In His presence . . . trust His direction.

OBEDIENT PATIENCE

Rest in the LORD, and wait patiently for Him. . . .
Do not fret—it only causes harm.
PSALM 37:7–8 NKJV

It is never wise to know God's will and disregard it. If the Father has insisted you wait for Him, then the only wise course is to remain patient until He shows you how to proceed. To do otherwise may mean delaying His blessings—or worse, forfeiting them altogether.

King Saul found this out the hard way. He was well aware that the Lord had appointed Samuel to make the sacrifices. However, with an enormous Philistine army arrayed against his small Israelite forces, he grew exceedingly fearful. The prophet had not arrived to administer the offering, his men were deserting him, enemy soldiers were growing restless, and Saul knew he couldn't defeat the Philistines without God's help. So he disobeyed God and made the sacrifice himself. And because of his impatience, the Lord tore the kingdom from his hands (1 Samuel 13:1–14).

Do not make the same mistake. Don't act out of fear. Whatever the decision, wait for God. He will show you what to do and bless your obedient patience.

Father, I will wait for You. I know You hear me and
will answer my prayers in Your perfect time, amen.

In His presence . . . wait with patient expectation.

ETERNAL YIELD

Those who live to please the Spirit will harvest
everlasting life from the Spirit. So let's not get tired
of doing what is good. At just the right time we will
reap a harvest of blessing if we don't give up.
GALATIANS 6:8–9 NLT

At times you may wonder if the time you spend in prayer, reading God's Word, and waiting in His presence has any real impact. Friend, it absolutely does. Though you may not feel any closer to Him, practicing these spiritual disciplines increases the Father's influence in your life—especially as you obey Him.

But like everything else in the Christian life, trusting the Father to transform you "by the renewing of your mind" (Romans 12:2) as you seek Him is an act of faith. You're sowing unseen seeds to the Spirit, who then grows an amazing, eternal harvest of love, joy, peace, patience, kindness, gentleness, goodness, self-control, and faithfulness in you. Often you don't detect that His fruit is showing through you—but others do. And they love the Lord more because of it.

So don't despair. Keep seeking God. And be confident that the time you spend with Him is yielding great eternal rewards.

Lord, thank You for transforming me during these
quiet times. May my life glorify You always, amen.

In His presence . . . trust He's transforming you.

THE PURPOSE OF BROKENNESS

When He has tried me, I shall come forth as gold.

JOB 23:10

If you keep experiencing the same type of trial repeatedly, it means the Lord is instructing you. Most likely you have a pattern of thought or behavior that is contrary to who you are as His child and He must bring it to the surface to heal you of it. In order to set you free, He targets areas of self-will, destructive attitudes, and anything in your life that does not honor Him.

Take heart. This is painful for the moment, but the Father is liberating you from your self-sufficiency so that He can demonstrate His sovereign power and wisdom through you. Unfortunately, it's only through brokenness that you'll truly stop depending on your limited resources and start relying wholeheartedly upon Him.

So what is it in your life that the Lord keeps addressing? What is keeping you from trusting Him fully?

Friend, He is God—wise, loving, and always working for your ultimate benefit. So surrender control of every area of your life to Him and allow Him to determine what can remain in your life and what must go.

> *Father, I don't want to keep going through*
> *these trials. Please teach me and help me*
> *rely upon You wholeheartedly, amen.*

In His presence . . . learn from your brokenness.

Absolutely Convinced

I know whom I have believed and I am convinced that He is able to guard what I have entrusted to Him until that day.

2 Timothy 1:12

Trust God. Believe with every fiber of your being that He will faithfully fulfill His promises. Do not just say, "I *hope* the Lord will come to my aid." Do not merely stop at declaring, "I know He *can* work everything out." Exhibit the highest level of faith by proclaiming, "I am *absolutely certain* my heavenly Father *will* help me—it's as good as done."

With such a profound confidence in the Lord, you don't have to worry. You realize you can endure no matter what happens because of who He is—your faithful God who is able to do all things on your behalf. Absolutely nothing is impossible for Him!

But what if I misunderstood Him? you may wonder. Then the Father will gently correct you. He wants you to know and do His will so He won't hide His ways from you.

So thank the Lord for answering your prayers. And trust Him completely. Certainly He *will* fulfill His promises and take care of you regardless of what happens.

> *Lord, I'm absolutely certain You will*
> *help me. Undoubtedly, Your promises*
> *are as good as fulfilled! Amen.*

In His presence . . . believe Him completely.

A WORTHY LIFE

Live a life worthy of the Lord.
COLOSSIANS 1:10 NIV

Friend, do not doubt your worth. Your life is important. The Father created you with love and wisdom for a purpose. And because His Spirit indwells you, what you say and do can have an enormous influence on others. The question is: Are you willing to live in a way that exalts Him?

Whether you realize it or not, your relationship with God can motivate others to seek Him. If those who know you could see how deeply He loves, comforts, and strengthens you, they would want to know Him as well (2 Corinthians 4:5–7).

So ask yourself, when others watch you face trials, do they witness your faith in the Savior's wisdom and provision? Could they say your relationship with Him is not in word only, but a very real part of your life? Can they observe His powerful activity in how you live daily?

Follow the Father obediently in faith and demonstrate your love for Christ to everyone you meet. He will work through you and everyone will see how precious your life and your Savior truly are.

Lord, help me live a life worthy of You.
May others know You as I bear witness
of Your loving character, amen.

❈

In His presence . . . reflect His character and love.

CHOOSE HIS PEACE

"Peace I leave with you; My peace I give to you;
not as the world gives do I give to you. Do not let
your heart be troubled, nor let it be fearful."

JOHN 14:27

When you focus on what you can accomplish instead of God's power, your life will be characterized by defeat and frustration rather than victory, peace, and joy. Perhaps you are discouraged right now. Maybe you've been disillusioned by unmanageable circumstances and delayed dreams. But this is a sure indicator that you're relying on the wrong foundation for your hope and security.

There is only one source of true peace—the Lord God Almighty, who holds the entire universe together. The tranquility of soul He gives is not dependent upon circumstances but upon your personal relationship with Him and your faith in His perfect power, wisdom, and love.

So today and every day, you have a choice. You can either dwell on your limited resources and negative circumstances, or you can choose to trust God. Friend, surrender to Him—because with the Father as your focus, you can face every day with His indescribable peace.

Lord God, I choose to focus on Your wisdom,
power, and love instead of my circumstances.
Thank You for being my peace, amen.

❦

In His presence . . . find true peace.

Right Hearing

"My people shall know My name; therefore they shall know
in that day that I am He who speaks: 'Behold, it is I.'"
Isaiah 52:6 NKJV

Sometimes the prevailing question that will continue to burden your soul is: *How can I know for sure I've heard God correctly?* You can trust the Father to show you His will. So in prayer and time in His Word, ask the following questions:

> *Lord, is what I've heard consistent with Scripture? Please show*
> *me Your will clearly through Your Word.*
> *Jesus, does this fit Your overall plan for my life?*
> *God, is this a genuine peace I have in my spirit or am I*
> *overlooking something You desire to show me?*
> *Father, am I honoring, obeying, and glorifying You in pursuing this?*

If the issue drives a wedge between you and the Savior, then you know it's not His will. So continue listening to the Lord carefully and do not ignore His promptings. And don't allow doubt, fear, or sin to keep you from obeying Him. Rather, continue seeking His face until you are absolutely confident you've heard His voice.

> *Father, lead me clearly, powerfully, and irresistibly to*
> *do Your will. Help me please You with my life, amen.*

In His presence . . . listen carefully.

ROCK BOTTOM

He brought me up out of the pit of destruction . . .
and He set my feet upon a rock.
PSALM 40:2

This is not the end. God knows exactly what He is doing. At times the Lord will allow you to hit rock bottom in order to separate you from destructive dependencies. It's only when He removes everything you usually count on that you discover the only real security is in Jesus.

This was the case for the people of Judah. Their land, inheritance, and history were the foundation for their national identity. But when they were deported to Babylon by an invading army and separated from all they knew, they realized their true security was in God alone. And when they had repented and the time was right, the Lord faithfully returned them to the land He'd promised them.

Likewise, the Father wants to set you free from the bondage you have to this world. So when trouble comes, remember that your smartest course of action is to turn to God. He has your best interest in mind, so praise Him and trust He's using exactly what's necessary to set you free and plant your feet on solid ground.

Lord, You are my Protector and Provider, my only
genuine refuge. Thank You for safeguarding me, amen.

In His presence . . . discover true security.

Restoring Your Passion

God has not given us a spirit of timidity, but of power and love and discipline.

2 Timothy 1:7

With enough pressure and disappointments, the passion you have for God can wane. The apostle Paul understood that Timothy was in such danger. Persecution against believers was rampant and false teachers were infiltrating Timothy's church, causing terrible division. Under such strain, anyone could become tired, dispirited, cynical, and could even question if efforts to serve the Lord were in vain.

But Paul taught Timothy how to stay strong, and you can benefit from his counsel as well (2 Timothy 1:3–14). How? First, acknowledge you're experiencing difficulty. Second, do as you did when you were really on fire for God—study His Word, praise Him, exercise your gifts, and fellowship with believers who encourage you. Third, repent of any sins, admitting that you need Him and want to live in a way that honors Him.

Like Timothy, stir up your passion for God and take hold of the Spirit of love, power, and discipline He's given you. He will not only restore your spiritual fire, He'll make you a shining light to a world that desperately needs Him.

Lord, I love You. Please restore the joy of Your salvation and my passion for Your presence, amen.

In His presence . . . regain your passion.

TRUSTING IN THE SILENCE

"If you believe, you will see the glory of God."
JOHN 11:40

When you are desperate for help and direction, God's silence can feel disheartening. You wonder if He has forgotten you or if He really cares at all.

Certainly, as Martha and Mary waited for their dear friend Jesus to respond to their pleas, they grew increasingly desperate. Their brother, Lazarus, was dying and they knew Jesus could easily heal him. If Jesus would just respond in time, surely Lazarus would be okay. But Jesus tarried. And Lazarus died.

However, do not think the delay was because Jesus didn't love them. He did. Rather, when He finally arrived, He used the opportunity to glorify the Father and deepen their faith by raising Lazarus from the dead (John 11:1–45).

Likewise, God's silence to you is not to dishearten you but to bring you to a new level of intimacy with Him. So do not despair and do not sin. Keep seeking Him passionately, knowing He will answer you. And He will reward your intense desire for His will with a greater revelation of His character than you've ever known.

Jesus, I will trust even when You are silent. I
want Your will more than anything, amen.

⚜

**In His presence . . . believe He will
answer you powerfully.**

SELF-CONTROL IN MEDITATION

I discipline my body and bring it into subjection, lest, when I
have preached to others, I myself should become disqualified.

1 CORINTHIANS 9:27 NKJV

Self-control is a necessary discipline in meditation. There are so
many things competing for your notice, it may be difficult to keep
your focus on God. But strive to do so anyway. When maintaining
your attention on Him is a problem, turn to Psalms and ask Him to
work through His Word to direct your mind. Pray, "Father, immerse
me in these psalms and reveal Yourself to me through them."

Read Scripture until the Lord speaks to you. Don't be discouraged if it takes a while. Soon enough, He will turn your mind to His
will and His ways. Think about Him. Become lost in His love and
grandeur. And when He shows you His truth, write it down.

Friend, there's nothing better, more productive, or more
rewarding than to align your mind with the Father and ponder the
great thoughts of almighty God.

Therefore, make the commitment. Take deliberate steps each
day to control your mind and focus your attention on the Lord.
Surely He will speak to you powerfully.

Father, help me control my thoughts and focus my
attention on You. I delight in Your presence, amen.

——————— ❈ ———————

In His presence . . . exercise
self-control and focus on Him.

THANKFUL ALWAYS

I will give thanks to the LORD with all my heart.
PSALM 9:1

If you desire to have deep and lasting joy, it's important for you to develop an attitude of appreciation. You must decide to see the good in situations and choose to be thankful regardless of what goes wrong.

So begin right now by counting your blessings. Think about what it cost Jesus to have a relationship with you. Be grateful for the amazing forgiveness He's given—pardoning your sins past, present, and future.

Meditate on your wonderful God, who would never leave or forsake you, but loves, protects, and provides for you always. Consider the Holy Spirit, your Advocate in all that concerns you. He empowers you to serve successfully and gives you all you need for life and godliness.

Finally, consider the wonderful plans God has for you and all the loved ones He's given you to share your life with.

Friend, you have so much to be grateful for. Surely the Lord is worthy of your praise. So worship God and give Him thanks in every situation. Because you're a child of God and truly, "praise is becoming to the upright" (Psalm 33:1).

Lord, I am so grateful for You! Thank You for
loving me and making me Your own, amen.

In His presence . . . give thanks and praise Him.

EAGLE-LIKE FOCUS

Those who wait for the LORD will gain new strength;
they will mount up with wings like eagles.

ISAIAH 40:31

Seeking and obeying God can be difficult, especially in a world that is often adversarial to believers. So when you're tired of the battles and just want some peace, what do you do? Do you give in? Compromise? Or do you find your strength in your Creator?

Scripture is clear—if you want to soar, you must take your eyes off of what everyone else is doing and focus on the Father.

The eagle is the perfect example. When fish come into view, eagles train their sights on their targets with amazing intensity. Regardless of wind currents or weather, they sweep in with power and precision—their mighty talons successfully gathering their prize.

In a sense, this is your goal as a believer—to set your full focus on God. He gives you the strength, precision, and perseverance so you can continue flying and receive your reward (1 Corinthians 9:27).

So when you're weary, remember to train your sights on the Father. With Him, the victory is always in view.

Lord, I wait on You. Give me Your energy, strength,
and focus so I can continue to obey You, amen.

❧

In His presence . . . gain strength to persevere.

JUNE

FOR THE LORD

*Whatever you do, do your work heartily, as for
the Lord rather than for men, knowing that
from the Lord you will receive the reward.*
COLOSSIANS 3:23–24

Are you being called upon to make challenging sacrifices? There
are times when you may be required to take on jobs or responsibilities that are difficult or you deem "beneath you," and you may
be tempted to nurse a bad attitude. But don't. Right now there's
nothing more victorious you can do than to give your best effort
for the Lord.

Friend, your mind-set about what you have to do makes a tremendous difference—directly affecting your task now, but also
impacting eternity. Why? Because one day you will stand in the
presence of Jesus and be judged for what you've done and how you
honored Him in what He gave you to accomplish.

Keep this in mind as you go about your day. You may have
many unpleasant responsibilities to take care of, but do them joyfully for God, knowing that He will reward your loving obedience.
That change in perspective alone will make all the difference in
your day—and also in eternity.

*Lord, whatever I'm called to do, I will do it joyfully and
with excellence, knowing I am serving You, amen.*

In His presence . . . do everything for His glory.

STOP, LOOK, LISTEN

My soul waits in silence for God only; from Him is my salvation.
PSALM 62:1

Growing up, I recall hearing my first-grade teacher remind us repeatedly to stop, look, and listen before crossing railroad tracks. That was before we had flashing red lights, warning bells, and those long arms that swing down and block entry onto the rails.

Of course her purpose for this caution was our safety. But through the years, I've often pondered the wisdom of her words. No doubt our impulse to hurry—rather than fully assess a situation—can harm us terribly. We have to be careful because with every passing year, it seems life accelerates a bit more.

So when you're in a rush, consider, "What am I missing by moving at such a pace?" By rushing through life, you may forfeit the best of what God has for you—the blessings of His presence, godly friendships and a strong family, and—worst of all—His will.

Do not make that mistake. Stop by waiting in His presence. Look for His activity and leading. And listen for His direction.

> *Lord, I will stop, look, and listen for Your*
> *instruction. Thank You for keeping me safe and*
> *leading me to life at its very best, amen.*

In His presence . . . wait for Him to lead you.

OVERCOMING MOUNTAINS

Every valley shall be raised up, every mountain and hill
made low. . . . And the glory of the LORD will be revealed.
ISAIAH 40:4–5 NIV

When you face a mountain in your life, you have a choice: be overwhelmed or be energized because you know the Savior will reveal Himself in a profound way to you.

Of course, your first thought may be, *If I were really in God's will, I wouldn't be facing obstacles—especially ones this enormous.* But that is not so. You have an enemy who will oppose you whenever he sees the Lord doing anything great through you. You can be in the center of God's plan, doing exactly as He says, and encounter a mount of opposition.

But don't focus on the mountain, friend. Look at almighty God who loves and provides for you. He can handle the troubles before you with ease (Matthew 21:21). And if you respond correctly—with faith—your relationship with Him will grow stronger and He will be glorified.

So don't give up! Look to God and trust Him. You'll be amazed at how He levels the mountains before you.

Lord, thank You for taking care of the
mountain before me—it is nothing to You.
I praise You, my Savior! Amen.

In His presence . . . watch for the Savior's deliverance.

YOUR UNASSAILABLE SALVATION

*It is by free grace (God's unmerited favor) that you are
saved (delivered from judgment and made partakers
of Christ's salvation) through [your] faith. And this
[salvation] is not of yourselves [of your own doing, it came
not through your own striving], but it is the gift of God.*

EPHESIANS 2:8 AMP

Remember this today whenever you doubt your relationship with
the Father: the enemy knows that if he can convince you that your
salvation is vulnerable, he can render you discouraged and ineffective. Any thoughts and feelings you have that God is mad at you or
no longer loves you are the evil one's lies. Do not listen to him!

Your salvation has never been based on your own goodness or
how you feel. Rather, it has *always* been unfalteringly founded on
Jesus' sacrifice on the cross. As a forgiven, beloved child of the living God, your position is safe, unassailable, and sure for eternity.

Friend, do not allow the enemy to discourage you. Stand on the
fact of your salvation and the perfect provision of your wonderful
Savior.

*Lord Jesus, thank You for being my Redeemer, loving me
unconditionally, and saving me permanently. I praise
You, my all-sufficient and unassailable Savior! Amen.*

**In His presence . . . give thanks that
your salvation is eternally secure.**

YOUR HIGH CALLING

Be sure to carry out the ministry the Lord gave you.
COLOSSIANS 4:17 NLT

Do you find God must constantly prod you to keep growing in your faith? Or perhaps you've progressed in your relationship with Him, but there's not much fruit and you wonder what's going on?

If so, then it may be that the Lord has called you to serve Him in a specific way, but you've refused. It's possible that you're not using your gifts to honor Him, or you are ministering in areas that make you feel comfortable rather than really obeying what He's asked you to do.

Friend, you may have your own goals, but remember, the highest, most wonderful purpose you can embrace is to faithfully carry out whatever He specifically created you to do (Ephesians 2:10). Those who follow Him in such a way encounter adversity, yes, but they also experience the power of the Holy Spirit—for guidance, faith, hope, and strength when doing the Father's will.

That is life at its very best. So don't settle for anything less. Be sure to carry out the ministry He gives you.

Lord, where would You have me serve You?
What did You create me to do? Lead me—
I will obey and glorify You, amen.

In His presence . . . discover all you were created for.

WHOLEHEARTEDLY

*"You will seek Me and find Me when you
search for Me with all your heart."*
JEREMIAH 29:13

Do not get frustrated or discouraged when it appears difficult to seek the Father. You may wonder why He doesn't just make Himself known to you. But don't despair, He is training you to find Him. How does He do so?

First God develops your trust by stretching you beyond your comfort level. Romans 8:24–25 explains, "Hope that is seen is not hope; for who hopes for what he already sees? But if we hope for what we do not see, with perseverance we wait eagerly for it." And so the Father remains silent for a time so you'll persist in seeking Him and increase in faith.

Second, the Lord teaches you to depend upon Him rather than any earthly crutch. He sustains everything in the universe with His power and He wants you to realize it. So He brings you to the point where you must rely upon Him for everything—even the timing and manner by which He reveals Himself to you.

So keep watching, and expect to hear your loving God. He will certainly be found by you as you seek Him wholeheartedly.

*Lord, thank You for deepening my relationship
with You. I give You my whole heart, amen.*

❦

In His presence . . . wholeheartedly seek His face.

HOW GOD SPEAKS TODAY

"I will put My law within them and on their heart I
will write it; and I will be their God, and they shall be
My people. . . . They will all know Me, from the least
of them to the greatest of them," declares the LORD.

JEREMIAH 31:33–34

Do you long to engage in direct and meaningful communication with God? Do you want to hear from Him and understand His path for your life?

The Lord is in the communication business. And His primary way of speaking to you today is through His Word.

In the Bible, you have the complete revelation of God—He doesn't need to add anything else to it. It is the unfolding truth of His character and ways throughout history—completely inspired by the Holy Spirit. And just as His Spirit controlled the minds of the men who penned its pages, He can and will teach you the truth through it.

So when you face difficulties or heartaches, rather than seeking the counsel of others, first go to Scripture and hear straight from your Savior. He wants to speak to you. Set your heart to listen.

Precious Lord, help me hear You speak
through Your Word today, amen.

———— ✚ ————

In His presence . . . listen for His
voice as you read His Word.

LED TO THE SOURCE

"Whom shall I send? And who will go for us?"
And I said, "Here am I. Send me!"
ISAIAH 6:8 NIV

Have you ever found that when reading your Bible or listening to a sermon, sometimes God will lead you to the same passage over and over again?

I recall an occasion when I was seeking the Lord's will about a decision I faced, and every morning I found myself reading Isaiah 6. I was into the third week of this before I realized I was being rebellious toward the Lord with regard to what He required of me. Somehow He would not let me escape verse 8. When I finally said yes to the Lord, Isaiah 6 was no longer prominent in my morning meditation.

One of the most rewarding experiences in the Christian life is to face a challenge and meditate upon Scripture until we know our heavenly Father has spoken. Through His Word He directs us, challenges us, warns us, and reassures us.

Will you be open to what He is saying to you today? Then be sure to pay attention to the verses that keep turning up.

Father, thank You for Your Word and Your
persistence with me as I seek to hear Your
voice and follow Your lead, amen.

❧

In His presence . . . let Him lead you.

SACRIFICES

"Because you have . . . not withheld your son, your
only son, indeed I will greatly bless you."
GENESIS 22:16–17

God will never ask you to sacrifice anything without giving you a greater blessing in return. Of course, the moment He asks it of you, it may be difficult to remember that.

It certainly was for Abraham. When he and Sarah were well beyond child-bearing age, the Lord miraculously provided them with Isaac. But then God commanded something very difficult, indeed—that Abraham offer his only son as a sacrifice (Genesis 22:1–10).

Abraham willingly complied, confident that the Lord would keep His promise to provide many descendants through Isaac. Though he didn't know how God would do so, Abraham absolutely trusted He would—and the Lord spared Isaac. And because Abraham was faithful, God blessed him beyond imagination.

Likewise, the Father may ask you to give up something important—not to wound you, but to make sure your trust in Him remains firm. No matter how difficult it is, do it. He will bless you in amazing ways that will both surprise and delight you.

Lord, I won't withhold anything from You. Fill me
with faith and help me always be obedient, amen.

∘⟡∘

In His presence . . . trust Him with
what's dearest to you.

COMPREHENDING THE TRUTH

I want to know Christ and experience the mighty
power that raised him from the dead.
PHILIPPIANS 3:10 NLT

God wants you to know the depths of who He is. He wants you to truly grasp His majesty, holiness, power, love, grace, and joy. Because when you begin to comprehend these mighty truths about His character, you are enriched, enabled, and energized (1 Corinthians 2:9–10).

Despite being stoned, beaten, shipwrecked, slandered, rejected, and imprisoned, Paul wrote that his ultimate aim in life was to "know Christ" (Philippians 3:10). And he surely did. This knowledge carried, encouraged, and strengthened him to the very end. And Paul was able to proclaim, "The Lord stood with me and strengthened me. . . . The Lord will rescue me from every evil deed, and will bring me safely to His heavenly kingdom; to Him be the glory forever and ever, amen" (2 Timothy 4:17–18).

When you know Jesus as your Deliverer, Comforter, Forgiver, Healer, and Prince of Peace, you can endure too, because you know the truth of His character and the certainty of His promises. So press on to know Him at all costs.

Lord, I want to know You—all of You—to the greatest
heights and the very depths of Your being, amen.

❖

In His presence . . . persevere to know Him.

THE TRUTH ABOUT YOU

*Christ made us right with God; he made us
pure and holy, and he freed us from sin.*

1 CORINTHIANS 1:30 NLT

Are you finding it difficult to overcome certain sins or destructive behaviors? Part of the reason may be because you don't fully understand all Jesus has done for you. You must comprehend your position in Christ before your actions can change.

So take hold of this truth today: at the cross, not only were your sins forgiven, but your nature changed. You're no longer a sinner; rather, you are now a saint who at times fails to seek God for your needs. The difference is not only how the Lord perceives you but how you view yourself.

If you still see yourself as a sinful individual, then you'll likely act like one. But if you accept your identity as a completely new person in Christ, then you can behave as His blameless, beloved child.

Friend, God has given you a fresh start by giving you a new nature and identity. So embrace it and rid yourself of the sins that no longer hold you captive.

*Lord, thank You for freeing me from sin. Help
me remember my position in You so that I may
always glorify Your holy name, amen.*

In His presence . . . rejoice in your new identity.

AGGRESSIVE LISTENING

[The people of Berea] searched the Scriptures day after
day to see if Paul and Silas were teaching the truth.
ACTS 17:11 NLT

There are two kinds of listeners: passive and aggressive. A passive listener takes what his pastor says as truth without much more consideration. On the other hand, an aggressive listener diligently seeks to know what God has to say—and grows much more quickly in his faith because of it.

Aggressive listeners are the ones whose Bibles are open and pens are ready. In Bible study, they demonstrate an inquisitive mind. In personal devotion, their notebooks are replete with insight into God's ways. They are always probing, searching, and comparing what they've heard with previous instruction. And the Father blesses their attentive hearts (Matthew 7:7–8).

So consider, are you sensitive to what God is saying? Do you persist in asking how the lessons you're taught apply to your own life? Do you take what you hear as truth, or do you investigate the Word, making sure the principles you've learned align with Scripture? What kind of listener are you?

> *Father, I want to be an aggressive listener who can*
> *identify Your truth and apply it to my life. Teach*
> *me to hear You and walk in Your ways, amen.*

❈

In His presence . . . commit to aggressive listening.

TRUE PEACE

Gideon built an altar . . . and named it The LORD is Peace.
JUDGES 6:24

It's not in the appeasement of evil, ungodly compromise, or by engaging in the false security the world offers that you'll ever find true and lasting peace. You will only do so by obeying God.

Gideon understood this firsthand. Judges 21:25 says, "In those days . . . everyone did what was right in his own eyes." This did not bring anyone tranquility. On the contrary, the Israelites' idolatrous ways invited continual assaults by surrounding armies. So God called upon Gideon to obey Him and to stand against the invaders.

Being from the smallest, weakest tribe, Gideon felt unprepared for the challenge. Wouldn't it be easier just to get along with the oppressing Midianites?

The Lord's answer? "Surely I will be with you" (Judges 6:16). Yes, Gideon's righteous stand would stir up the enemy, but God would be his abiding peace and lead him to triumph.

The same is true for you. Obeying the Lord may not be easy or popular, but you can have peace no other way. So stand firm in Him and trust that He will be your place of rest.

Lord, lead me—I will obey You. I praise
You for being my peace, amen.

❈

In His presence . . . find true and lasting peace.

TAKE HIM SERIOUSLY

The priests who bore the ark of the covenant of
the LORD stood firm on dry ground in the midst
of the Jordan; and all Israel crossed over.
JOSHUA 3:17 NKJV

After living in Egyptian bondage, being disobedient, and wandering the desert for forty years, the people of Israel turned to God with sincere and submissive hearts. And as they approached the promised land for a second time, they did so without complaint or hesitation. They were ready to obey—regardless of how unreasonable God's commands appeared.

So when the Lord told them to take their most precious symbol of His presence—the ark of the covenant—into the middle of the flooding Jordan River, they did it. And because they obeyed, He parted the waters and allowed them to cross on dry ground.

When you take God seriously, He will bless you for it. So regardless of what He instructs you to do today, trust Him to lead you. Mind the checks in your spirit, obey the principles of Scripture He shows you, and step out in faith when He calls. Take Him seriously because blessings always follow when you do.

Father, I want to live in obedience to Your will for
my life. Help me submit whenever You call, amen.

❧

In His presence . . . respect His authority.

RESTLESSNESS

*That night the king could not sleep; so he ordered
the book of the chronicles, the record of his
reign, to be brought in and read to him.*

ESTHER 6:1 NIV

Everyone, at times, deals with a restless spirit. There are many reasons for this, but one is because we're doing things our own way rather than aligning with God's will.

Esther 6 is a beautiful example of this. King Ahasuerus had been unwittingly deceived into signing an edict for the destruction of the Jews. Subsequently, the king could not sleep because of a restless spirit. So he called for the chronicles to be read, and through them discovered an error that ultimately led to the salvation of the Jewish people.

Friend, has God made you restless? You can't put a finger on it; you don't know why the agitation is there—but you have an uneasiness in your heart that won't go away?

Do not be surprised—the Father is actively seeking your attention. When such a time comes, the wise thing to do is to stop and ask the Lord what He is trying to say.

*Lord, when my spirit is restless, remind me
to seek You. I want to know Your will and
how You desire me to proceed, amen.*

❀

**In His presence . . . respond to
restlessness with obedience.**

WHEN OTHERS SPEAK

Like an . . . ornament of fine gold is a
wise reprover to a listening ear.

PROVERBS 25:12

In 2 Samuel 12, Nathan's confrontation with David serves as an example of how God gets our attention through others. The Lord gave insight to Nathan—instruction that David desperately needed to hear. And because King David listened, he was able to repent of his sin, and his fellowship with God was restored.

This still happens today. Realizing what is troubling us, the Father speaks to us through another person with the exact message we need. If we are proud or egotistical and refuse to take direction from wise counselors, we are destined for failure. But godly rebuke will lead to success in life if we'll take it to heart.

Of course you should not listen to just anyone without any discernment. Be extremely careful about who counsels you because even those with the best intentions can lead you astray if they are not walking daily with the Savior. While God speaks through other people, always examine both message and messenger carefully and be sure everything you're told aligns with Scripture.

Lord, please give me the discernment to know when
You are speaking to me through others, amen.

In His presence . . . ask Him to
identify the godly counselors.

SPIRITUALLY LEARNING

My dear children, I am writing this to you so that
you will not sin. But if anyone does sin, we have an
advocate who pleads our case before the Father. He
is Jesus Christ, the one who is truly righteous.

1 JOHN 2:1 NLT

What is the alternative to being united with Christ? It is despair and utter discouragement at all turns. However, by accepting Jesus Christ, we trade in our inadequacy for His adequacy and are born again. We have the opportunity to start over with a clean slate. And as God's spiritual offspring, He teaches us how to be victorious in every aspect of life.

Of course, the fact that the Lord calls us His children indicates that He knows we have a lot to learn—and in the process of growing in our knowledge of Him and His ways, we are going to fall occasionally.

But, friend, take heart. The Father understands that you are not going to be a perfect Christian. You will falter and fail, but He will not forsake or abandon you. His grace is sufficient for you— each and every day!

Lord Jesus, thank You for being such a wise
and patient Teacher and for forgiving my sin.
Truly, You deserve my praise, amen.

❈

In His presence . . . accept His grace and learn His ways.

UNCOMFORTABLE ANSWERS

*To keep me from becoming proud, I was given a thorn
in my flesh, a messenger from Satan to torment me.*

2 CORINTHIANS 12:7 NLT

The Father always responds to your petitions. However, His answers don't always come in the manner you expect or prefer. The apostle Paul understood this. The Lord didn't remove the thorn as Paul asked. Yet through his time in prayer, Paul received a new understanding of God's grace and a more profound dependence on His strength.

Likewise, there are times God gets your attention by being silent, answering no, or telling you to wait. During such seasons you are wise to conduct a spiritual self-examination. Are you requesting something for the wrong reasons or that's outside of His will? Have you disobeyed Him in any way?

Friend, when God answers your prayers in a manner that's uncomfortable, it is because He has something far better for you that He doesn't want you to miss. So if He doesn't respond in the way you expect, like Paul, allow Him to redirect your focus to the needful areas of your life—such as building your faith and character. Continue to listen and expect whatever He reveals to bless your soul.

*Lord, help me hear You clearly and accept Your
answer to me with gratefulness, amen.*

❀

In His presence . . . accept however He answers you.

INVOLVING GOD

Blessed is the one . . . whose delight is in the law of the
LORD, and who meditates on his law day and night.
PSALM 1:1–2 NIV

You have a choice every day: to involve God in your life through prayer and time in His Word, or to go it alone. One ultimately yields peace while the other brings anxiety.

But take note, you're not just promised tranquility when you meditate on Scripture—you're assured you'll be *blessed*.

This is because when you ponder the Word deeply—analyzing it, considering it thoroughly, and asking God for insight into it—your pattern of thinking is changed in the process. The Father gives you uncommon wisdom for your finances, relationships, and future. And when your mind is filled with His ways—His goodness, will, provision, power, and principles—you will have a peace and steadfast faith no storm can tear apart.

So today, make the choice—involve the Lord in your life by meditating on His Word and seeking Him in prayer.

> *Father, open Your Word to me—fill me with a*
> *passion for Scripture and Your holy presence. I*
> *commit my life to You and seek understanding*
> *into Your will and Your ways, amen.*

In His presence . . . allow Him to guide
your life and teach you His ways.

UNUSUAL CIRCUMSTANCES

He looked, and behold, the bush was burning
with fire, yet the bush was not consumed.

EXODUS 3:2

This story of Moses shows how God got the attention of a strong-willed man who needed to be broken. Moses had seen lots of fires and burning foliage, but he had never seen a bush that blazed and was not consumed. It was when he stopped his plans to investigate the phenomenon more closely that God spoke to him.

The Father often uses unusual circumstances to get us to turn our eyes and hearts to Him. There is no such thing as an accident in the life of a child of God, so we must learn to look for His presence in *every* situation that arises.

Job loss, illness, bills paid anonymously, even unexpected emergencies are not surprises to Him. The Father knows exactly what it takes to get our attention. And often it is through highly unusual circumstances that we will finally stand back and take note of what He is doing in our lives.

Lord, help me see all the circumstances that arise
in a new light. Make my heart open to what
you're trying to do in my life for my good.

In His presence . . . look for
Him in every circumstance.

FAILURE

*Joshua tore his clothes and fell to the earth on
his face before the ark of the LORD.*
JOSHUA 7:6

Having just defeated the great city of Jericho, the Israelites prepared to take Ai, a small town that seemed easy to conquer. But the Israelite warriors had disobeyed God and had become overconfident in their own abilities. So the Lord got their attention by letting them fail in their military endeavor against Ai. It was a terrible blow, but it reminded them of their dependence on God.

Of course there is a vast difference between failing and being a failure. A person only becomes a failure if he or she stops trying altogether. But being unsuccessful in an incident can actually prove to be the greatest stepping-stone to success in your life if you will turn your attention to God—as Joshua did after the defeat at Ai.

Friend, your failure today can actually serve to make you a success tomorrow if you're willing to acknowledge your mistakes and learn from the Father. Therefore, thank Him for getting your attention, forgiving you, and teaching you to respond properly. And be assured—by doing so, you pave the way to future victories.

*Father, thank You for keeping my pride
from inhibiting Your purposes. Help me
honor You in all things, amen.*

In His presence . . . learn from your mistakes.

FINANCIAL COLLAPSE

Midian so impoverished the Israelites that
they cried out to the LORD for help.
JUDGES 6:6 NIV

The theme of the book of Judges is "every man did what was right in his own eyes" (17:6). So when did the Israelites finally cry out to the Lord? When God took away every material resource they had. The Lord knew exactly what it would take to get their attention: the destruction of all their possessions.

Has the Father allowed your finances to dry up? Has He taken something of great value from you? This is difficult to endure, but the Lord wants you to understand that He is your security—not anything you could possess.

Of course, you may say, "But I thought God promised to supply all of my needs?" Yes, He did (Philippians 4:19). And He will continue to do so. But He also knows that your greatest need is to have a relationship with Him and listen to Him.

Your spiritual well-being is far more important than anything material. So God will bring you to utter dependence on Him rather than allow your possessions to become a destructive idol in your life.

God, strip away my self-dependence and materialism
so that I will always rest in Your provision, amen.

In His presence . . . find the supply for every need.

Using Illness for Our Good

*Hezekiah became mortally ill; and he prayed to
the Lord, and the Lord spoke to him.*

2 Chronicles 32:24

Persistent health issues can be disheartening. They drain us physically and make us realize how limited we are. However, we should not overlook the fact that sometimes God uses illness to get our attention and bring about self-examination.

Some years ago I experienced such an affliction. I was in the hospital for several weeks, and during that time, God dealt with me in a wonderful way. He used my malady to focus my attention on His voice and correct my thinking about several issues. If He had answered prayers to heal me, I would have missed what He wanted to say to me. But today, I give thanks for that season of infirmity because of how it increased my intimacy with Him.

Likewise, God cares about you—enough to use whatever is necessary to get you to listen to what He is saying. He wants to give you guidance and help you succeed in His wonderful plans for your life. So listen to Him. Certainly He will heal you in ways you never imagined.

*Lord, thank You for using all circumstances—even
times of illness—to get my attention. I know it's
because You love me and want what is best, amen.*

❖

In His presence . . . pay attention to Him.

How to Identify God's Voice

*"My sheep hear My voice, and I know
them, and they follow Me."*
John 10:27 NKJV

At times, seeking the Lord's direction about a decision can seem like a drawn-out process. We can become frustrated and confused, and wonder how much we can know for certain that we're hearing God's voice.

As believers who walk in the Spirit, it should be easy for us to distinguish whether the voice we hear is of the Lord, the flesh, or the devil—right? Yet understand, your Shepherd is constantly teaching you how to recognize when He beckons to you. Whether you've been with Him for many years or are just learning His ways, you can take heart because your tenderhearted Shepherd calls out to you in a way that you can recognize Him.

However, since Scripture teaches that all believers, young and old, should clearly be able to discern the voice of God, it's important for you to stop talking at times and just listen to Him. Grow still and quiet. Open His Word and learn to identify how He speaks. You will, eventually, recognize His voice and know exactly what to do.

*Father, as I talk with You, remind me
to stop and simply listen. I want to hear
Your voice above all others, amen.*

In His presence . . . practice the discipline of listening.

A COMMITTED MIND

"The seed falling on good soil refers to someone
who hears the word and understands it."
MATTHEW 13:23 NIV

The fertile soil in this verse is what I refer to as the *committed mind*—one that's been cultivated, is ready for the seed to take root, and will ultimately bring forth fruit. This person is teachable—God can instruct this faithful believer in any area.

So how can you cultivate a committed mind?

By listening carefully to His message—fixing "your thoughts on what is true, and honorable, and right, and pure, and lovely, and admirable" (Philippians 4:8 NLT). By resisting outside clutter—purposely refusing to entertain frivolous distractions. And finally, by asking the Savior to help you concentrate on His Word and apply it to your life. This can only be done by faith in the Lord Jesus Christ because He is the One who enables you to receive the Word in your inner person.

Friend, cultivate a committed mind by evaluating your life in the light of what God tells you. And be assured, when you obey His truth and submit to His leadership, you will grow into the productive, fruit-bearing believer you long to be.

Father, I devote myself to You—cultivate
my mind with Your truth, amen.

**In His presence . . . cultivate
your mind by dwelling on Him.**

CONQUERING YOUR FEARS

I sought the LORD, and He answered me,
and delivered me from all my fears.

PSALM 34:4

Anxiety can grip you at any time—it may arise from your situation, or it could be a spiritual attack from the enemy. Regardless of where it originates, it's absolutely crucial that when you're frightened, you go directly to the Father for help.

Ask God to identify the fear and bring it to the surface so you can confess its presence. Allow Him to expose its root cause. For example, an apprehension about the dark may be linked to feelings of abandonment. Therefore, ask Him to show you what is causing you to respond in the way you do.

Also, trust the Lord to help you conquer your fear—don't just accept it. Anxiety keeps you from becoming all God desires you to be, so He's committed to rooting it out. Therefore walk with confidence in His healing.

Finally, face your fear by hiding Scripture in your heart and acknowledging the Lord's presence with you at all times. He is with you wherever you go; so trust Him to help, protect, and provide for you every step of the way.

Lord, help me identify any fear that resides within
me and face it with Your strength and power, amen.

In His presence . . . live free of fear.

A SPIRIT OF CONTENTMENT

I have learned to be content in whatever circumstances I am.

PHILIPPIANS 4:11

If anyone had good reason to complain about life, it was the apostle Paul. He experienced brutal beatings, shipwrecks, imprisonments, infirmities, and he lived in constant danger. He went without sleep, food, or water on countless occasions, not to mention he was often criticized and falsely accused. And like all of us, he constantly struggled with sin.

So how could Paul find peace, joy, and contentment in such terrible circumstances? By yielding totally to Jesus and receiving strength, comfort, and assurance from the Spirit of the living God.

Friend, all that Christ offers is available to you as well—regardless of your circumstances. As you commit yourself to Jesus in increasing measure, the power of His Spirit in you grows more apparent—you have a greater desire to obey Him and reflect His character. And the more you submit to Him, the more your faith will mature—and that always results in greater peace.

Paul learned to be content in all circumstances by learning to trust God completely. You can too. So where are you in this learning process?

Jesus, I will obey You in every situation, knowing
You are greater than any difficulty I face, amen.

In His presence . . . discover true
contentment in all circumstances.

CASTING OUR CARES

Casting all your anxiety on Him, because He cares for you.
1 PETER 5:7

Problems are inevitable in life—they are woven into the fabric of our day-to-day living. So it's no wonder that we struggle with anxiety—sometimes to the point that it cripples us and prevents us from experiencing joy and fulfillment.

But God didn't create us to handle the troubles of this world on our own, which is why He tells us to cast our burdens on Him and allow Him to care for us.

How do you do this? How do you turn your troubles over to Him? It begins by simply talking to your heavenly Father. Why? Because prayer shifts your focus away from the problem to the One who can handle it, giving you the solution and revealing the next step for you to take.

Therefore acknowledge your anxiety and your need for God's peace. Confess any sin that you believe may be associated with your fears. Say to the Lord, "I need Your help, presence, comfort, provision, and direction." Then look heavenward to your Father and be confident that He will, indeed, take care of you.

*Father, I release my cares to You and ask that You bless
me with Your divine comfort and provision, amen.*

In His presence . . . cast your cares on Him.

KNOWING GOD'S VOICE

"The sheep follow him because they know his voice."

JOHN 10:4

Do you know how investigators are trained to recognize counterfeit money? They diligently study the true currency—the real thing. Then, when held against the standard, the counterfeit bills stand out.

Likewise, the best way to learn the Lord's voice is by studying the words He's declared to all generations—by reading the Holy Bible.

There are several principles you can apply to what you're hearing to gauge whether it is of God, but the most basic and most important is whether the message conflicts with Scripture. The Father won't tell you to do anything that counters what He already has recorded for all mankind.

Therefore, the best way to know His voice is to get to know Him. Spend time in His Word and immerse yourself in His truth. Because as you do, you'll be able to differentiate God's direction from the messages the world, the enemy, or your flesh are sending you. You will know His voice, and He will certainly lead you well.

Father God, thank You for Your Word and the guidance
it gives me. Impress it on my heart so that I will be
able to discern Your voice from all others, amen.

In His presence . . . study His
Word and listen for His voice.

INEXHAUSTIBLE RICHES

I pray that the eyes of your heart may be enlightened,
so that you will know what is the hope of His calling,
what are the riches of the glory of His inheritance.

EPHESIANS 1:18

What do you think of when you hear the word *heir*? Does it evoke images of wealth handed down through generations? Perhaps it reminds you of someone you love who has passed away.

The truth is, not many people inherit a vast estate or receive great gifts from wealthy relatives. But when Jesus becomes your Savior, He makes you a co-heir of all God's immeasurable riches (Romans 8:16–17). He wants to be your fullness and abundant supply for every aspect of your life.

Do you need strength? God has all power and gives you energy for every task. Do you lack wisdom? He provides discernment and insight that can cut through even the densest fog of confusion. Are you searching for contentment? Jesus gives you peace beyond human understanding.

Friend, material wealth can be depleted and taken away. But the inheritance you have in Christ is unchanging and inexhaustible forever. Therefore, embrace how rich you truly are in Him.

Jesus, I am so grateful for the inheritance
You've given me. You are all I need! Amen.

In His presence . . . embrace His abundant supply.

JULY

LED BY THE HOLY SPIRIT

*We have received . . . the Spirit who is from God, so that
we may know the things freely given to us by God.*

1 CORINTHIANS 2:12

Did you know that, as a believer, the Holy Spirit dwells within you?
And that the Spirit, who knows the mind of God, communicates
to you every truth He wants you to hear? The moment you receive
Christ as your Savior, the Holy Spirit begins teaching you the truth
of who He is.

Paul clearly stated this in 1 Corinthians 2:12, "We have
received . . . the Spirit who is from God, that we might know the
things that have been freely given to us by God"(NKJV). The Greek
word for "know" is *oido*, which means "fullness of knowledge."

Given over to a self-life, unbelievers are absolutely incapable of
understanding the things of God and therefore will not understand
why they do some of the things they do. But you have the mind
of Christ (1 Corinthians 2:16), and He offers you all the insight
you need. So commit to listening for the Spirit's direction—and be
confident He will reveal it to you.

*Heavenly Father, thank You for the gift of
Your Holy Spirit guiding me and filling
me with Your knowledge, amen.*

In His presence . . . submit to His leadership.

Victory Over Sin

God . . . will not allow the temptation to be more than you can stand. When you are tempted, he will show you a way out.

1 Corinthians 10:13 nlt

Do you realize the victory you have because of Jesus? As a believer, you have everything necessary to triumph over sin. How do you do so?

First, admit when something is a temptation and acknowledge that God can free you from it. When you're willing to accept your vulnerability and choose to depend on the Lord, you've taken an important step toward victory.

Second, look at the big picture. Ask yourself, *How will this affect my future? Will it distract me from God's will?*

Finally, recall the Father's promises and set your mind on what honors Him. Temptations are often powerful because they play into your anxieties. Don't allow disappointments and setbacks to lead you to sin. Trust that God can and will fulfill His word to you.

When you feel the lure of sin, conquer it by seeking the Savior. It won't be easy, and sometimes deliverance will take time. But always seek to honor Him and He will certainly teach you how to overcome.

Lord, You know my struggles, but I'm
confident You'll help me overcome them.
Thank You for the victory, amen.

In His presence . . . triumph over temptation.

JUST ASK

You don't have what you want because you don't ask God for it.
JAMES 4:2 NLT

Have you talked to the Father about the desire burning in your heart? You don't have to be embarrassed or think what you yearn for is too insignificant for His notice. God cares about you, and He's interested in what concerns you. But you'll miss His blessings if you refuse to open your heart to Him fully.

So talk to God as a friend—share your inmost hopes and desires with Him. The more specific you are about your goals and longing, the better you can see Him working in your situation.

The Father may say yes to your request immediately or He may instruct you to wait for His perfect timing. He may also show you that what you're asking for doesn't fit His plan for your life and that He has something much better for you.

Although God may not always answer in the way you think He will, the most important thing for you to understand is that He is willing and waiting to respond. So talk to your heavenly Father. And be assured—He loves you and He's listening.

Lord, thank You for listening to me and
hearing my heart. Certainly You are my
faithful, loving, and wise Provider, amen.

In His presence . . . ask freely.

PRAY FOR THE NATION

Rec. day this day 2021

Blessed is the nation whose God is the LORD.
PSALM 33:12

Our nation is always in need of prayer. In good times and bad, whether at war or at peace, during seasons of overflowing abundance or great need, it's always important for us to intercede for our country.

Why? First, because our fellow citizens need to accept Jesus as their Savior. If we desire for our nation to be characterized by godly families, wise and capable leaders, and strong communities, then we need to pray our countrymen will enthrone the Lord in their homes and hearts.

Second, we need the Father's favor and protection against threats such as terrorist attacks, natural disasters, epidemics, and economic downturns. If we wish for our country to remain safe, productive, and strong, we will need God's divine provision.

So today, kneel before the Lord, seek His face, repent from your sins, and ask Him to bless the nation. Only the Lord can truly transform our country. And He has promised to do so when we ask according to His will and act in obedience to Him (2 Chronicles 7:14).

> *Lord, today I pray for my country. May my*
> *fellow citizens accept You as Savior and may*
> *Your name be exalted across this land, amen.*

In His presence . . . ask God to heal the nation.

RECOVERING FROM REJECTION

Even if my father and mother abandon
me, the LORD will hold me close.
PSALM 27:10 NLT

When others are cruel and unloving, does their criticism distress you deeply, stirring up painful feelings of worthlessness? Do you ever torment yourself with thoughts such as, *I'll never be good enough,* or *No one will ever love me?* If so, you're likely wrestling with rejection. And when you internalize the brutal words of others and believe their lies about you, it can wound you profoundly.

However, as a believer, you belong to almighty God—who loves you unconditionally, accepts you fully, and enables you to accomplish great things. And because His Holy Spirit dwells within you, you have a powerful Helper in every situation.

So what is the best way to overcome your feelings of rejection? Believe what Scripture says about you and thank God for who He formed you to be. Affirm the truth with your words: "Lord, thank You for making me worthy, accepted, and competent through Jesus." Certainly He will heal your wounds and give you the sense of worth He created you to enjoy.

Jesus, You're the One who makes me worthy.
Thank You for loving me and giving my
life purpose and significance, amen.

In His presence . . . discover your true worth.

Overcoming Apathy

*Whatever you do in word or deed, do all in the name of the
Lord Jesus, giving thanks through Him to God the Father.*

Colossians 3:17

When apathy takes over, it can be difficult to get motivated. You have so much to do, but you just don't feel like proceeding. Why have despair and boredom taken such a profound hold of you?

Many answers are possible. Perhaps you're facing overwhelming pressures and you just want to give up. Maybe you're not where the Lord wants you. It could even be that you're angry at yourself for where you are in life. But realize, you don't have to allow discouragement to rule you. Instead, you can renew your passion by doing whatever is before you to God's glory (Colossians 3:17).

It is quite impossible to be where the Father wants you—doing your best and giving thanks from a grateful heart—and still be bored. So when you're disheartened, remember reaching God's potential for you is more about *who you are* than *what you're doing*—it's more about glorifying Him than past mistakes or pressures.

Therefore, close your eyes, focus on Him, and thank Him for everything you can think of. He will certainly inspire you.

*Lord, please motivate and inspire me. Please help
me serve You passionately and gratefully, amen.*

❧

In His presence . . . be inspired.

Impossible Circumstances

The Lord will rescue me from every evil deed, and will bring me
safely to His heavenly kingdom; to Him be the glory forever.
2 Timothy 4:18

The apostle Paul approached the end of his life in a prison cell. He could have felt sorry for himself. But instead, he encouraged his friends to trust in God, even when his own circumstances looked very dismal. How was he able to do this?

Peace is the last emotion in the world Paul *should* have been feeling, but the apostle was unshakably secure in his faith because of his profoundly intimate relationship with the Lord. Despite Paul's sufferings, the one foundational truth he knew was that God's supernatural power, wisdom, and peace—though impossible to comprehend rationally—were able to see him through the trials of life.

The same is true for you. God is with you—He is operating in you and in your situation in a manner far beyond your ability to understand. And the promise of His sovereign care—regardless of your circumstances—is all you really need to make it through whatever you're facing. So trust Him to sustain you as He did Paul.

Father, no matter my circumstances,
I trust in Your unfailing peace, power,
wisdom, and abiding presence, amen.

⚜

In His presence . . . invite Him to
guard your heart and mind.

SETTING YOUR MIND

*Set your mind on the things above, not
on the things that are on earth.*

COLOSSIANS 3:2

If you're wondering why it's so difficult to control your thoughts and maintain your faith, remember that your mind reflects what you feed it. For example, if you're constantly partaking of conflict-based or violent entertainment, it is no wonder that anger characterizes your interactions with others. If you're always indulging your fearful thoughts, then trusting God will be difficult indeed.

So if you desire to become all that the Father created you to be, you must fill your mind with His ways and principles from His Word. You must ask God to help you sift through everything that enters your mind each day and choose for His truth to take precedence. It is an act of your will.

This may appear difficult, but it's the most rewarding endeavor you will undertake because through it, you will know Him better and experience life at its very best. So don't wait. Begin refining your thoughts today. And take hold of all Jesus has given you by setting your mind on Him.

*Jesus, I want to honor You. Please reveal and
purge the thoughts that displease You, amen.*

**In His presence . . . focus on His ways,
principles, and unfailing character.**

YOUR LIVING HOPE

We have fixed our hope on the living God, who is the Savior.
1 TIMOTHY 4:10

You have a living hope in Jesus Christ. Take this truth to heart today—though all around you appears desperate and your dreams seem to have perished. No matter the present circumstances, you can take courage in the knowledge that your Savior is the triumphant Warrior who has defeated your every foe (Revelation 17:14). He helps you and will continue to fight for you regardless of what circumstances arise.

This is the strength and joy of your Christian life—it is always possible to live above the present because your future is secure. You have an incorruptible inheritance, an unwavering Defender, and your God's unfailing love. But you must choose to believe His promises (2 Corinthians 1:20).

So if you've experienced loss, do not despair. This defeat is only for the moment and what is truly important can never be taken from you. Focus on your living hope. Set your eyes on Jesus, your Lord and Savior, and expect Him to lead you to victory.

Lord Jesus, You are a mighty Warrior, my triumphant
Savior, and my Living Hope. You never fail.
Help me cling to you now and forever, amen.

In His presence . . . allow Him to restore your hope.

THE POWER OF THE WORD

*Christ loved the church. He gave up his life for her to make
her holy and clean, washed by the cleansing of God's word.*
EPHESIANS 5:25–26 NLT

Do you ever avoid reading the Bible because it makes you uncomfortable? Certainly God often works through His Word to reveal the areas of your heart He wants to heal—and that's not always easy (Hebrews 4:12). But Scripture is crucial for the well-being of your soul. The Holy Spirit speaks through it to help you move ahead spiritually, emotionally, and relationally.

Of course, you may be tempted to skip reading God's Word or dismiss what it says because it contradicts how you think. But don't. The Father does His greatest transformational work in you as you meditate on His truth (Romans 12:2).

So if you have any desire for God; any yearning for healing; any longing for a life of meaning, hope, and joy—then open Scripture, drink in its life-giving words, and do as it says. Not only does the Lord understand who you are, He will help you see how your life can be more fulfilling, healthy, and significant.

*Lord, transform me according to Your wonderful,
supernatural, life-giving Word. I want to know
You and the abundant life You offer, amen.*

In His presence . . . allow His Word to transform you.

CONFORMING TO THE TRUTH

Whom He foreknew, He also predestined to be
conformed to the image of His Son, that He might
be the firstborn among many brethren.
ROMANS 8:29 NKJV

God wants to conform each of His children to the likeness of His image. He does this by revealing Himself through His Word. As we are confronted with the truth about His character, we have a choice: refuse to adapt to God's mold, or yield to Him and be fashioned into His likeness. But as we accept His Lordship, submit to Him, and apply His Word to our lives, He liberates us and reveals His glory through us.

Friend, you are called to listen to the Father in order to comprehend His ways and be shaped and conformed to His truth. God doesn't speak just to entertain you; He communicates so you can be more like Jesus.

So today, consider, are you resisting being conformed by God, or are you being shaped and molded by His truth? Commit yourself not to merely hearing His Word but to obeying it. Do not simply allow Scripture to enter your eyes, but take hold of it so it will rule your heart.

Lord, teach me to hear and embrace Your Word so
that I may be fashioned to Your likeness, amen.

❦

In His presence . . . conform to His truth.

A Prayer of Direction

Guide me in your truth and teach me, for you
are God my Savior, and my hope is in you.

PSALM 25:5 NIV

The Father has given you the powerful gift of choice—the ability to select the direction of your life. In fact, every day you'll face a continuous series of options—some that honor the Lord and others that don't. Some that lead to His abundant life and others that divert you away from it to destruction.

One of the most powerful, life-changing decisions you can make is to invite God to guide you—trusting that everything He allows in your life is for the purpose of building your character and bringing you into His freedom.

Friend, God's plan for you is unquestionably the best. The question is: Will you allow Him to direct you? If so, pray:

Lord, change me and work through me in any way You please. I believe that You will form Your character in me, shape me into Your likeness through my circumstances, and lead me to life at its best. Thank You, dear Jesus, amen.

> *Lord, thank You for replacing my misery with*
> *Your joy, my fears with faith, my weaknesses*
> *with Your strength, and my selfish ways*
> *with grateful devotion to You, amen.*

In His presence . . . trust Him with your life.

SILENCE IN MEDITATION

Guard your steps as you go to the house
of God and draw near to listen.
ECCLESIASTES 5:1

When you pray, do you do all the talking? To have God speak to your heart is an awesome experience—one you may miss if you monopolize the conversation and never pause to listen.

But when you remain quiet, the Lord will transform you, changing how you think and conforming you to His ways. How does He do so? He may remind you of an important passage of Scripture, reveal a biblical truth for you to apply, expose unconfessed sin, or bring someone to mind that needs your ministry. In other words, He will direct your path (Proverbs 3:6).

This is why it is so important for you to sit before Him in silence and allow Him to pour Himself into you. He will reveal His will and bring peace to your inner being.

Friend, sitting before God allows Him to speak to your heart clearly, positively, and unmistakably—showing you what to do. You will know that the Lord has truly spoken to you—and that's the definition of life at its very best.

Lord, I will remain silent and listen for Your voice.
Speak to me, Father. Your servant is listening, amen.

❦

In His presence . . . be silent and
give Him time to respond.

READY TO CHANGE

Do not be conformed to the former lusts which were yours in
your ignorance, but like the Holy One who called you, be holy.

1 PETER 1:14–15

Do you sense something in your life needs to change? Are there areas that simply aren't working? Are you willing to say, "Lord, I want to exalt You. I've had enough of my own way—I want to live by Yours"?

If so, ask God to identify the areas where you're sinful, self-centered, and struggling rather than Christ-centered and victorious. Whatever He brings to mind, acknowledge that He is right and make the decision to turn from your ways. He will show you how as you read Scripture.

As He reveals principles from His Word, apply them to your life—even when they don't completely make sense—and trust Him to bless your obedience.

Answer all of the questions, dilemmas, and challenges you encounter with this: "Lord Jesus, what would You have me do? I want to obey You." Not only will doing so transform your life, it will build the most wonderful, profound, and indescribable intimacy between you and the Savior.

Jesus, please reveal if there's anything in my
life that displeases You. Show me the way I
should go—I want to obey You, amen.

———————— ⚜ ————————

In His presence . . . allow Him to transform you.

WHEN YOU'RE WEAK

"I do believe; help my unbelief."
MARK 9:24

Today you may feel as if your hope has failed—your faith is gone. You are trying to cling to God's promises, but the pain continues to return and you wonder if He's really going to come through for you when you're so weak.

Yet understand—the fact that you are turning to the Father is evidence of the faith necessary for victory. You still believe He has the answers and will help you (Hebrews 11:6). Good!

The focus of your faith should never be about how strong you are but about your utter dependence on God—who has the outcome under His control (2 Corinthians 12:9). The question is always: Will you trust Him, even in this? Will you choose to believe that no matter how confusing or excruciating this is, He is still sovereign and will cause "all things to work together for good" (Romans 8:28)?

Friend, you don't have to be strong, you just have to be His (2 Timothy 2:13). So declare your trust in the Lord and obey Him. Believe—for He will certainly bring your unbelief to an end.

Lord, I will trust You. You are the strength
of my heart and my portion forever.
Thank You for helping me, amen.

In His presence . . . cling to Him in faith.

FAITH TEST

In this you greatly rejoice, though now for a little while, if
need be, you have been grieved by various trials, that the
genuineness of your faith, being much more precious than
gold that perishes, though it is tested by fire, may be found
to praise, honor, and glory at the revelation of Jesus Christ.

1 PETER 1:6–7 NKJV

Sometimes you will face situations that are bigger than you are, making you feel as if you have no answers or resources to continue on. Everything in you says, "Give up!" But don't do it.

Friend, you're in the midst of a faith test. God isn't punishing you and He hasn't forgotten you. Rather, He is providing an opportunity for you to grow spiritually and believe Him for greater things.

So make a decision to believe the Lord in spite of everything. Don't look at your circumstances or pay attention to the opinions of others. Listen to the Father.

Open God's Word and trust what He says. He is teaching you that Jesus really is sufficient for every need you have. There's no challenge too overwhelming or pit too deep—He can always deliver you. So expect Him to prove Himself faithful in this difficulty.

Lord, I cannot overcome this—but You
can. So I will trust You, amen.

In His presence . . . believe He will be faithful.

THE REQUIREMENTS

*"Let your light shine before men in such a way that they may
see your good works, and glorify your Father who is in heaven."*
MATTHEW 5:16

When you feel inadequate to serve God or carry out His commands, remember that what He expects of you is different from what you think. You may believe He is looking for charisma, persuasiveness, and a brilliant mind. But what He really requires is:

Sensitivity to the Spirit. Be attentive and obedient to His promptings.

Service. Humbly glorify Him and edify others rather than promote yourself.

Sacrifice. Pour yourself out for His name's sake rather than what you can attain.

Self-denial. Seek His kingdom and goals instead of your own.

Suffering. Follow Him obediently even when it means pain and persecution, knowing that you are serving His eternal purposes.

In other words, the Savior wants to use your life as a platform for His power. So when He calls, don't worry about whether you're smart, talented, or beautiful enough. Just obey Him wholeheartedly. He will surely magnify Himself through you.

*Lord, thank You for choosing me to serve You.
May my life glorify You in every way, amen.*

❈

In His presence . . . reflect His glory.

THE POWER OF HIS WORD

The word of the cross is foolishness to those who are perishing,
but to us who are being saved it is the power of God.

1 CORINTHIANS 1:18

Have you experienced the power of God's Word in your life? Have you seen how the Father uses it to sustain your soul and transform your life? It's not only when He heals a disease or provides for your needs in a supernatural way that He's active on your behalf. Often the greatest miracles He does involve breaking you free of strongholds and destructive behaviors.

However, realize that God releases His miraculous truth in your life not only to liberate you but also as a testimony to those who don't know Him. Your unsaved loved ones see the Savior's power in your life and it inspires them to believe in Jesus and be saved.

So as you spend time in Scripture and faithfully testify of God's love, look for ways He exhibits His power in your life. Ask the Father to use you mightily as His representative to those around you. And then watch as He uses His Word to work miraculously through you.

Jesus, use Your Word powerfully in my life and help
me be a faithful witness of Your saving love, amen.

In His presence . . . allow His
Word to work powerfully.

ANYTHING?

"If you ask Me anything in My name, I will do it."
JOHN 14:14

Will God answer that deep desire of your heart that you've repeatedly taken to His throne? Will He really help you? Jesus placed only one condition on answering your requests—that they be made *in His name*. However, this doesn't mean merely affixing the phrase "in Jesus' name" to the end of every appeal.

As Christ spoke to His disciples, they understood that His name signified His character. So to pray "in the name of Jesus" meant that they would conform their requests to His mission, values, and will.

How do you do that? How can you be sure your prayers align with His character? Rely on the Holy Spirit. Romans 8:26 explains, "The Spirit helps us in our weakness. We do not know what we ought to pray for, but the Spirit himself intercedes for us" (NIV).

Praying in Jesus' name requires the help of the Holy Spirit. So allow His Spirit to guide your words and conform the desires of your heart to His will. And be assured—He hears you and will answer.

Holy Spirit, thank You for guiding my
prayers. Align my heart with God's will and
help me walk in Your ways, amen.

In His presence . . . pray with hope and boldness.

Time with Him

"Seek the Lord that you may live."
Amos 5:6

Do you desire a release from the stress you're experiencing? Do you wish something could quiet your fears or give you a fresh perspective on your struggles? If so, meditating on the Word of God can revolutionize your life.

The Father wants you to relate to Him—to be quiet before Him so He can speak to you and teach you His ways. Unfortunately, you will miss His activity, direction, and intervention in your circumstances if you don't take the opportunity to listen to Him and know Him through His Word.

Of course life is busy, and you may think you don't really have time to sit in His presence. But realize that when you forfeit your relationship with God, you lose much more than just time. You miss His joy, peace, power, love, and wisdom—and even the very purposes for which you were created.

Friend, the Father loves you intimately—with a depth that can never be measured. So spend time with Him and give Him the opportunity to have you all to Himself. You'll surely find all that you've been longing for.

Father, help me know You. Teach me Your ways so I
may love You more and obey You faithfully, amen.

❦

In His presence . . . learn from Him.

CALL OUT TO HIM

O God, have mercy! I look to you for protection. . . . I cry out
to God Most High, to God who will fulfill his purpose for me.
PSALM 57:1–2 NLT

Are there obstacles or difficulties that seem to block you from fulfilling God's purposes for your life? Perhaps you've worried, planned, and toiled but have ultimately failed to achieve what you desire, and despair is beginning to settle in. If so, it is time for you to stop *doing* and begin *asking*.

Friend, the Lord your God is sovereign. He can soften hearts that you could never touch, change circumstances beyond your control, provide resources you can't even dream of attaining, and untangle messes that seem unredeemable. And He is waiting for you to cry out to Him for deliverance.

Friend, it is sheer pride that keeps you relying on yourself rather than depending on and obeying Your heavenly Father, who wants to be your strength, your life, and your all. Stop trying to figure everything out. Kneel before Him and leave all that concerns you in His hands. He will not fail you.

Lord, You are my only hope and help. I count on You,
Father. Lead me in the way I should go, amen.

❦

**In His presence . . . trust Him to
fulfill His purposes for you.**

GRACE TO FORGIVE

Love each other deeply, because love
covers over a multitude of sins.
1 PETER 4:8 NIV

Whenever someone wounds you, it's common to think about what they've done and nurture your hurt feelings. This is normal, but it's not God's will for you. The Father wants you to forgive. And He gives you an amazing example of forgiveness in David.

If ever anyone had a right to be angry, David did. As a young man, he saved Israel from the Philistines by slaying the giant Goliath. He served faithfully in King Saul's court—playing music to soothe Saul's troubled spirit and always expressing his unwavering loyalty. David did nothing wrong. Nevertheless, Saul was so jealous of David that he sought to kill him.

Did David grow bitter? No. He understood that just as he'd received God's grace, he was also to extend it—no matter how hateful Saul was to him. And the Lord blessed David because of it.

Likewise, you're called to forgive as freely as Christ forgave you. So don't allow resentment to consume you. Instead, like David, let grace characterize your relationships. Because certainly, "love never fails" (1 Corinthians 13:8).

Jesus, please help me forgive freely. Fill my
heart with love so I may honor You, amen.

In His presence . . . accept and extend grace.

MAKING EXCUSES

I heard Your voice in the garden, and I was afraid
because I was naked; and I hid myself.
GENESIS 3:10 NKJV

Why did God call to Adam after he ate the forbidden fruit? Didn't
the Lord know where Adam was? Of course He did. But Adam was
hiding out of fear and shame—just as many of us retreat emotionally and spiritually after we've disobeyed the Father.

But understand, God didn't ask Adam questions to find out
information. Rather, He did so to receive a response—to reveal what
thoughts were driving Adam's decisions. He does the same for us.

Unfortunately, like Adam and Eve before us, we often give
excuses. We try to rationalize our disobedience instead of accepting the mercy and healing the Lord so freely offers (1 John 1:9).

But friend, the Father wants you to turn to Him so He can free
you of the shame and pain you bear.

God knows your past, future, personality, woundedness, and
everything that makes you who you are—and He loves you anyway.
So don't hide from Him. Return to the Lord. Seek His wonderful
presence, let Him heal you, and live.

Father, I've been hiding areas of my life
because of my shame. Please set me free and
restore the joy of Your salvation, amen.

⚜

In His presence . . . receive forgiveness and healing.

THE CONSEQUENCES OF DISOBEDIENCE

The LORD God sent him out of the garden of Eden
to till the ground from which he was taken.
GENESIS 3:23 NKJV

When Adam and Eve gave in to temptation, they lost their intimacy with God and their home in the garden of Eden. Hardships began to assail them. Ultimately, all of their suffering could be traced back to one cause—they didn't obey the Father. And humanity has been paying the terrible price ever since.

Likewise, when you fail to submit to God, you will always suffer the consequences. This is why it is absolutely crucial for you to learn to listen to the Lord and heed His direction. Because it can make the difference between life at its very best for you or life at its terrible worst.

Therefore, whenever you're getting ready to make plans or proceed in some endeavor, seek the Father and commit to walking in His will. Be wise and cautious enough to stop, face the Father, and ask, "Lord, lead me. I will obey You." He will certainly tell you the truth, steer you in the right direction, and save you a lot of pain.

Lord, if I'm headed in the wrong direction, please
show me. I want to walk in Your will, amen.

In His presence . . . seek His will
and commit to obey Him.

FIRST

I count all things to be loss in view of the surpassing
value of knowing Christ Jesus my Lord.
PHILIPPIANS 3:8

What is it that consumes your thoughts today? What holds the utmost place of prominence in your life? Your answer will say a great deal about what's truly important to you.

But be warned, the frustrations and discouragement you face often have more to do with what you're pursuing than anything else. Perhaps you desire to be loved or respected—to be appreciated and accepted for who you are. Maybe you yearn to feel whole, safe, or free from burdens. So you chase the goals, objects, and people who seem to answer your profound need.

But friend, these misplaced priorities will rob you of peace, energy, and joy. It is God alone who deserves the highest place of honor in your life. Do you spend time with Him daily, seeking His face and deepening your intimacy with Him? Do you pursue Him with greater passion than everything else?

If not, you will be disappointed. Nothing is as wonderful or worthy as He is. And nothing can satisfy your soul as He will.

Lord, I want You to be first in my life. Purge
anything that does not serve Your will or
help me follow You faithfully, amen.

In His presence . . . declare He is first.

KNOWING GOD'S WILL

Ask God to fill you with the knowledge of his will through
all the wisdom and understanding that the Spirit gives.

COLOSSIANS 1:9 NIV

Do you find that knowing God's will feels like a constant struggle? Do you weigh the pros and cons of your decisions, look for signs of His direction, but then continue to wonder if you're truly making choices that honor Him?

Friend, understanding God's will for your life is not as ambiguous as you may think. The Lord *wants* you to obey Him—He eagerly seeks to direct your path. So when you're walking with Him, He provides the wisdom you need for every step.

But how do you ensure you're staying in close fellowship with the Father? First, give yourself to Him completely, understanding that you are His beloved child and He would never steer you wrong. Second, refuse to be conformed to the world's standards or follow its strategies to achieve your goals. Third, be transformed by allowing the Holy Spirit to change the way you think.

Finally, trust that the God who saved you is able to teach you the way you should go. He will not fail you, friend. Trust Him.

Lord, speak to me strongly by Your Spirit. Teach me
Your will that I may walk in Your ways, amen.

In His presence . . . trust Him to lead you.

Count on Him

He who did not spare His own Son, but delivered Him up for
us all, how shall He not with Him also freely give us all things?
ROMANS 8:32 NKJV

You can depend on God. You can count on His loving provision as a fact because you know how much He gave to solve the greatest problem you have—the sin that separated you from His presence (Isaiah 59:2).

The Father understood your deep need to have a relationship with Him, so He gave no less than the One "far above . . . every name that is named" (Ephesians 1:21), His only Son, Jesus. If He would give His own precious Son so you could know Him, why is it you doubt He would want to help you with what you face? Of course your problem matters to Him—because it means so much to you.

The truth of the matter is, the God of all creation, the Great I AM, the King of kings and Lord of lords *loves you*. And He is wholeheartedly committed to you. So listen to Him and trust Him to help you with whatever you need today.

Lord Jesus, thank You for saving me. Thank
You for this trial and for teaching me Your
great provision through it, amen.

In His presence . . . rely on Him completely.

HE WILL

*"I am God Almighty; walk before Me, and be
blameless. I will* establish My covenant between Me
and you, *and I will* multiply you exceedingly.*"*

GENESIS 17:1–2, EMPHASIS ADDED

Do not miss the pivotal words in the covenant between the Lord and Abraham: "I will." From the beginning, God took the full responsibility for fulfilling His promise. It was up to Him to give Abraham a son and multiply his descendants.

Have you asked the Father to help you in some area? Is His answer taking longer than you expected? Does the attainment of your hope seem impossible? Don't make the terrible mistake of taking matters into your own hands. Sarah did so by offering her maidservant Hagar to Abraham, and Israel is still suffering because of her impatience.

Rather, remember that it's "God who accomplishes all things" for you (Psalm 57:2). Abraham's only responsibility was to follow the Lord obediently, and the same is true for you.

So stop trying to handle everything on your own. It's His responsibility. Trust that the Father has wondrous plans for your life and that *He will* bring them about.

*Lord, thank You for taking full responsibility. Help me
walk obediently and trust Your perfect plan, amen.*

---- ❀ ----

**In His presence . . . trust that
He will fulfill His promises.**

WHEN YOU'RE DRY

My soul thirsts for God, for the living God.
PSALM 42:2

Do you feel discouraged, dry, and weak—as if God has disappeared and you're merely surviving? At times, the Father allows you to face a season when you feel defeated and spiritually parched in order to draw you closer to Himself.

Although you might think the desert experiences of life would drive you farther from the Savior, they can actually mature your faith in Him greatly. Like a lost child looking for his parents, you seek Him desperately, listen intently for His voice, and long for His presence.

You also cast off anything that would hinder you from finding Him. In fact, more than likely you'll discover that when you don't feel the Father's presence, it's because you've unintentionally become focused on something other than Him. You are distracted and no longer drinking in His marvelous presence. He's not your first priority, so He creates a thirst for Him in you.

So return to the Lord and enjoy Him. It may take time to rebuild your relationship, but be assured, those who seek Him "shall be satisfied" (Matthew 5:6).

Lord, I am thirsty for Your wonderful
presence. Restore our fellowship, and help
me experience Your love, amen.

In His presence . . . your thirst will be satisfied.

OVERCOMING FAULTY FAITH

The righteousness of God is revealed from faith to faith; as
it is written, "But the righteous man shall live by faith."
ROMANS 1:17

The greatest barrier to your faith is not circumstances, your past, or anyone's actions. Rather, it's your lack of belief in God's sovereignty, wisdom, and love. You don't trust Him. And it's hindering His power from flowing in your life.

So how do you overcome faulty faith? First, ask the Lord to help you be so centered on Him that when difficulties arise, you immediately look for His aid. He will help you achieve this focus as you spend time with Him and meditate on His Word daily.

Second, relinquish your desire for control. Friend, it's scary to let go—there's no doubt about it. But whenever the Father calls you to follow Him in faith, He promises to support you every step of the way. He assumes full responsibility for your needs and is ready to equip you for whatever arises.

So overcome your faulty faith by releasing your need to direct your circumstances and trusting in your sovereign Savior. Obey God and leave the consequences to Him. He will certainly bless you.

Father, strengthen my faith. Help me trust
You fully whenever troubles arise and
keep my eyes fixed on You, amen.

In His presence . . . strengthen your faith.

CAUSE FOR FAITH

Let us run with endurance the race that is set before us,
fixing our eyes on Jesus, the author and perfecter of faith.
HEBREWS 12:1–2

Whenever you struggle with your faith in a particular situation, remember: you can place your trust in Jesus because of who He is and what He's done.

He is your Savior, Lord, Life-Giver, Protector, Provider, Counselor, Sustainer, and Redeemer. He knows everything about you—even details you don't know about yourself.

Because the Lord God is omniscient and omnipotent, He always knows what is absolutely best for you. And because He loves you, you can count on the fact that He will faithfully provide it for you.

Your wonderful Savior has forgiven you of all your sins (Colossians 1:13–14), made you complete (Colossians 2:10), and has given you everything you need for life and godliness (2 Peter 1:3). He is absolutely sovereign, unfathomably wise, and He cares for you perfectly.

Friend, you can trust Jesus to guide your steps. So place your absolute faith in Him, confident that He will honor your trust in Him and lead you to life at its very best.

Lord Jesus, I fix my eyes on You, confident You
will lead me in the best way possible, amen.

In His presence . . . fix your eyes on
Him and be filled with faith.

AUGUST

HE FILLS THE GAPS

"My grace is all you need. My power works best in weakness." So now I am glad to boast about my weaknesses, so that the power of Christ can work through me.

2 CORINTHIANS 12:9 NLT

When you struggle with a heavy load of any kind, isn't it wonderful when someone offers to help, or insists that you rest as they take care of things for a while? This is what happens with your life when you accept Christ and remain in relationship with Him. He says that as you grow in Him, He will work out His perfection in you. You don't have to struggle, strive, or wear yourself out. He will work in you—in His timing, using His methods, and all for His purposes.

Friend, be encouraged. Nobody can be the best always. Nobody gets it right every time. But it's in your times of weakness and failure that you have the capacity to grow the most.

When you have fallen short, you are in the perfect position to trust God to cover your failings. Therefore, take heart and rely on Him to help you succeed.

Heavenly Father, help me view my times of weakness as opportunities to grow in You, amen.

In His presence . . . His grace completes you.

LISTENING WITH PATIENCE

*"Those who, having heard the word with a noble and
good heart, keep it and bear fruit with patience."*
LUKE 8:15 NKJV

Nowhere in Scripture does God tell anyone to rush into a decision. Though there may be times when you need to hear from Him quickly, the Lord will never tell you to hurry forward blindly.

Satan, on the other hand, always encourages you to act immediately, because his desire is to rush you to destruction. The enemy knows if you back off and think long enough about a decision, you'll make a better choice—thwarting his ultimate plan.

Friend, if you feel an overwhelming urge to act spontaneously, pull in the reins. Be willing to listen to God persistently and patiently—even when doing so stretches your faith. Your loving heavenly Father has promised to speak to your heart, so you can expect Him to do so faithfully.

Just realize God most likely won't tell you everything the moment you desire the information. Instead, He will guide you one step at a time, waiting until all the details are in their proper places for your good, and then He will instruct you in how to proceed.

*Father, may Your Spirit work patience in me so I
can wait with joy for Your instruction, amen.*

In His presence . . . listen to Him with patience.

PURIFICATION

Create in me a clean heart, O God.
Renew a loyal spirit within me.
PSALM 51:10 NLT

When God points out areas of your life to work on, it's because He loves you. He wants to cleanse you so that you will be filled with His life and joy.

But be aware, these are the very times you will be tempted to run away from the Father, imagining He's angry with you or no longer loves you. Don't do it. Stay the course and develop your relationship with Him.

Because it is when you're willing to sit before the Lord and allow Him to expose your heart that your life is transformed. He prunes whatever isn't spiritually edifying from your life. So whatever He brings to your mind today, the best thing you can do is admit it, confess it, repent of it, and deal with it. That's the sure way to keep your sweet fellowship with the Father alive and healthy.

Friend, don't ignore God or rationalize your actions because that will only stymie your growth. Rather, humble yourself before Him, confess your transgressions, and ask Him to cleanse you. And be assured—He will never turn you away.

Lord, cleanse me so that I can enjoy uninterrupted
fellowship with You. Thank You for forgiving me, amen.

In His presence . . . be cleansed.

HIS GREAT LOVE

*See how great a love the Father has bestowed on
us, that we would be called children of God.*

1 JOHN 3:1

No one loves you more intimately and unconditionally than God does. He created you to be in relationship with Him—to glorify Him, have fellowship with Him, and be His beloved child forever.

He wants you to know how deeply and unconditionally He cares for you. There is nothing you could ever do to surprise or disappoint Him because He knows all things and is never shocked by your actions. Although He does not approve of sin, and may urge you to repent of ungodly behavior, He will always invite you back into His presence and accept you when you repent (1 John 1:9).

Therefore, when you do stumble, always remember you have an Advocate before the Father—Jesus Christ—who hears your prayers for forgiveness and cares when you are hurting. God may discipline you when you yield to temptation, but He will never withhold His love from you. You are His child. This truth never changes. And because He is righteous, loving, and steadfast, He will certainly never fail you.

*Lord, thank You for forgiving me. No matter what,
Your love is everlasting—and I am so grateful! Amen.*

In His presence . . . you are dearly loved.

ROOTED

"He has no firm root in himself . . . and when
affliction or persecution arises because of the
word, immediately he falls away."

MATTHEW 13:21

Friend, are there areas in your life where—because of past pain and self-protection—you will not allow the Word to take hold? If so, then it's likely that when the storms of life arise, you are completely devastated, you don't have anything solid to anchor to (Matthew 7:24–27).

This is why it is so crucial that you constantly renew your mind and allow the Lord to "plow up the ground" of your heart so that the Word of God can take root deep within you and you know what you believe without wavering.

So today, ask the Father to reveal the issues that are preventing you from accepting His Word—the areas where you've refused to trust Him. You may already know what they are because they are constantly causing you trouble. But acknowledge the rocky places and commit yourself to applying God's truth to your life. It will be difficult, friend, but it is worthwhile—because this is where your true healing begins.

Father, please reveal areas where Scripture hasn't
taken root. Make Your Word the foundation of
my life so that I may glorify Your name, amen.

In His presence . . . allow His truth to take root.

PRAYING IN FAITH

"I pray that they will all be one, just as you and I are one—as you are in me, Father, and I am in you."

JOHN 17:21 NLT

Jesus often went to the Father with concerns and petitions; and like Him, we are encouraged to make our requests known to God in all circumstances. We are to come boldly before the Lord with our specific needs—not timidly (Hebrews 4:16).

Friend, through Christ, your spirit has been forever joined to the One who has all answers, all solutions, all provision, all blessings. Therefore, your mind should be focused on the God who saves, delivers, heals, redeems, and restores you, regardless of your circumstances. He multiplies your resources, provides in ways you cannot even imagine, and is able to work miraculously on your behalf.

So pray! Turn your attention to the Father, who knows all, controls all, has all power, and is all-loving. He will help you be one with Him through the Spirit and walk according to His will. Thanks be to the Lord Jesus, whose ultimate sacrifice now allows us this sort of access!

Lord Jesus, thank You for making me one with You and giving me unlimited access to Your throne of grace, amen.

❀

In His presence . . . be confident in prayer.

AN INTIMATE COMPANION

Come close to God, and God will come close to you.
JAMES 4:8 NLT

God wants to build an intimate relationship with you, but do you desire the same thing? The intimate moments you share with the Savior—worshipping Him, sensing His closeness, and expressing your love for Him—are the very times when He reveals Himself to you. In fact, Exodus 33:11 describes the conversations God had with Moses "as one speaks to a friend." The word *friend* here means "intimate companion." This is the kind of relationship He desires to have with you as well.

The Lord never intended for you to merely know *about* Him. He wants you to know His ways and His unconditional love for you on a deeply personal level as you go through life—to see Him as your unfailing Companion and wonderful Friend.

Therefore, draw closer to the Father in fellowship. Because when you do, you'll trust Him more deeply and share the feelings and challenges you face with Him more openly. And you will get to know Him as Moses did—as your truly intimate, trustworthy Friend, who loves you, provides for you, and knows you best.

Lord, draw me close. May Your sweet
Spirit guide all my ways, amen.

———————— ❧ ————————

In His presence . . .
confidently draw near to Him.

GIFTS BY DESIGN

A spiritual gift is given to each of us so we can help each other.
1 CORINTHIANS 12:7 NLT

God doesn't act in a haphazard manner—He plans. And just as He strategically formed creation, He designed you carefully and gave you everything needed to carry out a specific purpose.

The Father has endowed you with distinctive gifts and talents to fulfill your special role in edifying the body of Christ. The Lord does this, not only to bless others and glorify His name, but to help you feel accepted, needed, and worthwhile by making you an integral part of His work.

So what did God have in mind when He created you—when He planned your purpose and gave you spiritual gifts? One thing is certain—if you ask Him, He'll not only tell you, but He will reveal the place where He wants you to serve.

So honor your heavenly Father by surrendering yourself to His plan and exercising your gifts in the service of other believers. It was the path you were created for and how you'll experience the depth of His joy, peace, and fulfillment.

Father, thank You for the gifts You've given
me and the wonderful plan You have for my
life. Help me serve You faithfully, amen.

In His presence . . . exercise the gifts He has given you.

THE IMPORTANCE OF FELLOWSHIP

Not forsaking our own assembling together, as is the
habit of some, but encouraging one another; and
all the more as you see the day drawing near.

HEBREWS 10:25

Have you ever questioned the necessity of being in fellowship with other believers? Perhaps someone in church hurt you or you didn't feel as though you fit in. Whatever the reason, you are missing out on genuine friendship, worship, support, opportunities for service, encouragement, instruction in your faith, and the love the Lord wants to show you through other believers.

Friend, no one can "go it alone" spiritually—and that's by design. God gathers His people into a community of faith and fellowship so that we can minister to each other and find the strength and courage we need for our daily burdens (Galatians 6:2).

So if you don't have a church to call home, ask the Father to lead you to a place He knows you'll thrive. Join a small group or Bible study. The important thing to remember is—don't try to go it alone.

Lord, I want to serve You and honor You in
all I do—and I know that means loving and
serving other believers. Help me be obedient
to wherever Your Spirit leads me, amen.

In His presence . . . find a place to serve and fellowship.

DRAWING NEAR TO GOD

Let me know Your ways that I may know You,
so that I may find favor in Your sight.

EXODUS 33:13

Moses loved and revered God. He sought out a relationship with Him that went much deeper than just believing the Lord exists—he wanted to live in a manner that honored his Creator. So Moses prayed and sought His face. And the Lord honored Moses greatly (Exodus 33:19–23).

Friend, learn from Moses' example. Set your heart to search out God's ways and experience an extraordinary blessing. As you understand how the Lord thinks and operates, you'll be amazed at the inconceivably awesome way He works in your life and the astounding depth of His love for you.

Eventually you will experience intimacy with the Savior in ways you never imagined. As it did for Moses, this will absolutely revolutionize your life. Undoubtedly, your desire to please Him will increase. You will learn to rest in the fact that He is God, and He is at work. But you will also have the right tools to live an abundant life—one that is complete, glorious, full of favor, and marvelously eternal.

Lord, I want to understand Your ways. Show me who
You are so I may find favor in Your sight, amen.

⁙

In His presence . . . you will discover His ways.

SUBMISSION IN MEDITATION

Humble yourselves in the sight of the
Lord, and He will lift you up.
JAMES 4:10 NKJV

If there is rebellion in your heart and you insist on having your own way, you will most likely find it very difficult to meditate. You won't want to be alone with God because He will expose the issues of your life that you prefer to keep hidden. Every time you go before Him, He will insist that you deal with the sin. Eventually you must either agree with Him and have your relationship restored or you'll quit going to Him altogether.

Friend, when you refuse to deal with a problem God has pinpointed, you don't lose your standing with Him—you are still saved. But your fellowship with Him is broken.

Don't miss out on a relationship with the Father because of sin and pride. Repent. Agree that you've been wrong and that He is right. Allow Him to free you from the stronghold. And enjoy the wonderful rewards of spending time alone with God, thinking about Him, obeying Him, and praising His holy name.

Lord, forgive me of my sins! I don't want anything
to come between us. Thank You for forgiving me
and drawing me back into Your presence, amen.

In His presence . . . confess any
rebellion and run to His arms.

INTIMACY IS ESSENTIAL

"Call to Me, and I will answer you, and show you
great and mighty things, which you do not know."
JEREMIAH 33:3 NKJV

At some point, we all wrestle with why God allows us to suffer and we wonder if it's because He no longer loves us. But the truth is, some of the greatest lessons we ever learn come as the result of hardship. During those painful times, if we'll cling to the Father, we'll gain tremendous insight into His heart and mind.

Friend, when you experience trials, realize that God doesn't want to hurt you (Lamentations 3:32–33). Rather, He has great things He wants to teach you—lessons that, unfortunately, can only be learned through sorrow (Hebrews 5:8). So when trouble strikes, be still and ask the Lord to show you what you can learn through the situation.

Your Savior is here—right now, right beside you. Your loving heavenly Father is beckoning to you, asking you to draw near and learn His ways. So call on Him. He will answer you. And He will teach you great and mighty things that you need to know.

Father, what would You have me learn through my
heartache? Teach me, my Lord—I am listening, amen.

In His presence . . . call to Him
and expect Him to answer.

LISTEN

Listen closely, Israel, and be careful to obey.
Then all will go well with you.

DEUTERONOMY 6:3 NLT

Why do you go to church, read the Bible, or attend Christian conferences? Most likely it is to hear what the Father is saying to you.

And if the Lord were to send you a personalized letter, address it, *Dear (your name)*, and sign it *YHWH God*, would you put it aside and read it after the evening news was over? Of course not. You would open the letter reverently, read it carefully, and probably reread it often.

Unfortunately there are many believers who never really give a second thought to what the Lord is saying. They are passive listeners—not involved in the hearing process and unchanged within. Sadly, they miss the joy and power of the Christian life.

Thankfully, that does not have to be you. You have a personal letter from God through the words of the Bible, and it will transform you as you apply it to your life. So today, don't miss out. Open the Word and listen to the Father with passion.

Father, I want to know You! Teach me to be an active
listener and increase my love for Your Word, amen.

In His presence . . .
apply His truth to your life.

NONE OTHER WILL DO

"You are my Lord, my goodness is nothing apart from You."
PSALM 16:2 NKJV

Within the heart of every man and woman there is a place that only God can fill. We may try to satisfy our longings with different things; but until we come to a point of full surrender to Him, we will remain vulnerable to fearful thoughts, feelings of discontentment, and selfish desires, as well as pride and lust.

But when you fellowship with God, He begins to transform the very core of your being—shifting your focus from yourself to Christ. He takes the throne of your heart—conforming you to His character, freeing you of sinful strongholds, and surrounding you with His eternal care.

Practically speaking, you cannot experience this unless you actively seek to walk in God's ways and surrender yourself to Him. As long as you hold Him at arm's length, you cannot know Him. This is because abiding relationships, including yours with the Lord, can only exist and grow through mutual intimacy.

Friend, the only relationship that can fill your longings, sustain you through difficulties, and bring you peace is the relationship you have with God. Don't hold Him back in any way.

Father, take the throne of my heart and
make me a vessel for Your glory, amen.

❦

In His presence . . . abide fully in His love.

UNREASONABLE

"My thoughts are not your thoughts, nor are
your ways My ways," says the LORD.
ISAIAH 55:8 NKJV

Sometimes God will require something of you that doesn't make sense. For example, Jesus said that if a fellow strikes you on one cheek, you should turn and offer him the other (Matthew 5:39). That's not exactly reasonable.

The Savior also said that if someone commands you to go one mile with him, you should cheerfully go two—giving above and beyond what is asked, even if it's inconvenient (v. 41). That's not necessarily practical either. But Jesus' wisdom far exceeds the world's, and He often did the opposite of what people expected because He understood spiritual realities they were too limited to see.

That's not to say that the Lord doesn't utilize human wisdom—He does. But quite often, He will ask you to accomplish goals that seem illogical to your rational mind. When this occurs, be mindful that God is purposeful, wise, and absolutely sovereign. His ways are far higher than your own. And He will certainly bless you as you trust and obey Him.

Father, equip me and make my paths straight so
that I may participate in Your work, amen.

———————— ✿ ————————

In His presence . . . believe He is
leading you with wisdom and power.

FAITHFUL IN EVERYTHING

"He who is faithful in a very little thing is faithful also in much."
LUKE 16:10

There will be opportunities today for you to take shortcuts and do less than your best—and you may have a million reasons for why you should do so. However, realize that whenever you choose to throw away any opportunity for honoring God, you're cutting yourself off from His best blessings. But if you glorify Him in even the minor issues, He will reward your faithfulness.

For example, when Joseph's brothers sold him into slavery (Genesis 37), he served in Potiphar's household, was falsely accused, and went to jail (Genesis 39). Yet he refused to feel sorry for himself. Rather, he chose to do the absolute best job possible—not just to bless the warden of the prison, but to honor God. And the Lord eventually used his dedication to place him as second in command of Egypt (Genesis 40–41).

Friend, don't look at your circumstances or try to cut corners. Do your best wherever God has placed you and trust Him to lift you up (1 Peter 5:5–6). Wherever you are, work with excellence, and trust He will lead you on the path of blessing.

Lord, help me do my best so You will
always be glorified in my life, amen.

❧

In His presence . . . be faithful.

PRAYING WITH THANKSGIVING

It is good to give thanks to the LORD and to sing
praises to Your name, O Most High.

PSALM 92:1

Do you pray to God with thanksgiving in your heart? Do you approach His throne of grace with praise? If so, you've likely found that doing so ushers you into His presence in a way nothing else can. You move from worrying about your problems to exalting the One who can solve anything that concerns you. And it is in these moments of adoration that the Father gives you the unshakable assurance that all will be well.

Therefore, right now, praise Him. Thank God that He has the power to resolve your problems, wisdom to know what's best for you, and mercy to forgive your failings. Worship the Lord for His love, for His wonderful purpose for your life, and for providing you with a home in heaven.

No doubt you'll have more reasons to voice your appreciation. But one thing is sure—there's no substitute for thanksgiving and praise to grow your intimate relationship with the Father. Therefore, don't wait. Worship the Lord for who He is right now.

You are my Savior, Redeemer, Victorious Warrior,
Healer, Deliverer, and Counselor. Thank You
for loving me, my Lord and my God!

In His presence . . . praise God with a thankful heart.

CHOOSING TO FOLLOW

"If anyone desires to come after Me, let him deny
himself, and take up his cross, and follow Me."
MATTHEW 16:24 NKJV

Are you in a situation that is not God's best for you? Are you facing the consequences of your decisions and wondering if He will ever help you again?

While the Father is always glad to provide the wisdom and insight you need, He will wait to answer you until you're in a position to accept His guidance. In other words, He wants you to be willing to do as He says.

If you think about it, Jesus made Himself available to His disciples, but they had to *choose* to follow Him and obey His commands. Some who heard the Savior speak went away unchanged. But those who submitted to His leadership experienced a dramatic transformation.

You have the same opportunity today. So present yourself to the Lord—knowing that He loves and accepts you completely—and do as He says. And, friend, be assured as He works on your heart, changes *will* come; some of them painful, some of them delightful—but all of them purposeful.

Father, I will trust Your ways for my life. Help
me graciously accept whatever changes or
opportunities You put before me, amen.

In His presence . . . allow Him to guide your steps.

UNSHAKABLE

I have set the LORD continually before me; because
He is at my right hand, I will not be shaken.

PSALM 16:8–9

Have you ever wondered why Mary wasn't afraid to risk public shame to obey God? Or why the apostle Paul didn't abandon his faith as he experienced severe suffering? Or how David not only survived but *thrived* during the years King Saul persecuted him?

Through trials, difficulties, heartaches, and deep sorrows, men and women like Mary, Paul, and David learned the ways of God. They found that His love never changes and that He is completely trustworthy. His wonderful, abiding presence kept them faithful even as the world fell apart around them.

Likewise, by learning His ways, you will have all you need to stand firm in your faith at every turn in life. When you understand—as they did—the power that's yours in Christ, you won't be so fearful. You'll realize that whatever comes your way first passes through the loving hands of your Savior. And His love, power, strength, and abiding care will strengthen your soul in times of great distress—regardless of what trials may come.

Father, You are continually before me. Because
You sustain me, I shall not be shaken. Thank
You for holding me steady, amen.

❀

In His presence . . . you have His power to stand firm.

SEEK GOD'S DIRECTION

This also comes from the LORD of hosts, who is
wonderful in counsel and excellent in guidance.
ISAIAH 28:29 NKJV

Do you trust God to lead you in a way that is beneficial—a manner that is absolutely best for you? If you're like a lot of believers, you say you do, but your actions may tell a different story.

Often we may say we believe the Lord is all-wise and knows what is best for us, but then we look for advice from people around us. Our pride or refusal to be open to His plan can bring misery and regret.

My friend, listen: only one Person has absolute knowledge, and that is the Lord. And He has promised to provide all the guidance you need. You can worry, fret, and fume about an issue that God has already dealt with—and continue to be miserable. But if you will set your heart to trust Him, He will help you obey Him each and every time. He will guide you step by step, even when you don't see His omnipotent hand.

Lord, the next time I start to turn to friends
for direction, stop me! I want to hear from
You first to know my certain path, amen.

In His presence . . . accept
that His is the best plan.

YOUR FULL POTENTIAL

"Before I formed you in the womb I knew you,
before you were born I set you apart."
JEREMIAH 1:5 NIV

Many people wonder, *God, can You really use me? Can You really make something of my life?*

Yes, friend—He can! No matter how old or young you are, the Father has wonderful plans for you and is—even at this moment—training you by His Spirit.

How can you know this for sure? Because in Christ, you are God's beloved child. You have been given the spiritually miraculous opportunity to have a personal relationship with the God of the universe. And because of that—not your strengths, intelligence, or talents; rather, your relationship with Him—He can work through you in astounding ways that will thrill your soul.

You may not understand why the Lord directs you on a certain path, but if you are willing to obey Him and learn His ways, you will gain insight into His heart. Then His Spirit will enable you to carry out all the good works He planned for you to accomplish even before you were born.

Father, mold me, lead me, and use me to fulfill
Your purpose for me in this life, amen.

———————— ✙ ————————

In His presence . . . discover
your full potential.

The Ways of God

Blessed are those who keep my ways.
PROVERBS 8:32 NKJV

Sometimes when God is revealing Himself to you, He may move in your life in a miraculous way. But friend, take note—He not only wants you to understand His divine, omnipotent nature, He also wants to teach you about His attributes and character, and for you to desire the same things that He does.

This means God shows you not just to do good works but to be fully devoted to Christ and His purposes. Yes, there is a difference. You can perform acts of charity without ever loving those you serve. But when you're influenced by the Spirit of the living God, you have a deep, passionate love for souls that transcends their physical needs or how they respond to you.

You see, when God is at work in your life, He brings *eternal* change. He lifts you up, prepares you for His service, and gives you a greater understanding of why He gave so much to redeem humanity. Knowing who He is in such a profound way will transform your life, inspire you to reach others, and bring about a greater sense of peace and security than this world can ever deliver.

*Lord, please align my desires with Yours as
I fellowship with You today, amen.*

In His presence . . . experience and reflect His love.

PEACE THROUGH OBEDIENCE

I will hear what God the LORD will say; for
He will speak peace to His people.
PSALM 85:8

There's one thing I can tell you with certainty: I've never met a person who regretted obeying God. Sadly, too many people live in a storm because they're running from Him. They think that if they drink enough, dull their pain with drugs, acquire plenty of money, or have the right relationships, somehow they will be able to silence the raging waves of fear within them. But they're wrong. They may block out the tempest for a while, but it always comes back with a vengeance.

But when you express a true desire for the Lord to help you, something inside of you changes. He takes you to a deeper level of intimacy with Him and transforms you—changing your very nature to quiet the storm within you.

Friend, you can't find true joy and satisfaction by knowing just a little about the Savior. They are discovered through learning His ways, walking in fellowship with Him daily, and asking Him to make His desires yours. So don't run from Him. Obey Him and allow Him to speak peace over your life.

Jesus, keep me close so I can follow Your lead
and learn more about Your ways, amen.

———————————————— ❧ ————————————————

In His presence . . . trust Him to quiet the storms.

CLING TO HIM

The LORD is my shepherd, I lack nothing.
PSALM 23:1 NIV

At times, God's ways can seem perplexing. One reason is our lack of understanding of how He works. Another reason is our desire to be set free quickly from trouble, heartache, or disappointment. We may accept the challenge when trouble first appears, but after a season or two, we are ready to be freed of our pain. Unfortunately, the enemy will take the opportunity to tempt us into thinking that the Lord is not working in our best interests, so we end up questioning His wisdom.

When we know someone intimately, however, we know what that person likes, how he responds, how deeply he loves us, and whether we can truly trust him. The same is true in our relationship with the Savior.

Friend, when you understand *why* Jesus does certain things in your life, then you will develop true insight into how greatly He cares for you. God loves you profoundly—beyond what you can fathom. And if you will continue to cling to Him through the troublesome times, you will discover the depth of His love in ways beyond human expression.

Lord, I will cling to You. Thank You for the
opportunity to know and love You beyond
what words can express, amen.

⚬⚬

**In His presence . . . seek to understand
the depth of His desires for you.**

TIME WITH GOD

My soul longs for You, indeed, my spirit
within me seeks You diligently.
ISAIAH 26:9

Do you desire more time with the Lord but can't seem to make it work out? The day gets away from you, and the next thing you know, it is time to start all over again.

We are commanded to seek the Savior—to have a desire to know Him and His ways. He also tells us that if we will pursue Him, we will find Him. But it doesn't just happen—we must make Jesus a priority. A demanding schedule or busy personal life is no excuse. We must be careful not to pursue urgent or immediate goals while we miss the one thing that is absolutely essential to our spiritual health and, ultimately, our enduring success: intimacy with God.

So set boundaries—let nothing interrupt the time you have apportioned for the Father. He will teach you about His nature and His eternal care, and will give you the strength to meet the challenges of life. Then when problems come, challenges increase, or sorrows deepen, you will instinctively go to Him for wisdom and guidance with the confidence that He will provide only the absolute best for you.

Lord, help me set aside time to
spend with You, amen.

❈

In His presence . . . make Him your priority.

DON'T MISS HIM

"Martha, you are worried and upset over all these details!
There is only one thing worth being concerned about."
LUKE 10:41–42 NLT

In today's verse, Jesus' goal was not to discourage Martha; He understood her desire to prepare a wonderful meal for those present. But He wanted to make a point concerning our fellowship with God. Martha was so distracted by her duties that she couldn't grasp the importance of simply *being* with the Savior. Her service was very important but paled in comparison to how crucial it was for her to experience God's presence.

Are you guilty of doing the same thing? Do you focus on what you must do so much that you miss who you're doing it for? The Holy Spirit is drawing you close, but you can block fellowship with Him by becoming involved in too many activities—including the godly ones.

So set your heart to fellowship with Jesus today. Certainly reading and studying His Word, and engaging in sincere prayer and worship are very important to knowing Him. But simply being alone with Him and experiencing His presence are also crucial. Friend, your Savior loves you. Turn to Him, be silent, and draw close.

Lord, I'm so grateful for You! Draw me close and bless
me with the knowledge of Your presence, amen.

In His presence . . . know Him.

A Glimpse of Heaven

"Worthy are You ... for You were slain, and
purchased for God with Your blood men from every
tribe and tongue and people and nation."

REVELATION 5:9

Do you long for a glimpse of heaven? The Lord allowed the apostle John to see the glories of heaven, and what he found was that first and foremost, it is a place of praise for the One who bought our salvation.

Of course, when John saw his risen Savior, he was overwhelmed by a desire to worship. And he wasn't alone. John reported seeing myriads of angels, living creatures, and elders saying, "Worthy is the Lamb that was slain to receive . . . honor and glory and blessing" (Revelation 5:11–12).

Take this to heart today as you think about your Savior. When you are called to stand in His presence, everything else—even the troubles that appear overwhelming today—will seem small and insignificant in comparison. There will be only one desire in your heart: to bow down and worship your Savior.

Friend, you can enjoy a glimpse of heaven here and now. Enter God's presence with a grateful, worshipful heart as you meditate on His goodness to you.

Jesus, thank You for Your salvation and goodness to
me. I worship You, my beloved Redeemer, amen.

—————————— ෨෨ ——————————

In His presence . . . worship Him unreservedly.

NONE LIKE HIM

The LORD gives strength to his people; the
LORD blesses his people with peace.

PSALM 29:11 NIV

At times, people hesitate to build a deep relationship with the Lord because they think He will require painful sacrifices from them. They assume that they have troubles because the Father doesn't care about them or is punishing them. But once they submit themselves to Him, the pressure they once felt lifts. They understand they can trust Him—and that He only wanted what was absolutely best for them.

God is God. There is none like Him, and He doesn't have to hound us to make His point or gain our attention. He may allow trouble to come as the result of sin or as a way to teach us more about Him. But the Father also understands that if we never experienced times of adversity, we would miss one of the most important aspects of His love: His ability to work in our lives in the ways we need Him to the most—delivering us from spiritual bondage; helping us rely on His faultless wisdom and power; and teaching us that nothing can touch our lives apart from His divine purposes.

Lord, thank You for loving, teaching, providing for,
and protecting me. I know You are truly good, amen.

In His presence . . . know He is good.

CROSSROADS

How blessed is the man who has made the LORD his trust.
PSALM 40:4

Are you standing at a crossroads, wondering whether you can really trust God? He is pointing you in a particular direction and outwardly you may say, "I believe He will help me." But deep inside you wonder whether He will really come through for you.

Friend, you may be standing at the brink of a blessing, and the only thing standing between you and what your heart desires is a step of faith. Of course God understands that you feel torn about the future. He knows that trusting Him more is a process—one that's often long and challenging. But you can do it! You can put your complete faith in Him, knowing He has never failed to keep any of His promises—not one of them (Joshua 21:45).

You may not fully comprehend what is ahead because God's ways are beyond your human ability to understand them (Isaiah 55:8). But be assured that His Holy Spirit is there to guide you every inch of the way (John 16:13). So take His direction, step out in faith, and receive all He has for you.

*God, thank You for giving me Your Holy Spirit to
guide me and help me understand Your ways, amen.*

⁂

In His presence . . . find wisdom and guidance.

MAKING IMPORTANT DECISIONS

For Your name's sake You will lead me and guide me.

PSALM 31:3

Did you know that the Lord has your best interests at heart every second of your life? There is never a moment when He stops caring about you or doesn't work to provide His very finest for you. In Psalm 16:11, He guarantees to show you the path of life as you follow Him. Then in Psalm 32:8, God promises to instruct you in the way you should go, and to guide you with His eye upon you.

While we can only see the present, the Lord sees the beginning, middle, and end. Why, then, would we not ask Him to lead us—not only in major decisions, but also in our daily choices?

So consider, do you prayerfully submit your choices to the Father and rejoice in the fact that He has given you His Holy Spirit as a Navigator in your search for direction? If so, instead of telling Him what you wish to do, make it a practice to ask Him first instead. And trust Him to lead you to blessings that are better than you could have imagined.

God, thank You for guiding my decisions,
no matter how big or small, amen.

In His presence . . . turn to Him for all decisions.

LOVE THROUGH FORGIVENESS

"Her many sins have been forgiven—
as her great love has shown."

LUKE 7:47 NIV

There are many reasons why people fail to experience God's love, and one of them is unforgiveness. When we don't forgive, a barrier of bitterness grows and obstructs His love from entering in.

Friend, are you harboring resentment? Then you're hurting yourself without reason. Jesus came to set the captives free (Luke 4:18)—and He did so through His love on the cross. He came, not to injure you, but to heal your wounds. And He calls you to forgive those who've hurt you because it's a crucial part of liberating you fully.

He asks you to have an accurate view of all you've been forgiven so you can understand others (Luke 7:47). You sinned out of pain, unawareness, fear, and self-protection (Luke 23:34). The same is true for those who've hurt you—they sinned out of ignorance; they couldn't possibly know the full effect their actions would have on you.

Friend, don't remain captive to your hostility any longer. Express Christ-like mercy to your offenders and be free of the prison. Because then you'll be able to fully experience His love in return.

Jesus, give me the strength to forgive so I can
experience Your peace and love to the fullest, amen.

꩜

In His presence . . . choose forgiveness.

SEPTEMBER

THE FUTILITY OF REGRET

*If we confess our sins, he is faithful and just and will forgive
us our sins and purify us from all unrighteousness.*

1 JOHN 1:9 NIV

Is there anything in your life that brings you shame? Are there
any memories or choices you've made that you hide from others
because of how much they embarrass you?

Perhaps you've tried to run from those sins, but time has not
healed you. You still feel the disgrace. The biting feelings of regret
and unworthiness won't go away.

Friend, God never intended for you to live this way. When He
forgives you, He does so in a manner that takes away your terrible
shame forever (Psalm 103:12). Sin is no longer part of who you are.
You are clean, redeemed—a person who is loved and valued.

So don't get stuck in the past. Don't allow memories of your
failures to keep you from what your heavenly Father created you to
do. Ask God to pardon you.

Then forgive yourself and embrace your true identity in
Christ—forgiven, cleansed, and a powerful vessel of His grace.

*Lord Jesus, thank You for Your forgiveness and
grace! I can move forward with no regrets because
You, my Savior, make me new, amen.*

In His presence . . . is where you are made new.

A Christ-Centered Life

To me, living means living for Christ.
PHILIPPIANS 1:21 NLT

When the Lord doesn't answer your prayers in the way you hope, do you accept His will? Or do you get angry, doubt Him, and question His character? When circumstances turn negative, do you immediately accuse Him of being unloving? Or do you voice your trust that your sovereign, wise, and loving God has allowed the adversity for a purpose—for your good and His glory?

The reason for these questions is to ascertain if there is any self-centeredness in your life—to determine whether you're more concerned with your wishes and goals than you are with God's will.

If so, do not be surprised or discouraged. This is part of the sin nature the Father is purging from your life. He wants you to trust Him fully—with absolute faith that He provides the absolute best for you regardless of what happens. And His ultimate goal is to bring you to the point of saying, "What God wills is what I want. What pleases Him is what I desire. Because for me, to live means exalting Christ who saved me."

Jesus, thank You for saving me and cleansing me
of self-centeredness. Help me live in a manner
that reflects You and Your desires, amen.

In His presence . . . dedicate your life to Christ.

ANXIETY

"Do not worry about your life."
MATTHEW 6:25 NIV

Has anxiety become a way of life for you? Are you living in a constant state of uncertainty and worry? Fear will arise whenever you respond to a problem or troubling situation on your own—without going to God first and seeking His help and power.

The Lord gives you the gift of free will—you can choose what you do, how you feel, what you think about, and even how you'll respond when faced with a problem.

With this in mind, the Father may allow an overwhelming situation to arise in your life in order to develop and strengthen your faith, mature you spiritually, or to change a bad habit or negative attitude. Through your circumstances, He gives you the opportunity to seek Him, trust Him, obey Him, and cast your cares into His able hands.

Therefore, understand your anxiety is an indication that you need God. Every time you sense fear rising up within you, go to your all-powerful, infinitely wise Father. And give Him thanks that He is at work, teaching you to trust Him more, obey Him faithfully, and receive more of His blessings.

Father, I won't be anxious, for You are with me. Thank You for releasing me from the bondage of fear, amen.

In His presence . . . find freedom from anxiety.

LISTEN WITH CONFIDENCE

"Keep on asking, and you will receive what you ask for.
Keep on seeking, and you will find. Keep on knocking,
and the door will be opened to you. For everyone
who asks, receives. Everyone who seeks, finds. And to
everyone who knocks, the door will be opened."

MATTHEW 7:7–8 NLT

When you want to hear from God about a matter, listen with confidence and know that He will reveal everything necessary for the path ahead of you. He always answers with your best interest in mind. He may not always respond in the manner you prefer, but God communicates to you what is essential for your walk with Him.

Would you withhold information from your children that they need in order to be obedient to your instructions? Would you tell them, "Here's what I want you to do," and then not provide them with clear guidance? Certainly not. And neither does your heavenly Father (Matthew 7:11).

Trust Him completely, both in instruction and provision.

Lord, I trust You to know what is best for me.
Therefore, I will trust Your decisions, Your
instruction, and Your provision, amen.

In His presence . . . be confident in Him.

OBEY ANYWAY

Master, we worked hard all night and caught
nothing, but I will do as You say.

LUKE 5:5

Today, recognize that God's ways are not your ways, which means He probably won't lead you in the way you think He will (Isaiah 55:8–9). If your common sense were enough to successfully follow Him, there would be no reason for His Spirit to indwell you or His Word to inform you. But it's not. His plans will always confound your understanding (Proverbs 3:5–6).

Such was the case for Peter, who fished all night and caught nothing. When Jesus instructed him to go back out on the Sea of Galilee, he was reticent. After all, he was weary, he'd just cleaned his nets, and Jesus wasn't a fisherman. Frankly, what the Savior asked made no sense from his human perspective.

Thankfully, Peter obeyed Jesus anyway, and it changed his life forever (Luke 5:1–11).

The same will be true for you when you submit to the Lord. Do as He says even when His direction seems illogical. Because when you do things His way, you'll get His results. And friend, those are miracles you don't want to miss.

Lord, I will obey You. I don't understand Your plans,
but I acknowledge that Your way is always best, amen.

In His presence . . . obey Him without fear.

ABOUT SUBMISSION

Incline your ear [submit and consent to the divine will]
and come to Me; hear, and your soul will revive.

ISAIAH 55:3 AMP

Today, before you even begin to listen to the Father, decide to be submissive. Often the Lord may instruct you in ways that are challenging in order to set you free from bondage and grow your faith. So do not be surprised that responding in obedience to Him will be difficult at times. He asks you to work against the very patterns that hold you captive, and that hurts.

But obey anyway, realizing that your Father understands the struggle you feel. He knew your wounds and spiritual strongholds before you ever came to listen to Him, and He knows exactly how to free you from the pain you feel.

So friend, today, trust that Your Savior works for your best interest. You may not understand how or why God is instructing you to do something—but you can be absolutely certain that blessings will result if you obey Him. So be as submissive as you know how to be and depend on Him to lead you.

Lord, I submit to You daily, so I may hear, trust, and
obey You, even when I don't understand, amen.

In His presence . . . submit to His authority.

RASH DECISIONS

*The plans of the diligent lead surely to plenty, but
those of everyone who is hasty, surely to poverty.*

PROVERBS 21:5 NKJV

When we try to make a decision quickly or without asking God for direction, Satan will be right there saying, "Go ahead! You'll be fine! Don't worry!" But he conveniently leaves out any mention of consequences. This is because Satan wants you to fail—his ultimate goal is to destroy you.

The Father, however, is always concerned about the ramifications of our actions. As we look back on our lives, how many of us, if we had considered the consequences of our decisions, would have made the same choice? Surely we all have a few we'd like to do over.

But whenever God speaks, He has your future in mind. This is why He encourages you to ask, "If I make this decision, what will happen to my family, to my job, to my walk with the Lord?" You see, your loving Savior isn't just the God of today—He also reigns over tomorrow. And when you follow Him, He ensures that your future is bright and hopeful (Jeremiah 29:11). Listen to Him.

*Lord, help me seek Your counsel first. Thank You for
blessing me and keeping me from harm, amen.*

In His presence . . . wait patiently for His response.

TRANSCENDING PEACE

*The peace of God, which surpasses all understanding, will
guard your hearts and minds through Christ Jesus.*

PHILIPPIANS 4:7 NKJV

When God speaks, one of the most prevalent results will be an undeniable sense of peace in your spirit. You may not feel tranquil at first when you approach Him. In fact, you may be full of conflict and strife. But the longer you listen to Him, the quieter your spirit will become. You will begin to possess what the apostle Paul called a tranquility "which surpasses all understanding." It is a calmness that surrounds you like a fortress and keeps you from being overwhelmed with anxiety, worry, and frustration.

Now, it bears mentioning that you will never have God's peace about disobedience in your life. You may be able to justify what you're doing with your mind, but you'll never convince your spirit, and it will hinder you from exercising your faith.

But when God's peace comes to you, you'll know it without a doubt. You have confidence your Father has spoken. You've heard from Him and you believe Him. And you're calm because you know whatever He says to you, He will accomplish.

*Father God, keep my mind and heart fixed on You so
that I can experience the fullness of Your peace, amen.*

⁂

In His presence . . . seek His peace.

MEDITATION

King David went in and sat before the LORD and prayed.

2 SAMUEL 7:18 NLT

Today, notice the phrase "David . . . sat before the LORD." This signifies that David was meditating—focusing on the Father's ways and character. And it made sense for him to do so. As a man after God's own heart, David wanted to know the Lord's will for his life. And to a large extent, God revealed it to him as David persistently meditated before Him—and He blessed David greatly.

Likewise, meditation should be a daily priority for all believers. Of course, it is the one discipline Satan will doggedly keep us from observing because of all the Lord accomplishes through it. But it is of immense value if we are to know the Father, listen accurately to Him, and walk in His will.

So consider, what dilemma has you confounded today? What need is there that isn't being filled or task that you're hesitant to accomplish? Spend time today meditating upon God and His Word and He will certainly show you what to do.

Lord, help me make time with You my first
priority of each day, and keep my mind
fixed on all You teach me, amen.

In His presence . . . focus on Him.

PEACE WITH OTHERS

Depart from evil and do good; seek peace and pursue it.
PSALM 34:14

Hebrews 12:14 instructs, "Pursue peace with all men." However, this does not signify compromising your beliefs or acting in a sinful manner that dishonors God. Rather, it means practicing loving, godly communication and an attitude of forgiveness.

How do you do so? You prayerfully seek to understand where others are coming from—especially when their words or actions confuse or upset you. Why? Because it's far too easy to misread people's intentions. This is why you should always give others the benefit of your doubt. You don't know what's motivating them to respond as they do.

Pursuing peace with all people isn't easy, and the only way to succeed is to seek the Father's understanding about who they are, what burdens they bear, and what they struggle with rather than relying on your own limited view (1 John 4:20).

Therefore, as you go about your day, make sure that your heart is right with God and that you are not operating out of hurt or anger. Rather, treat others with love, because "love covers a multitude of sins" (1 Peter 4:8) and is the sure path to peace.

Lord, help me always be loving—a peacemaker
who brings You honor and glory, amen.

❁

In His presence . . . seek God's view of others.

RESPONDING TO CRITICISM

"God blesses you when people mock you and persecute
you and lie about you and say all sorts of evil things
against you because you are my followers."
MATTHEW 5:11 NLT

There's no escaping criticism, nor the wounds it can cause. But moments of censure can be opportunities for you to experience God's power if you'll respond in a manner that honors Him.

The truth is, when you're living in obedience to the Savior, others will persecute you for it. Instead of retaliating, Scripture admonishes you to respond by doing good to, praying for, and forgiving the people who attack you—in the hope that they'll "come to their senses and escape from the snare of the devil, having been held captive by him to do his will" (2 Timothy 2:26).

This isn't easy, but you can trust God to work through your obedience to Him. He promises to vindicate you, heal you, and give you a deeper understanding of all Jesus did for you.

So when others criticize you, don't lose heart or strike back. Rejoice that it's an opportunity for Him to reveal Himself powerfully—both to you and to your accusers.

Lord, whenever people persecute and criticize,
help me respond in a manner that glorifies
You and leads them to repentance, amen.

In His presence . . . forgive those who persecute you.

RESTORING RELATIONSHIPS

"If you forgive others for their transgressions, your heavenly Father will also forgive you."

MATTHEW 6:14

Have you been hurt by someone you love? If you don't deal with the problem quickly, it is likely that bitterness will take root deep within your spirit—and this is never good. It produces emotional bondage, leads to broken relationships, and hinders you from experiencing the joy and freedom God created you for. It can have a paralyzing effect on every aspect of your life.

Of course, the worst consequence of unforgiveness is that it erodes your fellowship with God. He provided the ultimate sacrifice for your sins through Christ's death on the cross, and you're called to demonstrate your gratefulness by graciously extending forgiveness to others. When you refuse to do so, you are not reflecting His character, which then hinders your relationship with Him.

Friend, don't harbor unforgiveness. Be kind-hearted to the one who has offended you—just as Jesus was to you—and allow Him to restore your relationship. He will give you an even more profound love for that person and a deeper appreciation of what He did for you at Calvary.

Father, help me forgive and accept forgiveness. I want to demonstrate Your love to others and glorify You, amen.

In His presence . . . seek to be as forgiving as He is.

FEAR OF THE LORD

Fear of the LORD is the foundation of true knowledge.
PROVERBS 1:7 NLT

When you read in the Bible about having a "fear of the Lord," it means to respect Him greatly, with the awareness that God governs all creation and is absolutely righteous. Having this awesome understanding of His sovereignty and reverence for His character produces humility and obedience.

Friend, God never intended for you to be afraid of Him. On the contrary, He loves you and provides what's best for you.

However, He does expect you to obey His instruction. You see, fears will arise that prevent you from doing as He asks—proclaiming the gospel, reaching out to those in need, and submitting to His will. But the fear of the Lord—your respect for Him—should motivate you to obey Him anyway.

So today, no matter what He calls you to do, do it, even if you're afraid. Allow your reverence for Him to overcome your earthly anxieties. Make a decision that you are going to believe your loving God, who is always available to you and is in control of your life at all times.

Father, help me overcome my fears and trust in You.
Help me obey You every step of the way, amen.

⸘

In His presence . . . respect His holy name.

LISTEN TO HIM

Who is among you that fears the LORD, that obeys the voice
of His servant. . . . Let him trust in the name of the LORD.

ISAIAH 50:10

Are you intently listening to the Lord so that you can hear even His hushed whispers? Or must He use extraordinary measures to gain and hold your interest?

Certainly, most would agree it's far better to be receptive to the Father's tender call than to wait until He must shout. But often our insensitivity to Him forces the Lord to use methods that command our undivided attention.

The point is, God *is* speaking to you—even now. He is constantly drawing you into His presence to experience an intimate relationship. But the question is: Are you listening?

Friend, don't ignore your Savior, who has great things to show you. Read His Word to discover His will and allow the Holy Spirit to speak to your heart. He desires to guide (Psalm 48:14), comfort (John 14:16), and protect you (Genesis 19:17–26); teach you obedience (Joshua 6:18–19); and express His unfailing love to you (John 16:27). So don't allow the incessant noises of life to drown out His voice. Listen to Him.

Lord, tune my ears so that all You need to
get my attention is a whisper, amen.

In His presence . . . listen intently for His whisper.

UNITY OF THE SPIRIT

Make every effort to keep yourselves united in the Spirit.
EPHESIANS 4:3 NLT

The structure of the human body is complex and endlessly fascinating. All of the body's components work together in a beautiful, intricate harmony that surpasses understanding. When something goes wrong with one part, the entire organism is affected.

This is the way the body of Christ functions as well. As believers, we all work together and operate as one unit when we submit to the leadership of the Holy Spirit and recognize Jesus as our Head. However, when one part of the body is wounded or hurting, the entire body suffers.

This is why we cannot ignore when fellow believers are in distress (Hebrews 3:13). Rather, we are challenged to be "kind to one another, tender-hearted, forgiving" (Ephesians 4:32). In other words, we express the fruit of the Spirit so His unity can be restored (Galatians 5:22–23).

Friend, is there a believer who could use some love and godly counsel? Then take the opportunity to minister to your brother or sister in Christ and by so doing, build up the body to the glory of God.

Father, by Your Spirit, join me in unity, love,
and service to Your church, amen.

In His presence . . . be unified with fellow believers.

TRUE VICTORY

This is the victory that has overcome the world—our faith.

1 JOHN 5:4

When life sends us reeling in pain and confusion, our response to our struggles will reveal how mature we are in our relationship with Christ. Of course, what He desires to see is our unshakable trust in Him, regardless of what happens. That is the measure of true victory—our unwavering faith. We realize that as children of our sovereign God, we are never victims of our circumstances. He is in control and will ultimately use whatever touches our lives for our good and His glory.

This is the goal. However, it's easier said than done. And if we drift in our devotion to God, the tragic events that unfold can leave us jaded.

Friend, don't allow the storms in your life to discourage you; rather, cling to the Lord and invite Him to fill you with His strength and hope. Hold tightly to Him and to the promises He's given you—no matter what the cost or how circumstances appear. Have faith to the end. Because you know that with God, you'll be able to endure anything that comes your way in life and emerge triumphant.

Lord, I cling to Your promise that You
will prevail on my behalf, amen.

In His presence . . . anticipate true and lasting victory.

ENGINEERED BY GOD

My salvation and my honor depend on God;
he is my mighty rock, my refuge.

PSALM 62:7 NIV

Thoughts of failure will almost always stir up feelings of anxiety and fear: *If I fail, what will others think of me?* But realize that failure is sometimes engineered by God for a purpose—so you'll recognize your need to trust the Lord in every aspect of your life. Whether your failure relates to a particular sin that seems impossible to conquer, a disastrous relationship, or an unsuccessful venture into ministry or business, it helps you understand how absolutely dependent you should be upon God in every detail.

Of course, this is often a hard-learned lesson. As fallen, sinful human beings, we're used to striking out on our own—even when we're attempting to do something in the Savior's name. But when we do so in our own strength—rather than trusting in Him—failure is imminent.

Friend, don't make that mistake. Learn the invaluable lesson and depend upon God in everything you do. Because when you trust Him for your success, you'll experience an incredible freedom and peace. And reaching that point will make every failure worthwhile.

Lord, help me depend fully on You. Thank You
for always leading me to victory, amen.

⁂

In His presence . . . acknowledge
your dependence on Him.

THE BLAME GAME

Temptation comes from our own desires,
which entice us and drag us away.
JAMES 1:14 NLT

When questioned by God in the garden, Adam demonstrated a common response to sin: he redirected the blame (Genesis 3:12). He tried to say that Eve was responsible for his act of rebellion. How often we still employ this tactic today—accusing others instead of admitting our need for the Lord's forgiveness.

At the root of this, of course, is our guilt over our wrongdoings and desire to protect ourselves from punishment. In desperation, we attempt to blame whoever is readily accessible. But this only keeps us imprisoned in our transgressions.

Friend, you cannot be forced to sin—and you cannot fool God. Yes, another person may create the circumstances that make it easier for you to stray, but ultimately, how you react is your responsibility. As Jesus did, you can *always* choose to respond in a godly manner because His Holy Spirit dwells within you.

So today, instead of playing the blame game, confess your sins to Him. He stands ready to forgive you and will lead you to freedom when you admit your need.

Lord, thank You for not condemning me, but
leading me to truth and freedom, amen.

In His presence . . . be honest and seek forgiveness.

Healing Our Hurts

*Be kind and compassionate to one another, forgiving
each other, just as in Christ God forgave you.*

EPHESIANS 4:32 NIV

Whether it is the driver who cut you off in traffic, a friend who betrays you, a boss who overlooks you, or a loved one who makes you feel inferior, there will always be someone in your life who needs your forgiveness. Sadly, sometimes the deep roots of hurt prevail and the bitterness tightens its grip on your spirit, making reconciliation very difficult.

But friend, when you remember the immense debt that Christ has pardoned you of, it is so much easier to forgive. Jesus freely relieves you of your sin debt and heals you because of His unmatchable love for you. However, He also teaches you to forgive others because He understands how absolutely devastating bitterness can be. He doesn't want you imprisoned—He desires for you to experience the perfect freedom He bought you on the cross.

Therefore, friend, out of thankfulness to Jesus for His great gift of salvation, reflect the grace that you have been shown to others. You will never resemble your Savior more than when you do what He did for you: forgive.

*Lord, grant me the courage to relinquish my resentment
so I can reflect Your grace and forgive, amen.*

In His presence . . . forgive others.

OVERCOMING PERFECTIONISM

All glory to God, who is able to keep you from
falling away and will bring you with great joy into
his glorious presence without a single fault.

JUDE V. 24 NLT

If you struggle with perfectionism, take heart in today's verse: you are appraising yourself by the wrong standard. You don't have to feel worthless. You don't have to succeed at all costs. Jesus is your adequacy. Therefore, today read these truths out loud: *No one can live up to God's perfection or do what is right all the time. No one can live a totally sin-free life or escape all temptation. Jesus has paid my debts—I am blameless and can have great joy.*

Living in a fallen world, you will have temptations and struggles—including the urge to give up or to resist God's Word. But the good news is that you don't need to live with a spirit of inadequacy.

You are covered with Jesus' identity. This means that when the Father looks at you, He sees Christ's strengths, His perfection, and His uncompromising goodness. And friend, that's all you ever really need.

Father, help me release my fears by
knowing blameless perfection is achieved
through Your Son, Jesus, amen.

In His presence . . . accept you are
blameless and secure forever.

CLASH WITH THE FLESH

The mind set on the flesh is death, but the
mind set on the Spirit is life and peace.
ROMANS 8:6

God will never tell you to do anything that gratifies the flesh—to do just as you please without thought of the future. Yes, He wants you to enjoy life—but in a way that pleases Him and brings you wholesome fulfillment, not in a manner that will ultimately destroy you.

Friend, be cautious and wise. If what you hear urges you to feed your sinful nature, then it is not of God. His Holy Spirit within you always speaks in such a way that results in the "fruit of righteousness" (Philippians 1:11), not the indulgence of your flesh. In fact, your old sensual nature is constantly warring against the Spirit within you, and you must consciously work to bring it under His control (Romans 8:13).

Therefore, friend, set your mind to satisfy the yearning of the Spirit. His voice will build you up, edify you, and lead you on the path of God's will. Trust Him, obey His Spirit, and live.

Lord, lead me. I want to obey Your Spirit today,
not my flesh. Reveal where I have failed to
follow You so I may repent and live, amen.

In His presence . . . be sensitive to His Spirit.

TRUST GOD'S PROMISES

Not one word has failed of all His good promise.
1 KINGS 8:56

God always keeps His word. If He has given you a specific promise, you can be assured He will fulfill it. It may not be according to your timetable or expectations, but it will always be right in line with His will for your life.

Many times people become disillusioned with God because they do not actually see Him at work. They realize that He is leading them in a certain direction so they trust Him, walk closely beside Him in faith, and believe that He will fulfill His promise. But when nothing changes, adverse circumstances arise, or conditions move in the opposite direction, they panic and give in to thoughts of defeat.

If you are in such a situation, take courage. This waiting time and the seeming hindrances to God's promise are simply an opportunity to build your testimony of faith. The Lord has not failed or forgotten you. He is simply operating in the unseen—working everything out in a manner too wonderful for words.

Therefore, rest easy. He has never gone back on His promise and never will. His fulfillment is coming. Praise His name.

Father, I know You will always fulfill Your promises to me—therefore I will wait for You in hope, amen.

―――――――――――――― ✺ ――――――――――――――

In His presence . . . trust His promises.

Deliverance Assured

*Lord God! Behold, You have made the heavens
and the earth by Your great power and by Your
outstretched arm! Nothing is too difficult for You.*

JEREMIAH 32:17

From the confines of prison, the prophet Jeremiah clung to a single hope—the Lord's promise that He would release Judah from its captivity and bring the people back to the land after seventy years.

This appeared impossible, of course. Although the Jewish people had been restored to the promised land after their bondage in Egypt, it seemed unfeasible that it could happen again. No other people had ever successfully recaptured their territories after so many afflictions and such a long time away—especially a nation as small and weak as Judah.

But *God* had made a promise. And because He had never failed them before, Jeremiah knew that the Lord would be faithful to fulfill it. And sure enough, after seventy years, the people were supernaturally released to reenter their nation.

Friend, take this to heart. God can do anything in your life—even what looks absolutely impossible. So trust Him to keep His Word to you regardless of how challenging your circumstances may appear.

*Father, I trust You! Nothing is too difficult for
You. Thank You for delivering me, amen.*

In His presence . . . appreciate who He really is.

STATE OF PEACE

He will redeem my soul in peace from
the battle which is against me.

PSALM 55:18

When was the last time you experienced deep peace in your heart? How long did that time of tranquility last? Although God promises enduring peace, we may wonder, *Can I* really *feel abiding security in my spirit?*

The Greek word for "peace," *eirene,* means to "bind together" something that has been broken or disjointed. This is a superb illustration for how we—so often feeling empty and disconnected from each other and God—can find a way to unity and wholeness. The Lord's peace comes to us when we are united by faith with Him.

This Greek word, *eirene,* also refers to a prevailing sense of quietness and rest in a person's heart—unperturbed, unruffled. Peace is synonymous with being tranquil, serene, untroubled, and calm. It is a very real state of the soul when you are submersed in the Father's love and presence.

Therefore, friend, seek Him and enjoy the security He offers you. Let His peace be the norm in which you live day by day.

Precious Lord, thank You for Your peace, which
overcomes all trouble, binds my soul to You,
and leads me to Your perfect rest, amen.

In His presence . . . abide in the spirit of His peace.

SEEKING HIS GUIDANCE

Point out anything in me that offends you, and
lead me along the path of everlasting life.

PSALM 139:24 NLT

When seeking God's guidance about a matter, do you ever have trouble sensing what He would have you do? Have your feelings become so dominant that it is difficult to sense His direction?

If so, then pray and ask the Lord to give you promises from Scripture to cling to when your faith is challenged. Don't react to situations immediately when they arise. Rather, take time to seek the Father by opening His Word and asking Him to give you understanding about your circumstances. As you do, He will give you verses that will become anchors for your soul. Soon enough, you will begin to see how He is leading you.

Continue to lay the matter out before the Lord until you are not only certain about the path but have arrived at the destination.

Friend, God knows your heart and He realizes the depth of your feelings toward the situation that is on your mind today. You can trust Him to lead you wisely—even when the way is unclear. Have faith in His ability to teach you.

Lord, reveal the verses that You want me to cling
to and help me clearly hear Your voice, amen.

⁓

In His presence . . . trust His guidance.

LEAD THEM TO THE CROSS

He Himself bore our sins in His body on the cross,
so that we might die to sin and live to righteousness;
for by His wounds you were healed.

1 PETER 2:24

As believers, Jesus commissioned us to continue His work on earth—sharing the good news about the salvation He provided for us on the cross (Matthew 28:19). However, obeying this command isn't always easy, especially when we come across people whose lifestyles are questionable to us. It often feels more reasonable to befriend those who share our values and morals.

Yet understand, Jesus ministered to those whom society avoided. And He explained that He "did not come to call the righteous, but sinners" (Mark 2:17).

Remember, sin enslaves its victims. With despair and confusion as constant companions, the captive doesn't know the way to freedom. But believers do—and we should share the message of hope with them.

So today, as you come across those who need God's grace, tenderly point them to the cross. Jesus ministered to the needy, addicted, and downtrodden so they could be freed from sin's grasp. And because we are His, we should as well.

Father, work through me to lead
others to Your salvation, amen.

In His presence . . . reflect His love to others.

The Value of Defeat

He holds success in store for the upright.
PROVERBS 2:7 NIV

How many times have you tried to do the right thing but failed anyway? Maybe you were caught in a no-win situation. Perhaps your emotions undermined what you were trying to accomplish. It could even be that you thought you were pursuing the correct course of action but were simply wrong. When this happens, don't condemn yourself. This experience can teach you invaluable lessons about victory.

For example, God sometimes engineers defeat because He desires for you to depend on Him rather than your own gifts, skills, resources, and power. Likewise, brokenness is essential for the Lord to fulfill His purposes in your life. He will break your self-will and teach you to pursue His goals rather than your own. Finally, failure exposes your weaknesses and inadequacies. You allow Him to work through you because you realize your best efforts are never any match for what He can do.

Friend, defeat in your life isn't final; it's God's way of pointing you to true success. So don't be discouraged. Rather, learn from Him and trust He will lead you on the path to ultimate victory.

Lord, help me remember that defeat is simply a signpost pointing me to ultimate victory through You, amen.

—————————— ⚜ ——————————

In His presence . . . find victory in defeat.

TRUE JUSTICE

The LORD loves justice and does not forsake His godly ones.

PSALM 37:28

Is there someone God has brought to your mind that you need to forgive? Perhaps you're worried that if you pardon that person, the Lord will go too easy on them and it won't be fair.

The conflicting feelings you're dealing with aren't new. Throughout history, people have been challenged to forgive as Christ did. In fact, one of the most stunning examples is how the early church pardoned Paul. Before he was saved, he persecuted Christians viciously (Acts 8:1–3).

But after Paul accepted Christ, God challenged the church— the very people Paul had terrorized—to reach out to him in love (Acts 9:10–16). Thankfully, the people in the early church obeyed God and forgave him, freeing Paul to become a powerful witness.

You should forgive too. There is no telling what God wants to do through you or through the person who hurt you. The one thing you do know is that as long as you harbor unforgiveness, you're not going to be free. So don't be afraid to let God handle the situation. His plan of justice for your offender may surprise you.

Father, this is a helpful reminder to me to overcome
evil with good—to forgive as You would, amen.

❖

In His presence . . . relinquish retribution to Him.

TURNING OBSTACLES INTO VICTORIES

Shout! For the LORD has given you the city.

JOSHUA 6:16

As Joshua looked at the fortifications of Jericho, he realized that taking the city would be no small task, especially with the seemingly impenetrable wall that stood before him.

However, God promised Joshua that Israel would triumph, and Joshua believed Him. And for generations to come, the children of Israel would ask about the onslaught at Jericho, to which their parents would respond that it was by shouts and trumpet blasts that the walls were destroyed, because the Lord's power was with them. No battering ram, no warfare strategy was necessary—only obedience (Joshua 6).

Friend, is there a problem impeding your progress today? The lesson for you is that God will show you how to overcome every obstacle by His power. It may not be what you expect—in fact, the Father's methods will certainly surprise you. But He knows exactly what is needed to lead you to triumph. Therefore, do exactly as He says. Then shout His praises and trust Him to give you the victory.

Lord, I give You all my obstacles, for I know that You alone can lead me to victory over them, amen.

❀

In His presence . . . praise Him for leading you to triumph.

CORRECT SELF-APPRAISALS

God's judgment is right, and as a result you will
be counted worthy of the kingdom of God.
2 THESSALONIANS 1:5 NIV

Do you ever question if you are really worthwhile—lovable, acceptable, or competent? Have you ever felt as if you don't measure up enough to be of any true value to others?

These feelings of inadequacy are just that—feelings, not facts. And they blind you to who you really are in Christ. This is why you should always base your opinions on what God's Word says about you.

The Lord's judgment of who you are and what you are worth is more accurate than what you think of yourself because His view is eternal. He doesn't appraise you by investigating temporary issues such as who you know, where you live, your title, your income, or how you look. Rather, He sees you through the blood of Jesus and desires for you to seek Him wholeheartedly.

Friend, take your focus off of what you think—or what others think about you—and embrace what the Father says. No doubt your self-esteem will automatically improve because God's opinion is the only one that really counts—forever.

Lord Jesus, in You, and You alone, I am worthy!
Thank You for making me worthwhile, amen.

In His presence . . . understand your true value.

OCTOBER

HAVE YOU BEEN WITH JESUS?

When they saw the courage of Peter and John and realized that
they were unschooled, ordinary men, they were astonished
and they took note that these men had been with Jesus.

ACTS 4:13 NIV

Do you have a passion for obeying the Lord? Or do you merely engage in Christian activities because it's "the right thing to do"?

Friend, your heavenly Father wants you to obey Him out of love, joy, and gratefulness—not out of obligation. He wants to pour Himself into you, shine through you, and give you a genuine love for all that He is doing so you'll join Him in His kingdom mission.

This is what people saw in Peter and John—men who served with a joy, wisdom, and power that was not their own. It was obvious the Savior was working through them.

Likewise, when you make time alone with Christ the priority, it affects and influences every single facet of your life—He gives you His energy, wisdom, and strength to fulfill His purposes and make you fruitful for His kingdom.

Therefore, spend time with Him. Soon people will recognize you too as "having been with Jesus."

Lord, my greatest hope is that others would see You in
me. Magnify Yourself through me, my Savior, amen.

In His presence . . . make Him your foremost focus.

IT'S NOT ENOUGH TO LISTEN

"Of the tree of the knowledge of good and evil you shall not eat."
GENESIS 2:16–17 NKJV

True listening has a crucial companion: obedience. Sadly, today's verse illustrates what the Lord said to Adam was heard, but not heeded. There was no way for Adam to mistake what God said— He was very clear and concise.

But this is how the enemy operates—he tempts you with the one thing you have no business doing. Satan focuses your attention on the objects forbidden to you and stirs up dissatisfaction in all the blessings God has given.

But realize, every "you shall not" in the Bible is a promise of God's protection. He is not preventing you from enjoying life; rather, He is saving you—keeping you from destroying yourself. Every command in His Word is an expression of divine love to you, His beloved child. He wants to protect and preserve your life so you can enjoy all the blessings He's planned for you.

Adam and Eve didn't understand this and the world is still paying for it. Don't you make the same mistake.

Lord, forgive me for the times I've heard You
speak but have not obeyed. I want to follow
Your voice faithfully from now on, amen.

❦

In His presence . . . commit to listen and obey.

EASY DECEPTION

Has God indeed said, "You shall not eat
of every tree of the garden"?

GENESIS 3:1 NKJV

Satan is the master of deceit. Notice how he used *almost* the same words to entice Eve that the Lord had used to bless her. Sadly, Eve's response to the enemy was cataclysmic.

Friend, choosing to ignore God when you know He is speaking to you is an act of rebellion (James 4:17). It will lead you to failure every time. And the more you allow the enemy to influence you, the less distinct God's voice will be. You'll find yourself confused, thinking illogical thoughts, rationalizing, and tolerating attitudes and actions that you know are wrong.

Don't be fooled—redeem your focus. Listen to the Lord.

Tune in to the Father and obey Him. Because by doing so you will be mentally sharper than those who don't. Particularly on spiritual and moral issues, you will have a perception, awareness, and attentiveness that others do not possess. This is because "the fear of the LORD is the beginning of wisdom, and the knowledge of the Holy One is understanding" (Proverbs 9:10). The Lord gives you supernatural discernment and insight that can only come by His hand.

Father, help me stay focused on You and You
alone so my way stays pure and right, amen.

In His presence . . . stay focused on Him.

HE IS ALWAYS PRESENT

[Jesus] arose and rebuked the wind, and said to the sea, "Peace,
be still!" And the wind ceased and there was a great calm.

MARK 4:39 NKJV

An oceangoing craft can be tossed in great storms, but underneath the surface, there is no storm; all is perfectly quiet. No sound. No tumult. Not even a ripple of turmoil. The sea is perfectly calm.

This remarkable fact illustrates what our Lord must have been talking about when He promised His disciples His peace. He told them that because they were His followers, they would have trouble in this world. In fact, He declared that some of them would be persecuted because they were His disciples.

But He also made the promise that He would never leave those who followed Him, and that His constant presence would be the means whereby they could experience His peace.

Friend, do you see how His presence brings you His peace? He is the inner stability, security, and comfort that never leaves you. Storms may rage against you, but you can always take heart because the One who has overcome the world dwells in you and defends you (John 16:33).

Thank You, Lord Jesus, for Your constant
presence and the peace You bring me, amen.

❧

In His presence . . . claim His
promise to always be there.

PEACE BEYOND CIRCUMSTANCES

The one who is in you is greater than
the one who is in the world.

1 JOHN 4:4 NIV

As hard as it is to face suffering and rejection, your trials can actually be opportunities to experience the Savior's power, love, ability, wisdom, and peace that transcends understanding. This is because deep down inside, you learn—with an abiding assurance—that God is with you, that He is in control, and that He can give you joy far greater than any circumstance you can experience.

Of course, the comfort and assurance you experience from Him is not a denial of reality, nor an escape from it—on the contrary, it is supernatural and sustaining in ways no one can ever fully understand. His indwelling Spirit gives you a sense of security so deep and in such great measure that nothing can shake it.

Friend, all of God's children go through crises, and it's during times of adversity that His peace is most clearly manifested. So give thanks for these times—even though they're painful—because they'll serve to bring you closer to Him.

Lord, thank You for this time of adversity
and that when I'm struggling, I can lean
on You to carry me through, amen.

———— ❧ ————

In His presence . . . rest assured He is
with you in your circumstances.

INTIMATELY CONCERNED

*Although the Lord has given you bread of privation and
water of oppression, He, your Teacher will no longer
hide Himself, but your eyes will behold your Teacher.*

ISAIAH 30:20

Events may occur that make you feel isolated and insignificant. Perhaps loved ones fail to understand the pressures you face, or obstacles arise that make your goals appear unreachable. Even commonplace aspects of your life may suddenly become unmanageable—stealing your joy and making you feel defeated. You wonder if you've wasted your time trying so hard when no one seems to appreciate your sacrifices.

Friend, God has not abandoned you—and your love for Him is never in vain. He is hemming you in so you will seek Him and so He can reveal Himself to you in a more profound way than you've ever known. Don't underestimate what He can and will do through the difficult circumstances of your life. He wants you to realize that He is intimately concerned with even the most seemingly common, insignificant matters of your life. So seek Him. He can and will show you His glory. Allow Him to speak to you powerfully through the adversity.

*Father, thank You for guarding even the smallest
details of my life and working through this
adversity to help me know You better, amen.*

❦

In His presence . . . learn what He's teaching you.

EXTEND HIS LOVE TO OTHERS

You are all one in Christ Jesus.
GALATIANS 3:28 NLT

God's love is extended to *every* person who accepts Jesus as his or her Savior. This is true for people of all ages, cultures, nations, and throughout all generations. The Savior does not promise His love and then take it back. He does not offer a gift and then fail to deliver it. But take note—He has chosen to demonstrate His divine care through you.

God wants to make you an ambassador of His love to others—next door and across the globe—caring for them as He would. Even though other believers may be different outwardly, they are your brothers and sisters by the blood of Jesus. So don't judge them by their financial situation, skin color, language, customs, or even their faults. You are the same—you are one in Christ.

Therefore, as Galatians 6:10 instructs, "While we have opportunity, let us do good to all people, and especially to those who are of the household of the faith." Your Father will certainly work through you to give them a greater revelation of Himself.

Father, thank You that Your love knows no
boundaries. Help me be an ambassador of
Your care to those around me, amen.

In His presence . . . receive His
love and extend it to others.

COMMUNICATING THE TRUTH

*"You shall receive power when the Holy Spirit
has come upon you; and you shall be witnesses
to Me . . . to the end of the earth."*

ACTS 1:8 NKJV

One reason God speaks to us is so we may communicate His truth to others. The blessings He gives us are meant to be shared.

In fact, before His ascension, Jesus declared that all He had taught His disciples during His three years with them was not to be kept secret. They were to faithfully proclaim the truth they'd received—and His Holy Spirit would help them every step of the way.

Jesus promised, "Go therefore and make disciples of all the nations, baptizing them in the name of the Father and the Son and the Holy Spirit, teaching them to observe all that I commanded you; and lo, I am with you always, even to the end of the age" (Matthew 28:19–20).

The same is true for you. He is with you—filling you with power and giving you His words. So don't be afraid of sharing what you know. Tell others about your Savior and trust Him to communicate His truth to their hearts.

Lord, help me apply Your truth by sharing it with others. Thank You for giving me Your words, amen.

**In His presence . . . freely
give what you've received.**

Enemy Attacks

Submit therefore to God. Resist the devil
and he will flee from you.

James 4:7

Have you ever felt attacked by the enemy? He uses various means to cause you to lose faith in the Father. He stirs up your doubts and anxiety with questions such as, "If God is with you, then why has this happened?" Do not listen to the enemy—stand firm against him. His goal is to paralyze you with fear and lead you to destruction. Resist him.

How do you do so? By voicing your faith in Jesus. The best way to stand against the evil power that seeks to thwart the plan of God in your life is to speak about your faith in the Lord out loud. Your powerful, all-knowing, loving Savior is your peace—there is no need to live in fear. You *will* trust Him, and the Father *will* deliver you.

Your enemy cannot stand hearing the Lord exalted, so when you do this, he flees from you. Therefore, in moments when fear, doubt, and anxiety arise, recognize the devil's attack and defeat him by praising the name of Jesus!

Father, thank You for loving me, saving me, and
delivering me! You are my perfect Protector. To
You be all power, glory, and praise, amen.

In His presence . . . you always
have hope and victory.

CHANGE WITHIN

The LORD gives wisdom; from His mouth
come knowledge and understanding.

PROVERBS 2:6

The people, conflicts, and circumstances may be different—but it's the same challenge you've faced for years. Why can't you break free from these ever-repeating issues?

Your situation is just like the baker who set out to make a delicious cake, but used salt instead of sugar in his recipe. He tried different mixing techniques, pans, and ovens, but every cake turned out inedible. And he continued to fail until he finally realized that he had to change the ingredients.

The same is true for you. You may seek different ways of solving your problems, but until you change what's inside of you and how you respond to those problems, you'll never alter their outcome. The good news is, the Lord wants you to know the truth, and He takes responsibility for making it come alive in you.

So ask God for insight. Allow Him to transform your inmost being. He is able to teach you to respond to your circumstances in a manner that honors Him. And be assured, when you obey Him, He will fill everything that proceeds from you with sweetness.

Lord, help me stop making the same mistakes. Teach
me Your ways so I may live and honor You, amen.

༄

In His presence . . . be transformed from within.

FOR A SEASON AND A REASON

The disciples went and woke [Jesus], saying, "Master,
Master, we're going to drown!" He got up and rebuked the
wind and the raging waters; the storm subsided, and all
was calm. "Where is your faith?" he asked his disciples.

LUKE 8:24–25 NIV

Jesus, our Master, was a realist. He never called those who followed Him to live in denial of trouble and He did not shield them from adversity. He allowed the tempests to assail them and called them to have faith in the midst of the worst storms.

Friend, all trials are passing in nature—for a season and for a reason. Do not make the mistake of thinking your circumstances will never change or that they will destroy you.

Because God is with you, you do not have to give in to, sink beneath, or become defeated by troubles. You can face them, confront them, challenge them, deal with them, and—in the end—overcome them. You can have the victory because your all-sufficient God is with you!

Today, allow that truth to bring joy and consolation to your heart.

Father, I will live my day in confidence, knowing You
are watching, directing, caring for, and loving me, amen.

In His presence . . . remember He is
the source and strength of your faith.

GOD IS SOVEREIGN

He will call on me, and I will answer him; I will be with
him in trouble, I will deliver him and honor him.

PSALM 91:15 NIV

When troubles assail you, do you envision the most negative out-
comes to your challenges? Perhaps it starts by wondering what
will happen, but quickly deteriorates to imagining the very worst.
Subsequently, your situation seems more severe than it really is.

But friend, realize that God has never been out of control over
His creation for one fraction of a second since the beginning of
time. Recognizing and accepting His sovereignty is vital for your
inner peace—it means that nothing related to you is beyond His
watchful eye and loving care.

God is your Protector. He is responsible for carrying out His
purposes for you and meeting your needs as you obey Him. No
matter what happens, the Lord has a plan to bless you and reward
you in eternity. This means everything you experience—even the
"bad" things—He will turn for your good if you'll trust Him as
your sovereign Lord. Therefore, stop imagining the worst. Instead,
praise your Savior for always giving you His very best.

Father, You are in control—always. Thank
You that nothing can touch my life apart
from Your loving care, amen.

In His presence . . . praise Him for His sovereign care.

YOUR PROVIDER

Those who seek the LORD shall not lack any good thing.
PSALM 34:10 NKJV

It is not part of God's plan for you to lie awake at night, tossing, turning, and wondering, *How am I going to pay my bills? Have I saved enough for retirement? How am I going to provide for my family?* or any other concern that you may have.

Friend, be assured that the Lord—the Owner of heaven and earth—supplies all your needs. None is too massive, problematic, or severe for Jesus to meet it (Philippians 4:19).

So why do you still lack peace? The problem may be that you accept the idea of the Lord's provision in your head, but you don't believe in your heart that He will really take care of you. Perhaps somewhere within you, you don't feel worthy of His blessings.

Settle the issue once and for all in your heart and mind. God is your Provider. He *will* meet your needs as you trust and obey Him.

So whatever it is you require today—emotional healing, employment, a friend, reconciliation—trust your heavenly Father to meet your need and give Him the praise.

Lord, thank You for providing me all that's
required for a full, satisfying, and purposeful
life. I will trust in You, amen.

In His presence . . . wait expectantly for His provision.

ABUNDANT SUPPLY

*"I have come that they may have life, and that
they may have it more abundantly."*

JOHN 10:10 NKJV

Isn't this verse comforting? Not only does Jesus provide eternal life
when we accept Him as our Savior, but He also gives us an abundant life here and now—overflowing with every good blessing so
we can accomplish all that He has called us to do.

In a practical sense, what does this signify? It means if you
lose your job, God has an even better opportunity for you. If your
source of income changes, He has countless other means for supplying your needs. Just think of the many ways He provided for His
people throughout history: manna from heaven (Exodus 16:35),
water from a rock (Exodus 17:6), multiplying a boy's simple lunch
(Matthew 14:14–21), to name a few. His resources are unlimited.
He will not fail you (Habakkuk 3:17–19).

Friend, God is the same today as He was in Bible times, and
He works through everything that touches your life for your good.
Therefore, no matter how dire your circumstances may appear—
or how far He stretches the last of your resources—trust Him to
supply your needs.

*Lord, thank You for loving me and supplying
my needs so abundantly, amen.*

In His presence . . . there are no limits to His provision.

MADE PURPOSEFULLY

He made from one man every nation of mankind . . .
having determined their appointed times and the
boundaries of their habitation, that they would seek
God; . . . in Him we live and move and exist.

ACTS 17:26–28

Have you ever wished to be more like someone else? Do you see their beauty, success, skill, or intelligence and envy what the Lord gave them? Or do you embrace who He made you to be and see your looks, gifts, culture, language, and everything about you as His purposeful choices?

Friend, you are special. God gave you certain characteristics, personality traits, talents, and aptitudes for a reason—for you to fulfill a unique role in history. And when you accepted Jesus Christ as your Savior, He gave you certain spiritual gifts to use in ministry, for His glory (Ephesians 2:10).

Therefore, today, embrace who your Creator says you are—His beloved child who is "fearfully and wonderfully made" (Psalm 139:14). No one who has ever lived before, is alive now, or will be in the future has been just like you. So enjoy who God made you to be!

Father, help me embrace and accept myself
just the way You made me, amen.

In His presence . . . discover
who God created you to be.

INADEQUACY BY GOD'S DESIGN

Not that we are adequate in ourselves to consider anything
as coming from ourselves, but our adequacy is from God.

2 CORINTHIANS 3:5

Do you feel inadequate for the tasks before you today? Do you fear you'll fall short?

Realize that the Lord has brought you to the point where you admit, "I can't do this in my own strength" for an important purpose. As the Author and Finisher of your faith, He understands all the potential He has built into you, but He also knows how crucial it is for you to rely on Him completely. With the talents and gifts He's given you, you can achieve good goals. But that is not enough. He wants to do the extraordinary through you so that others can see His power at work (2 Corinthians 12:9).

Friend, you feel inadequate today so you can learn what it means to allow the Savior to be your adequacy—for Him to accomplish what He alone can do.

So today, don't say, "I can't." Instead, express your faith in Him and proclaim, "By the grace of God and with His help, I can do this."

Lord Jesus, I will trust You to be my adequacy in
whatever task You call me to accomplish, amen.

--- ❦ ---

In His presence . . . accept
Him as your adequacy.

ASSURANCE OF SALVATION

Everyone who calls on the name of the LORD will be saved.

ACTS 2:21

Three big errors I often hear about salvation are: "I've sinned too much to be saved;" "I've committed the unpardonable sin;" and "I don't think my salvation will last."

If you've struggled with any of these, be encouraged—Jesus took care of all these concerns at the cross. First, He's forgiven *all* transgressions committed throughout *all* history. There's no such thing as "sinning too much"—His sacrifice is more than adequate for whatever you've done. In fact, His redemption is sufficient for the whole world (John 3:16).

Second, the only "unpardonable sin" is to reject Jesus as your Savior. This is what is meant by "blasphemy against the Spirit" (Matthew 12:31)—you refuse God's provision of salvation. Once you're a believer, you're no longer capable of committing this sin.

Finally, just as you didn't earn your salvation—you accepted it as a free gift from Jesus—you cannot "undo" it (Ephesians 2:8–9). No matter how badly you fail, He still saves you.

Friend, Jesus is your eternal security. Don't worry about issues He's overcome. Rather, live your life as a "thank You" to Him.

Father, thank You for making me eternally secure.
I praise You with my life forever, amen.

———————— ❧ ————————

In His presence . . . surrender completely.

DISAPPOINTMENTS

*Should we accept only good things from the
hand of God and never anything bad?*

JOB 2:10 NLT

When you are faced with a big disappointment, do you get angry and blame God for letting you down?

When Job went through his intense time of suffering, Satan used Job's wife to stir up his despair and bitterness. But the godly man would not listen. Job's response to her—and toward the extreme heartache he was experiencing—was amazing trust in the Lord. And because of his humble and submissive attitude, God honored Job greatly (Job 42:10–17).

Likewise, the way you respond to disappointment is extremely important. Do not listen when the enemy tells you you're not worth anything or that God doesn't love you anymore. Your merciful heavenly Father may actually be saving you from ruining your life. It may well be that the Lord, in His loving plan, has stopped a particular situation to keep you from destruction—and what seems a setback is actually His rescue.

So when trials occur, react like Job. Honor God, and ask Him to make clear whatever He is teaching you.

*Father, what do I need to learn from this?
Give me peace, in spite of my pain, amen.*

⸙

**In His presence . . . accept
disappointments with a new perspective.**

LIVING WITHOUT REGRETS

To You, O Lord, I lift up my soul. For You, Lord,
are good, and ready to forgive, and abundant in
lovingkindness to all who call upon You.

PSALM 86:4–5

Regret is rooted in unresolved guilt—in a choice you made recklessly, a person you treated unlovingly, or an opportunity you squandered unwisely. You had the chance to influence a situation in a manner that would bless others, exalt God, and benefit your life. But you messed up—and now you're paying the consequences for it.

Does this sound like you? Friend, you don't have to continue living with regret. Go to your loving Savior, ask for forgiveness, and lay down your feelings of guilt.

He may direct you to rectify the mistake, make amends to those you've hurt, and forgive anyone who has wounded you. If He does, then obey Him immediately. But then move on. Don't continue to beat yourself up over something that God has forgiven.

True, you may still have to live with consequences related to your choices. But the Father doesn't want you to live with unresolved guilt, shame, or regret. Seek Him and be free.

Precious Father, thank You for forgiving me,
healing me, and leading me to wholeness, amen.

**In His presence . . . experience
His liberating forgiveness.**

A MESSENGER OF VICTORY

The Lord spoke to Paul in a vision and told him,
"Don't be afraid! Speak out! Don't be silent!"

ACTS 18:9 NLT

Ancient Corinth was a difficult place to live, especially for believers. It was a port city—one that embraced visitors from all over the known world. However, its atmosphere of open commerce brought with it paganism, wicked practices, and every kind of immorality.

But Corinth was also a place that desperately needed the gospel and could become a strategic communication center for the good news of salvation. Therefore, God sent Paul there—and the apostle faithfully proclaimed the message despite opposition.

Likewise, you may be in a place that appears somewhat hostile to the gospel. Friend, do not abandon the post the Lord has given you or hide your faith. The Father is aware of your situation—including your fears, failings, and enemies.

So take courage and obey Him in teaching His truth. You are His messenger to those who need it most, and—just as He did for Paul—He will make you victorious in your labors.

Lord, let me be a light in darkness, bringing the
gospel to those who need it most. Help me stay close
to You and obey so others can be saved, amen.

<hr>

In His presence . . . be bold in
proclaiming His salvation.

NEVER ALONE

*"As the Father has loved Me, I have also
loved you; abide in My love."*

JOHN 15:9

When feelings of loneliness engulf you, there is something you can do right away to overcome those feelings—turn your focus away from what you don't have toward what you do have. What do you have? God Himself!

Friend, you'll never be alone once you've trusted in Jesus as your Savior. His Holy Spirit comes to dwell within you permanently when you receive Him as a guarantee of your salvation. You are connected to Jesus just as a branch is grafted to a vine—His divine power giving you everything you need to live.

Friend, God is dwelling in you, and you are to abide in Him. You share with Him the most profound relationship possible—an eternal spiritual intimacy. But realize the depth of your closeness with Him is—to a great extent—up to you.

So turn to the Lord and say, "Father, I need You! Only You can fill my heart." In so doing, you invite Him to reveal His presence to you and express your faith that He does, indeed, take away your loneliness.

Jesus, thank You for Your wonderful presence.
You are more than enough for every need I feel!
Draw me close to You, my Savior, amen.

In His presence . . . enjoy His companionship.

EMOTIONAL BAGGAGE

*"Take my yoke upon you and learn from me, for I am gentle
and humble in heart, and you will find rest for your souls."*
MATTHEW 11:29

Today, everyone you know is "poor"—or lacking—in spirit in some
way. They may be brokenhearted over a trial or ruined relationship,
captive to negative memories of the past, or disappointed by unfulfilled dreams. This emotional weight is not only a burden in their
everyday lives, it's indicative that the enemy has a stronghold.

Whether your heartaches, afflictions, and trials stem from
external or internal causes, the pains are real. And unless you deal
with them, they will keep on harming you. Those feelings, thought
patterns, and past experiences will continue to traumatize you each
time you recall them and will ultimately keep you from experiencing the freedom that Christ Jesus offers.

Friend, do not be ashamed. All of us struggle. But you must
turn your burdens over to Christ and allow Him to liberate you. He
will teach you a different way to live. So do not be afraid or discouraged. Rather, trust Him and find rest for your soul.

Jesus, I am broken and poor in many ways.
Through Your Spirit, liberate me from my
emotional baggage so I may be truly free, amen.

In His presence . . . be freed from your burdens.

LISTEN DEPENDENTLY

*"The Holy Spirit . . . will teach you all things, and
bring to your remembrance all that I said to you."*
JOHN 14:26

There's no way for you to hear from God apart from the ministry of the Holy Spirit. When the Lord speaks to you through His Word, others, or circumstances, it is the work of the Spirit giving you insight into His will.

You have a living, divine Receiver within you through the Person of the Holy Spirit. Prayer isn't God up there and you down here—separated and distant. Rather, it is the Holy Spirit speaking within you, ministering to your soul, and bearing witness to your spirit so that you may know the mind of Christ and accomplish the will of the Father.

But how can you know what the Spirit is telling you? By listening and believing that He is completely able to answer your petitions, speak to your heart, and give you direction. As fully as you trust Jesus to save you, have faith that the Spirit will lead you.

Therefore, today come humbly before God—dependent upon the work of the Holy Spirit within you—and hear what He has to say.

*Lord, thank You for Your Spirit, who lives
in and guides me each day, amen.*

**In His presence . . . obey
the promptings of His Spirit.**

PERSONALIZING MEDITATION

"This Book of the Law shall not depart from your mouth,
but you shall meditate in it day and night, that you may
observe to do according to all that is written in it."

JOSHUA 1:8 NKJV

Meditation is the foundation of obedient, victorious living. Of course, many don't see the benefits of focusing on Scripture and the Lord's character in this secular world where strife and competition reign. Yet it is in the midst of such constant turmoil that the believer finds the greatest need to sit quietly before the Father—so he can identify God's voice above the commotion and find victory over the trials that assail him.

Therefore, the Father calls not just preachers but all His children to focus on Him daily. He wants us to better relate to Him and triumph in the challenges of life.

Friend, personal meditation isn't difficult. It begins when you simply get alone with the Lord and sit quietly before Him. So don't wait any longer. Focus on the Father. Listen to His voice, be filled with His peace, and find His direction and purpose for your life.

Lord, help me set aside my daily stresses and
give You first place in my life. Fill my mind and
heart with Your truth and wisdom, amen.

❧

In His presence . . . find direction.

ALL YOU NEED

"Come to me, all you who are weary and
burdened, and I will give you rest."

MATTHEW 11:28 NIV

When you feel tired and defeated, remember: everything in your life flows out of your relationship with God. The more stressful and trying your circumstances, the greater your need is to experience His presence—not less.

So if you are weary and burdened today, spend time with your heavenly Father. You may think to yourself, *I can't possibly fit one more task into my schedule.* But you will be amazed at how your fellowship with the Lord will increase your effectiveness.

Therefore, be emotionally transparent with God and allow His Spirit to speak to your heart. Confess your sins and disappointments. Permit Him to expose the places where you are reticent to trust Him, and acknowledge when He reveals your fears. Finally, ask Him to increase your love for Him and your stamina for the tasks before you.

Only the Father can give you the strength, energy, and wisdom you need today. So go to Him and rest in His grace. Surely you will find all you need in His presence.

Lord, You know I'm weary. Strengthen me with
Your glorious presence. Thank You for making Your
wisdom, power, and presence available to me, amen.

In His presence . . . receive His wisdom and strength.

FROM DARKNESS TO LIGHT

*"I am the Light of the world; he who follows Me will not
walk in the darkness, but will have the Light of life."*

JOHN 8:12

Is there an area of darkness in your life—something that continually causes you fear, such as the future or a challenge you must face? Do not despair. The Father wants to relieve the dread you feel by shedding light on your circumstances.

Remember, in the beginning it was God who spoke light into existence—and He did it before creating the sun, moon, and stars (Genesis 1). This is because His very presence gives light (Revelation 22:5)—not just physical radiance, but spiritual illumination.

Of course, you may wish to overcome the uncertainty you feel by seeking your own solutions. Just understand that only God is light. And when you fight the dark with more darkness, all you get is deep despair.

Friend, God wants you to see not just the path ahead, but the profound spiritual realities that are affecting your life. He is ready to help you! So when you sense the dark fears encroaching, run to Him. Because when He is your light, you will have nothing to dread.

*Lord, free me from my anxieties. Shine Your truth in
my heart and help me walk by Your light, amen.*

In His presence . . . the darkness flees.

FINDING GOD

Teach me Your way, O LORD,
And lead me in a level path.

PSALM 27:11

Most people don't like to admit when they don't know something. Even if it means going in circles for hours, many of us would rather stumble upon the right answer ourselves than ask for help.

The same can be said of our Christian walk. We may believe that the Father has a specific purpose for our lives and unique blessings set aside for us, and yet not seek Him to tell us what He has planned. But how can we arrive at God's destination if we do not consult the only One who knows where we are going and how to get there?

Friend, God's will is not something that you can find through trial and error. Rather, you discover it through your intimate relationship with Him—through prayer and Bible study as you strive to know Him better.

If you have been on a quest to "find God" or "track down His will," stop searching and simply talk to Him. He knows where you are, and He knows exactly where you need to go. No roadmap could promise more.

Father, may I not waste precious time
wandering when I can go directly to You
and seek direction for my life, amen.

❦

In His presence . . . find direction.

TRANSFORMED BY THE TRUTH

Offer your bodies as a living sacrifice, holy and
pleasing to God—this is your true and proper worship.
Do not conform to the pattern of this world, but be
transformed by the renewing of your mind.
ROMANS 12:1–2 NIV

What does it mean to be transformed by the truth? Romans 12:1–2 can be divided into three goals for us to pursue: present your body as a living sacrifice; do not be conformed to the world; be transformed by the renewing of your mind.

Being a living sacrifice is how we honor God—we are to live in a way that glorifies Him. Not conforming to the world means that we refuse to live according to the faulty standards and practices of our fallen peers.

Transformation of our minds signifies that we adopt a new way of thinking—replacing our selfish and distorted thought patterns with God's truth.

And all together, it indicates that you are made better—gloriously changed as *the Lord* directs. This will be challenging, but is totally worthwhile. So be a living sacrifice and trust Him to do astounding things in you.

Lord, mold my life and transform my mind so that I
may become the person You created me to be, amen.

In His presence . . . your life will be transformed.

EVERY NEED

It is better to take refuge in the LORD than to trust in man.

PSALM 118:8

God is the only One who can truly satisfy your heart's desire for wholeness. When you feel lonely or disconnected, what you're really sensing is your soul's longing to be one with Him. And He alone knows how to bring that profound intimacy about in your life.

Once you recognize this and turn to the Lord to satisfy your loneliness, you are in a healthier position to receive the love and affection of the people God sends to you. Rather than become emotionally dependent on them, you are able to contribute to their lives and be involved in a wholesome, caring, mutual relationship with them.

However, understand the Lord is a jealous God. He wants a relationship with you, and if He sees that you're relying on another person to do what only He can, He often finds a way to end that relationship as it once was.

Only the Savior can provide everything you need to live a peaceful, joyful, fulfilling life. So look to Him first and foremost to satisfy the needs of your heart.

Father, please forgive me for looking to others
to fill my needs. Refocus my heart on Your
wonderful presence and provision, amen.

❧

In His presence . . . take refuge
in His perfect provision.

WHAT GOD IS REALLY LIKE

"The Son of Man has come to seek and
to save that which was lost."

LUKE 19:10

What is God like? Although you may be tempted to base your view of Him on what you've been taught or on your experience with your earthly father, have you learned who He really is?

God incarnate, Jesus always treated people with the utmost kindness, respect, and generosity. We can see this in His relationship with Zaccheus—who was often despised by others because he was a tax collector for Rome and was dishonest in his dealings. But Jesus didn't condemn Zaccheus. No, Jesus told him to climb down from the sycamore tree so He could draw him to salvation.

Likewise, throughout the Gospels we see Jesus healing, comforting, restoring, and delivering people from bondage. He wept when His friends were hurting, laughed with them in their joys, and forgave their sins so that they could enjoy eternal life with Him forever.

Thus is the character of God—the One who calls you into a profound relationship with Himself. He is holy, kind, powerful, and loving. So draw near to Him and experience what He's really like.

Lord, thank You for accepting me just as I am!
I love You. Reveal Yourself to me, amen.

In His presence . . . experience who He really is.

EXPERIENCING HIS PRESENCE

*How precious is your unfailing love, O God! All
humanity finds shelter in the shadow of your wings.*

PSALM 36:7 NLT

Have you ever experienced the security of being enveloped in God's everlasting arms? You may wonder if it is really possible to feel His company in such a powerful way. But you can.

We know God's presence and understand His protection, in part, through the friends and loved ones He brings into our lives who care for us just as Jesus would if He were physically present with us today.

At other times, however, God simply envelops us—almost as if He reaches down and covers us with His presence. This overwhelming sense of comfort can be so real that it's just as if we are being cradled in His arms. And indeed, we are! The feeling is one of total satisfaction, fulfillment, and security—what He longs for each one of us to have.

So if you need to sense the Savior's nearness today, seek His face. Wait before Him until you experience His loving presence, and trust He will reveal Himself to you. You'll be surprised at how profoundly real He will become to you.

*Father, embrace me. Hold me in Your loving arms
so I may feel Your presence and protection, amen.*

———— ❧ ————

**In His presence . . . be
enveloped in His loving comfort.**

November

EXAMINING YOUR HEART

If we confess our sins, he is faithful and just and will forgive
us our sins and purify us from all unrighteousness.

1 JOHN 1:9 NIV

Unforgiveness can be the source of a great deal of conflict and stress in your personal relationships. Therefore, examine your heart now to see if you need to forgive anyone.

Do you secretly hope that someone will get what he or she deserves? Do you talk negatively about anyone to others? Do you indulge in fantasies of revenge—even seemingly harmless ones? Do you spend time mulling over what others have done to you? How do you feel when something good happens to a person who has wronged you? Do you blame anyone for how your life has turned out? Do you find it difficult to be open and trusting with people? Are you frequently angry, depressed, or bitter? Do you find it diffi-cult to thank God for anything that's happened in your life?

If any of these is true of you, you may be harboring resentment. Let the Lord examine your heart. Does He find any unforgiveness there? If so, confess it immediately and allow Him to heal you fully.

Lord, help me forgive wholeheartedly,
just as You have forgiven me, amen.

In His presence . . . confess any unforgiveness.

God's Plan for Your Future

*"I know the plans I have for you, . . . plans
to give you hope and a future."*

JEREMIAH 29:11 NIV

Are you aware that God knows exactly where you are and what you are doing right now? Contrary to popular thought, you are not bouncing haphazardly through time and space.

The Creator who formed the universe and everything in it has a specific plan for every person on earth—and He has already set everything in place to provide you with a bright future. This is not just in heaven, but also here on earth. The Lord God has great purposes for you. There is hope!

Friend, your eternal future is secure—and because of that you can rejoice. However, God is also intimately interested in your day-to-day living. All of those details, joys, and troubles you yearn to share with another—He wants you to take them to Him because only He can truly be trusted to guide your daily steps. So invite Him into your decisions. He knows how to get you where He wants to take you.

*Father, I am so thankful that You are interested in my
day-to-day living. Lead me where You would have
me go and what You would have me do, amen.*

❧

In His presence . . . entrust your future to Him.

RIGHTEOUS INDIGNATION

There is forgiveness with You, that You may be feared.

PSALM 130:4 NKJV

Sometimes well-meaning believers proclaim that their anger is "righteous indignation"—noting that even Jesus overturned the tables of the temple money changers and often rebuked religious leaders.

The problem is that *righteous indignation* is anger directed at an offense committed against God and His people, not necessarily the wrongdoing we experience. It motivates us to stand for what is right and defend the powerless as Jesus did. It serves to cleanse others, restore them, and magnify the Lord's goodness.

Unfortunately, we often don't do anything to make unjust situations right; we just allow resentment to build and demand vindication. Friend, be warned. If this is you, you are not experiencing righteous indignation. You are merely harboring anger—and God's holy ire may come against you.

The Savior expects you to forgive those who've sinned against you—just as He did. So don't allow pride to dictate your reaction toward them or hide behind religious wording. You are not honoring God with your emotions. Rather, deal with your anger immediately and allow Him to show you His forgiveness.

*Lord, bring to mind anyone I need to release so
that I may honor You by forgiving them, amen.*

In His presence . . . forgive your offenders.

REFLECTING MERCY

The wages of sin is death, but the free gift of God
is eternal life through Christ Jesus our Lord.

ROMANS 6:23 NLT

Who hurt you this week? Did their actions appear to be intentional? How are you supposed to respond to them?

Naturally we all want to retaliate when wronged. We believe that we deserve to be treated with forgiveness, kindness, love, and respect. But how easily we forget how hurtful, malicious, and rebellious we have been throughout our lives.

Moreover, we have all offended the Lord far worse than any individual has ever hurt us personally. Our rebellion against the Father deserved only death because we have dishonored Him as our holy, sovereign Ruler by sinning against Him.

Thankfully, we serve a merciful God and are beneficiaries of His grace. And it is for this very reason that Ephesians 4:32 ends with the command to forgive others "just as God through Christ has forgiven you" (NLT).

Friend, you have been mercifully forgiven—though you did not deserve it. Now, out of gratefulness to Him, go out and show His compassion to others—even if they don't merit it either.

Lord, thank You for forgiving me. Please help me to
always show Your grace and compassion to others, amen.

———————— ✺ ————————

In His presence . . . reflect your Savior's mercy.

RELINQUISH CONTROL

"The cup which the Father has given Me, shall I not drink it?"
JOHN 18:11

Admit it—the reason certain situations bother you so deeply is because you feel out of control. Life hasn't turned out the way you planned and you're desperate to regain your influence.

Perhaps this was the problem for Peter. After all, how could a man brave enough to fight for Jesus in Gethsemane (John 18:10–11) suddenly become so fearful that he denied the Savior three times (vv. 25–27)? Could it be because his plans had fallen apart and he felt out of control? He could handle fighting Rome with swords. But he didn't comprehend the far greater victory Jesus' resurrection would have over sin. Had Peter understood Jesus' true purpose, certainly he wouldn't have been so fearful.

Like Peter, you may want God's will but are unsure about how He is accomplishing it—and you prefer to manage life according to your terms. But, friend, it just doesn't work that way. So let go of your fear and allow the Savior to work. He has a better plan than you can imagine. Accept that He's in control, and rest in the knowledge that He's always victorious.

Jesus, Your ways are far wiser than mine.
I will trust Your purposes, amen.

In His presence . . . rejoice that He is in control.

ALWAYS WILLING

"I am willing; be cleansed."
MATTHEW 8:3

Leprosy was a curse to this poor man. In fact, it was such a painful and terrible disease that people suffering with it were made to wear bells around their necks so others could avoid contact with them and not become infected. It was isolating, humiliating, and absolutely excruciating.

So when Christ came near, this brave leper immediately knelt before Him and said, "If You're willing, make me clean." They were words of tremendous faith spoken by a man who most likely didn't doubt God's ability, but who probably feared he would be overlooked.

But friend, take note: *Jesus is always willing.* And the Savior went beyond healing the leper's physical issues to ministering to his soul by touching him.

Perhaps you've suffered for a long time and wonder if Jesus can restore you too. Take heart, the Savior can heal your infirmity. He may choose to do so completely, or He may change your circumstances so that you can find peace in your suffering. But the point is—don't let the Savior pass by. Step forward in worship and allow Him to work in your life. He is willing. Trust Him.

*Lord, don't pass me by. Work in my life as I
humbly bow in worship before You, amen.*

———————— ❧ ————————

In His presence . . . find healing.

THE FINE IS PAID

You were bought at a price; therefore glorify God in your body.

1 CORINTHIANS 6:20 NKJV

There you are, driving down the interstate. And suddenly, there it is—you zoom past a police car. It is a moment of self-realization. Drivers aren't supposed to surpass the speed limit, and when you see that officer, you feel the guilt. What will the penalty be if he catches you?

But consider, how often do you go about your day and suddenly find yourself caught in a moment of *spiritual* awareness? You're doing what you shouldn't—pursuing lusts, gossiping, giving in to anger, or feeding your mind with things that don't honor God. If the Lord appeared before you, how would you respond?

The truth is, God is always beside you—seeing *everything* that you do. And there are always consequences to your disobedience. Thankfully, you can take joy in the fact that the eternal penalty for your sin has already been forgiven—Jesus paid your fine on the cross. But that is never a reason to continue in sin. Rather, declare your gratefulness to Him by honoring Him with your body.

Lord, thank You that my spiritual debt has been paid in full. Please help me obey You so others may know You as their Savior too, amen.

❧

In His presence . . . honor Him with your actions.

FACING LIFE'S MOUNTAINS

*"If you have faith the size of a mustard seed, you will
say to this mountain, 'Move from here to there,' and it
will move; and nothing will be impossible to you."*

MATTHEW 17:20

As a follower of Jesus Christ, you are not guaranteed an easy life.
You may face many mountains—trials, difficulties, and hardships—
throughout your life. So how do you respond when facing what
appears to be an overwhelming obstacle or problem? Do you panic?
Do you give in to discouragement? Do you give up?

Absolutely not.

When God calls you to a task or allows a trial, He assumes full
responsibility for removing the hindrances that would keep you
from succeeding. Therefore, you must respond in faith.

So what do you feel is looming before you like an impossible
mountain today? Work, relationships, finances, or health? No matter what you are facing or how seemingly difficult the task may be,
always look toward God for victory. He is your eternal, unfailing
hope who can move any obstacle when you trust Him.

*Lord, the mountain that is before me is overshadowed
by the victory I have in You. Thank You for making
a way for me and leading me to triumph, amen.*

———————— ✿ ————————

**In His presence . . . hope in His
eternal, unfailing provision.**

RELEASED FROM BONDAGE

"Even if they sin against you seven times in a
day and seven times come back to you saying
'I repent,' you must forgive them."
LUKE 17:4 NIV

Can you think of a conflict in your past that remains unforgiven?

When people wound us, it's easy for bitterness to creep into our hearts if we aren't careful. Far too often, we ignore the Bible's wisdom and seek out destructive means for justice.

But understand, when your mind is consumed with resentment, it is fertile soil for the enemy. He amplifies your anger by saying, "You've been hurt; it's all right to be upset. Keep punishing that person in your heart—it's what he deserves." And as long as you allow Satan's bitter, unforgiving messages, you will continue to sink into the mire of self-pity and bondage.

But friend, that's not Jesus' desire for you, which is why He always commands you to forgive. You are not punishing the offender or holding him accountable. You are only hurting yourself—it is you who have been prisoner all along.

Therefore, if you're holding grudges against people, loose the chains of anger that bind you to them. Forgive them and find freedom.

Lord, reveal any unforgiveness I'm harboring. Free me
from any chains that have held me captive, amen.

In His presence . . . find freedom through forgiveness.

His Power Will Triumph

"God has given Midian and all the camp into his hand."

JUDGES 7:14

Gideon understood fear and hopelessness. Accompanied by a very small army, God called him to defeat the numerous and mighty troops of Midianites. The task seemed absolutely impossible and doomed to failure. Then the Lord gave Gideon the news: his small, insignificant band of soldiers was to be reduced even further. Why? To bring God more glory when the tiny army of Israelites gained the victory over the vast legions of Midianites.

Have you ever encountered such a challenge—where your meager resources were cut even further and your only recourse was to trust the Father? Take heart—the more impossible your circumstance seems, the more glory God will receive when your situation is rectified.

Therefore as conditions become more unbearable and the odds build against you, do not be discouraged. The Lord faithfully gave the victory to Gideon, and He will do so for you as well. Trust Him and watch Him triumph.

Lord, I will trust that You are unlimited in power,
wisdom, and love and will never fail to help me, amen.

In His presence . . . be
equipped for the impossible.

CHOKING YOUR FRUIT

*"The worries of the world, and the deceitfulness of
riches, and the desires for other things enter in and
choke the word, and it becomes unfruitful."*

MARK 4:18–19

If you are feeling somewhat unmotivated and ineffective today,
realize that anxiety nearly always results in a person becoming less
productive. When bound by insecurities and apprehensions, we
simply cannot be effective for the kingdom of God or in our daily
tasks.

So consider, are you feeling somewhat paralyzed today? It may
be because of some fear hidden in your heart. But friend, you aren't
going to feel secure about anything in life until you are confident of
your relationship with the Lord. That's because, by design, there's
a part of you that God made for Himself. Nothing else can fill that
void or occupy that part of you except Him.

Until Jesus is the priority of your life, you will always fear
the unknown and be "choked" by the worries of this world. It is
a relationship with Him and being connected to His power that
enables you not to be anxious and fearful, but rather to grow and
be victorious.

*Lord, I don't know what my future holds, but You
do. So I trust You with all that lies ahead, amen.*

In His presence . . . you are secure.

SEEK TO KNOW GOD

"Seek the Kingdom of God above all else, and
he will give you everything you need."

LUKE 12:31 NLT

Once you become a Christian, what does God require of you? How does the Lord want you to live with Him and in relationship with others?

You find answers to these questions by reading God's Word. Begin by meditating on the Gospels—especially the book of John. Get to know who Jesus is. Enjoy His presence. Understand His character, His words, His mission, and His profound love for you.

And then read the Psalms. You'll discover that David experienced many of the hardships and challenges that you do, asked similar questions, and felt the same intense emotions. You'll realize that you are not alone in your difficulties and worries, and that God can and will meet you where you are.

Friend, no matter what you're struggling with today, seek the kingdom of God. In other words, learn how the Lord operates. Because as you begin to read Scripture and absorb it into your life, the Holy Spirit will move to fill your heart with more of Himself and will give you the answers you need.

Jesus, help me seek You first always. I trust that You
have the answer to every question in my heart, amen.

⚜

In His presence . . . get to know Him.

THE BEST YOU

The woman . . . said to the people, "Come, see a man who told me everything I ever did. Could this be the Messiah?"

JOHN 4:28–29 NIV

It's tempting to get caught up in the comparison game—to look at others and say, "At least I don't sin like that guy," or "I'm doing better than she is." But God doesn't judge us based on what others are doing.

The woman at the well had been married five times and was presently living with a man who wasn't her husband. But Jesus didn't say to her, "You're a sinner. Don't talk to Me." Instead, Jesus told her He would provide her with water that never runs dry (John 4:4–41). And that notorious woman ultimately brought many Samaritans to Jesus.

Every person has potential and only God knows fully what that is. In the end, He rewards you on the basis of three criteria: how much truth you know, what opportunities He gives you to express it, and what your response is in those moments.

Therefore, don't compare yourself to others. Rather, obey Him faithfully in whatever He gives you to do, and He will do the rest.

Jesus, help me honor You by becoming everything You created me to be, amen.

❊

In His presence . . . reach your full potential.

MADE WHOLE

He will give . . . a joyous blessing instead of
mourning, festive praise instead of despair.

ISAIAH 61:3 NLT

Are your painful, out-of-control emotions keeping you from being all God wants you to be? Are you paralyzed with doubt, fear, or shame? Do you ever wonder how you've missed the freedom Jesus promised you?

Some wounds pierce us so deeply we wonder how we will ever survive them. At times we give in to them, allowing them to poison our lives. At other times we ignore them, forcing the painful emotions below the surface and never truly dealing with them. Either way, we do not respond to them in a healthy manner, so they control our thoughts and actions.

Friend, it takes courage to put down the burdens from your past—especially if they've become part of your identity. But if you're wise, you will release them to the Father so He can set you free from the bondage they cause and make you whole.

So today, trust God to liberate you from any debilitating emotions. Certainly He will complete His good work in you and teach you to experience life at its very best.

Father, please free me from any unhealed
emotions so I can become the whole
person You created me to be, amen.

❦

In His presence . . . be made whole.

JESUS IS YOUR FRIEND

The LORD was pleased to make you his own.

1 SAMUEL 12:22 NIV

When you feel isolated, forsaken, misunderstood, and unwanted, remember the great love Jesus has for you. He is always drawing you into His presence to remind you how He cares for you.

How can you know this for sure? Because that's been His character throughout history. In the Old Testament, the Lord was constantly reaching out to His people, revealing Himself to them. He desires companionship, fellowship, and communion with those who will respond to Him in like manner.

In the New Testament, we find that Jesus knew what it was to be lonely, but He also knew what it was to be comforted even in the face of abandonment (John 16:32).

Friend, the Lord is intensely concerned for you and He wants you to know with certainty that He is closer to you than the very breath you breathe. Though you may *feel* lonely at times, you are never actually alone. Jesus is one Friend you will always have—who will be with you always—because He is "the same yesterday and today and forever" (Hebrews 13:8).

*Lord Jesus, thank You for the comfort I feel knowing
I am never alone—You are with me always, amen.*

In His presence . . . be comforted by His friendship.

Erase the Messages

"Neither do I condemn you," Jesus declared.
"Go now and leave your life of sin."

John 8:11 NIV

The woman must have been terrified. According to the Law, she was to be stoned to death, for she had been caught in adultery. Did Jesus condemn her? No. He simply told her to move forward and *leave her past behind.* But often that's easier said than done.

This is because there are constantly messages that are playing in our minds—reminding us of past mistakes and the unkind ways others have judged us. To turn off these painful thought patterns that drag us down, we must have a close, personal relationship with Jesus and allow Him to teach us who we really are.

Friend, it's time to move forward and leave your past behind— taking action against those destructive messages. When old thoughts arise, causing you to trust God less, despise yourself, or doubt that He has a great future planned for you, decide, "I'll not have any more of that!" Make the choice to accept what Jesus says about you and trust that His truth will set you free.

Thank You, God, that I can claim full
freedom and victory over my past. Help me
turn off destructive messages permanently by
replacing them with Your truth, amen.

❧

In His presence . . . embrace the truth.

OUR DAILY NEEDS

My God shall supply all your need according
to His riches in glory by Christ Jesus.

PHILIPPIANS 4:19 NKJV

God is your all-wise, all-powerful, and all-loving heavenly Father who loves you so much, He sacrificed His Son for your eternal salvation. After having given so much, you can certainly trust Him to provide everything you need to live from day to day.

Friend, it is God's responsibility to supply what you require. Your duty is to trust Him, obey Him, and keep your focus on Him—not on what you perceive is missing from your life.

Unfortunately, when we shift our attention to what we don't have, we typically try to fulfill our needs on our own. What we pursue is never as good as what the Father has for us, and is usually a sure path to sin.

Therefore, trust the Lord to be the Source of everything you need. Keep your eyes on Him. Whether through opportunities to work, the generosity of others, or His miraculous supply, God not only can, but will, make His provision available to you. It is His character to be faithful—so have faith He will come through for you.

Father, You have been so faithful! I will continue
to trust in You for all my needs, amen.

In His presence . . . praise Him for His provision.

Your Security

"I am the Lord, I do not change;
therefore you are not consumed."

MALACHI 3:6 NKJV

Do you trust God to be your security today? Do you keep your eyes on Him instead of the world situation—the country's mounting debt, the increasing political and spiritual division among people, or the constant threat of terrorist attack?

If you take your eyes off God and focus on what's happening in the world, you'll find plenty to be insecure and anxious about. The earth is in upheaval. The painful signs of the end seem to be coming faster and faster.

But we can be secure in the knowledge that we are anchored to our unchanging, omnipotent, omnipresent, and omniscient God—the Sovereign of this universe. He knows our hearts, what we need, and what we face. And He is in ultimate control.

Friend, we can't change the world, but we can trust the Father to guide us and help us make the right decisions in our relationships, our finances, and our vocations. So no matter what happens today, trust Him. He alone sees the future and will keep you absolutely secure as you walk in the center of His will.

Lord, thank You for being my unshakable
security in this troubled world, amen.

In His presence . . . trust Him for your security.

WHEN OTHERS FAIL US

The first time I was brought before the judge, no one
came with me. Everyone abandoned me. . . . But
the Lord stood with me and gave me strength.

2 TIMOTHY 4:16–17 NLT

In times of trouble, why are we sometimes forsaken by those we trust? Why don't our loved ones stand by us?

There are many reasons that others fail us, of course. They underestimate how the simple, loving support and prayers of a close companion can encourage the soul. However, even when it seems like everyone's walked out, you are never truly alone.

Abandoned by his friends, the apostle Paul was left to face his final court trial by himself. But the Lord took the opportunity to bless Paul with an even more powerful and profound experience of His presence.

The same is true for you. God offers you peace and support just as He did to Paul. Even if all others leave, He remains faithful. Your Savior will never abandon you. So when you feel forsaken, draw near to Him and find all the strength, comfort, and friendship you need to make it through.

Father, thank You for the peace I have in knowing
You will never leave me or forsake me, amen.

❀

In His presence . . . you are never alone.

VICTORY IN LIFE'S CHALLENGES

"We have no power to face this vast army that is attacking us. We do not know what to do, but our eyes are on you."

2 CHRONICLES 20:12 NIV

Jehoshaphat had a choice to make. In 2 Chronicles 20, we read how the enormous armies of the Moabites, Ammonites, and Meunites defied the nation of Israel with one intention: to destroy the people of God. But instead of plotting their survival, Jehoshaphat chose to lead the people in a prayer that confessed their total dependence on the Lord. He was wise enough to know that his nation wouldn't survive without God's intervention.

Likewise, you may encounter situations when you feel like there aren't any options—defeat is certain. This is because the enemy wants to dishearten you and make you ineffective for God. Don't listen to him. You should always do as Jehoshaphat did and turn to the Lord for the victory.

So when challenges come, don't run away in fear. Go to the Savior in prayer. Humble yourself before Him. Confess your inability to handle the situation and how much you need Him. Then trust God to do the impossible in your situation and lead you to triumph.

*Father, thank You for leading me in
the path to victory, amen.*

**In His presence . . . trust God
regardless of your circumstances.**

BECAUSE HE'S GIVEN

*Every good thing given and every perfect gift is
from above, coming down from the Father.*

JAMES 1:17

Today, be grateful for what you have. It may not seem like much—
and it may not appear to be enough at the moment. But give the
Lord thanks anyway. Why? Because He is God and deserves your
praise. Apart from His goodness, you wouldn't have any of it.
Deuteronomy 8:18 is clear: "Remember the LORD your God, for it
is he who gives you the ability to produce wealth"(NIV). It's crucial
for you to acknowledge He is the source of all your provision.

Also remember: "He who trusts in his riches will fall, but the
righteous will flourish" (Proverbs 11:28). In other words, what
matters is not *how much* you have, but *how obedient you are* with
what's been entrusted to you. You may be poor according to the
world's standards but wealthy by God's because of your faithfulness to Him.

So today, no matter how much you have, praise the Father for
His provision. And remember: "They who seek the LORD shall not
be in want of any good thing" (Psalm 34:10).

*Lord, thank You for all You've given me. I know
You will provide all that I need, amen.*

———————— ✤ ————————

**In His presence . . . be grateful
for all He's given you.**

Choose to Worship

Exalt the LORD our God and worship at His footstool.
PSALM 99:5

If worship is the utmost expression of who we are as believers, why does it seem so difficult to fall at God's feet and genuinely adore Him? Why is it easier to complain about life's problems rather than voice our praises?

One reason is pride—we focus on ourselves rather than on our wonderful Savior. Another is sin—we insist on meeting our needs in our way instead of trusting the Lord. Yet these are the very issues that cause us to feel weak, trapped, depressed, dirty, and forsaken.

But when you worship in humility, repentance, and obedience, you find a deep, abiding, and life-giving freedom. You focus on God and see His holy splendor, unlimited power, unfaltering wisdom, and unfathomably deep love for you. You encounter the joy of forgiveness and realize His faithful care for all your needs.

Friend, do not allow your rebellious heart to lead you away from God. Return to your heavenly Father today and worship Him in sincerity, humility, and repentance. Enter into His wonderful presence and experience the One you were created to enjoy.

Lord, I confess my sins and worship You in
humility and sincerity. You are God and
fully worthy of all my praise, amen.

In His presence . . . fall on your face in worship.

A SPIRIT OF PRAISE

"True worshipers will worship the Father in spirit and truth."

JOHN 4:23

During worship services and in your own quiet times with the Father, do you connect with Him? Do you sense His nearness? Perhaps you see people exalting God, but what they appear to feel escapes you. You wonder if you can truly have that deeply personal experience of His presence and love.

But understand that worship is a spiritual matter. Just as you can acquire facts about God without truly knowing Him, you can likewise go through the motions of adoring Him and never really bring Him glory.

Genuine praise comes from a heart submitted to the Father—you cannot work it up. In fact, Paul precedes the command "speaking to one another in psalms and hymns and spiritual songs, singing and making melody with your heart to the Lord" (Ephesians 5:19) with "be filled with the Spirit" (Ephesians 5:18). In other words, praise flows from those who are Spirit-filled. You must allow God to have control.

Friend, if you desire to truly worship, don't try to work it up. Yield yourself to God. Celebrate Him with your life. Undoubtedly, the praises will flow.

Lord, show me how to genuinely worship You. I
give You my life—show me Your glory, amen.

In His presence . . . exalt Him with all that's within you.

A SACRIFICE OF THANKSGIVING

"He who offers a sacrifice of thanksgiving honors Me."
PSALM 50:23

Today, offer the Father a sacrifice of thanksgiving. Even if everything is awry and you're feeling discouraged, praise Him anyway. How do you do so?

Deliberately look for reasons to be grateful even in the most difficult of your circumstances. Review all the ways He's helped you in the past. Rejoice in His character, His love for you, and the salvation He's freely given you. List all the blessings you can think of which are yours in Christ. Personalize the promises the Lord has made you in His Word. And ask the Spirit of God to bring His truth to life as you seek to exalt Him throughout the day.

As you consider the great blessings the Father has given, you will certainly find your heart full of thanks and praise—not only for what God has done for you, but for what He will continue to do in the future. So set your heart to worship God and expect Him to honor you for exalting His name.

Father, You have blessed me with life, salvation,
and, best of all, Your abiding presence. Help
me glorify You today and every day, amen.

In His presence . . . make the sacrifice and praise Him.

As He Is

Blessing and glory and wisdom and thanksgiving and
honor and power and might, be to our God forever.

REVELATION 7:12

There is absolutely nothing so wonderful as simply abiding in the presence of holy, almighty God—learning about Him and getting to know Him better. Of course, if you have no idea who He is, it will be difficult for you to be still and worship Him. But when you see Him as He really is, you won't be able to keep quiet about Him. You'll want to praise Him with everything in you.

So right now, clear your mind of troubles and concerns. Imagine yourself before His immense and glorious heavenly throne. Think of His astounding beauty, His unfailing power, His magnificent wisdom, His overwhelming love.

Not only do you serve the gracious and sovereign King of kings, but He has invited you to be with Him for eternity and you have constant access to His mighty throne.

So thank Him. Gratefully recall all the ways He's shown you His love and provision. Worship Him and sing His praise. Know Him deeply, friend. And catch a glimpse of the joy of heaven.

Lord, You are worthy, powerful, and magnificent! Help
me know You in the fullness of Your glory! Amen.

In His presence . . . praise His glorious name.

GIVE THANKS ANYWAY

*Rejoice always. . . . In everything give thanks; for
this is God's will for you in Christ Jesus.*

1 THESSALONIANS 5:16, 18

Sometimes giving thanks may be the last thing you want to do.
There are challenges you face that are so negative and painful that
they affect every aspect of your life—stealing your joy and taking
your focus away from God.

But if you will ask the Father to make you thankful, He will. If
you tell Him you want to praise Him in the midst of your difficulties, He will bring blessings to mind and change your focus.

Why? Because God wants to help you honor His commands
and reveal His good purposes in your circumstances (Romans 8:28).
Though your trials may seem to be impeding your progress from
your earthly perspective, He will show you how He is actually
accomplishing great goals through them—like growing your faith.

So ask the Father to make you thankful today and voice your
gratitude to Him. You'll find that when You take your eyes off the
problems and focus on Him, the challenges you face don't seem so
overwhelming anymore. You'll also realize He's already given you
the victory.

*Lord, I give You thanks. Bring Your blessings and good
purposes to mind so I may always praise You, amen.*

In His presence . . . be grateful.

THE POWER OF PRAISE

Rejoice in the Lord always; again I will say, rejoice!
PHILIPPIANS 4:4

Giving thanks to God is one of the most powerful things you can do as a believer. The Lord works mightily through the praises of His people. This is because when you tell the Father how much you love and appreciate Him, you acknowledge you're dependent upon His provision and strength. And that's exactly the attitude necessary for Him to exhibit His power through you.

Take, for example, Paul and Silas who were imprisoned in a Philippian jail (Acts 16:16–34). Beaten and imprisoned unjustly, they began to praise the Father. And God responded to their thanksgiving by sending an earthquake to shake the prison doors open. The jailer was so moved by the Lord's powerful deliverance, he and his household accepted Jesus as Savior.

It was to that congregation—to the eyewitnesses of the miracle at the Philippian prison—that Paul would write, "Rejoice in the Lord always." And the people knew the truth of his instruction because they'd seen how God works mightily through praise.

You can too. So exalt the Father regardless of your circumstances. Delight in Him, for certainly His deliverance is at hand.

Jesus, I praise You! Even when my situation seems bleak,
You hold my life perfectly in Your loving hand, amen.

◌◌

In His presence . . . rejoice!

THE CHOICE TO PRAISE

I will rejoice and be glad in Your lovingkindness,
because You have seen my affliction.

PSALM 31:7

As you ready yourself to face the day, you have a choice: you can either grumble about your troubles or you can turn your mind to the Father in praise. Before you decide, realize this important truth: *there is power when you give thanks to the Lord.* Not only do you honor God as He deserves, but you also refocus your attention to His positive attributes rather than your negative circumstances— and that sets you up for victory.

Of course, if you're facing a painful trial, this may be a difficult principle to practice. It takes an act of your will. However, be assured, you do untold good to your spirit when you place your trust in the Father through praise.

So don't wait—make the choice to exalt Him, confident that He'll turn your situation from hopeless to triumphant. The Father is in absolute control and He won't let you down. And when you understand what His ultimate purpose is for you, you'll see why it's so wise to thank Him in every circumstance.

Lord, I adore You! You are magnificent—
worthy of honor and always triumphant!
How grateful I am for Your love, amen.

In His presence . . . exalt Him.

THE BLESSINGS IN LIFE

*"Blessed are those who hunger and thirst for
righteousness, for they shall be satisfied."*

MATTHEW 5:6

Everyone wants the good things in life. But God's idea of blessings are often much different from our own. Whereas some may pursue material gain or relationships for their happiness and are left disappointed, our heavenly Father understands that real contentment originates elsewhere.

In fact, Psalm 34:10 promises, "Those who seek the LORD shall not lack any good thing." Those who pursue God daily find a fulfillment that transcends what this world has to offer. The more you understand your wonderful Savior and Lord, the more you will yearn to know Him better still.

This is what motivated the apostle Paul to say, "Everything else is worthless when compared with the infinite value of knowing Christ Jesus my Lord" (Philippians 3:8 NLT).

Friend, the best, most enjoyable blessings you will ever experience are those that bring you closer to Christ and fit you for His plan for your life. So seek Him with your whole heart, because assuredly, with Him are the best blessings, and you shall be filled.

*Jesus, I hunger for Your presence. Draw me
close to You today and every day, amen.*

❧

In His presence . . . be satisfied.

GODLY DISCIPLINE

*"God did not send his Son into the world to condemn
the world, but to save the world through him."*
JOHN 3:17 NIV

Have you ever made a mistake and been harshly judged by other believers? Experiencing someone's self-righteous condemnation can be absolutely disheartening, if not downright painful.

Many people caught in sin have turned away from Christ as a result of being cruelly attacked by other believers when they could have—and should have—been restored by godly, loving discipline. Sadly, some believers miss the fact that discipline is always directed toward a specific behavior and is rooted in compassion.

Condemnation, on the other hand, is directed toward the person and is often based on misplaced anger, fear, or hatred. Spitefully accusing someone because of their bad choices could result in even more bondage and resentment in their lives rather than helping that individual know and embrace God's liberating grace and love.

Therefore, whenever you feel led to rebuke another person, make sure you're motivated by love and are committed to helping them find freedom from their sinful behavior. Remember, Jesus came to free the captives, and that's to be your aim as well.

*Lord, make me an instrument of Your
peace leading others to You, amen.*

In His presence . . . extend God's grace toward others.

DECEMBER

A Cluttered Mind

"This is the man who hears the word, and the
worry of the world and the deceitfulness of wealth
choke the word, and it becomes unfruitful."
MATTHEW 13:22

We've all experienced times when we've listened to a sermon or read our Bible, but moments later couldn't remember what we just heard or read. That's what happens when we have a cluttered mind. Worldly worries—about yesterday, today, and tomorrow—consume us, making it difficult for the Father to speak to our hearts.

Of course, it's normal to think about daily demands and challenges, but Satan will do all he can to make us obsess over them, turning our attention away from what God has to say. So we must prepare our hearts, lest we miss the important truths that the Lord desires to share with us.

Friend, don't fixate on your troubles; focus on the Father. When your mind drifts, turn to Psalms and begin reading. Consciously praise God, acknowledging His character and attributes. You will find that doing so is not only one of the best ways to break the bonds of your wandering mind, but will also give you peace about your problems.

Father, I give all my burdens to You, knowing You are
faithful to accomplish all that concerns me, amen.

In His presence . . . praise His name and character.

SECLUSION IN MEDITATION

*While it was still dark, Jesus got up, left the house
and went off to a solitary place, where he prayed.*

MARK 1:35 NIV

If the Lord Jesus Christ, who was perfect in His relationship with
the Father, felt it necessary to seclude Himself for His times of
prayer, then shouldn't we make provisions for such solitude?

The Lord wants you to be alone with Him so He can have your
undivided attention—free from the competition of others—where
you can share your heart, joys, and sorrows with Him without res-
ervation. This is because you are His delight. He wants you all to
Himself to put His loving, divine arms around you and remind you
of His unwavering commitment and care.

God loves you. But unless you are willing to dedicate time alone
with Him, your mind will always be divided. You will not experience the ultimate blessing of having the Creator of all that exists to
yourself in deep, intimate, profoundly satisfying communion.

Friend, the Lord Jesus Christ wants to have you all to Himself.
So guard your private time with Him, because it will certainly be
precious.

*Father, thank You for wanting time alone with me.
I will seek Your face with all my heart, amen.*

**In His presence . . . give Him
your undivided attention.**

LET GO

Don't you realize that you become the slave
of whatever you choose to obey?

ROMANS 6:16 NLT

It can be painful to give up what you've become attached to—and even more excruciating when your desire is not sinful, but God requires you to let go of it for His reasons.

But understand, the aim of the Holy Spirit is to help you abandon yourself to Christ in every area of your life. Only then can His power flow unhindered through you into the lives of others.

So consider—is there anything that you don't want to give Jesus access to? Is there anything you're unwilling to leave behind for His sake?

Remember, to follow Christ requires that you release everything to His care. What He allows you to keep will be for your good and His glory. But all else must go if His power is to flow through you.

So today, pray until you're willing to say, "Everything I am and all that I have are Yours, Lord Jesus." Because that, friend, is true freedom.

Lord, I give myself to You wholeheartedly.
Reveal any area that I've reserved for
myself and help me let go, amen.

In His presence . . . give everything to Jesus.

GOD'S CHOICE TOOL

*I am well content with weaknesses, with insults, with
distresses, with persecutions, with difficulties, for
Christ's sake; for when I am weak, then I am strong.*

2 CORINTHIANS 12:10

Just as pressure turns coal into a beautiful diamond, adversity can
be the catalyst for God's miraculous work in our lives. Through it,
He transforms our hearts, changes our attitudes, teaches us what it
means to trust Him, and helps us walk in true victory.

However, to make sure we don't grow embittered or distrust-
ful of the Lord, we must look beyond our present struggles and
recognize this: adversity is God's choice tool for building character, deepening our relationship with Christ, and equipping us for
future ministry. This is because adversity hits us in our weakest
areas—the very places where we need God most and He can shine
through us.

Friend, the Father has a purpose for every trial that touches
your life, and He can bring a tremendous victory from each one if
you'll trust Him. Therefore, instead of hardening your heart when
you experience challenges, seek to discover the changes God is trying to make and give Him full authority to make them.

*Lord, I thank You that when I'm at my weakest, You are
strongest, and are working all things for my good, amen.*

In His presence . . . learn through adversity.

PRIDE AND INDEPENDENCE

*God knows that in the day you eat of [the tree
of knowledge] your eyes will be opened, and you
will be like God, knowing good and evil.*

GENESIS 3:5 NKJV

Satan deceived Eve by using a subtle form of manipulation. First
he said, "Eve, you're going to be like God, knowing good and evil."
Unfortunately, he didn't go on to say, "But you're going to despise
the day you learned the truth about sin and death."

Every time you choose to disobey the Lord, you are exhibiting
pride—the attitude that declares to omniscient God that you know
better than He does. Isn't that foolish?

But be warned—everyone is capable of falling. Just as Satan
deceived Eve into feeding her pride, he can lure you with the
promise of pleasure without penalty—of meeting your own needs
without seeking God's provision. Don't fall for his tricks.

You will never know better than your heavenly Father. So turn
to Him often, obey Him, and always make sure to stay in the center
of His will.

*Father, I confess my curiosity, independence, and
pride. Let my attention be always on You, amen.*

───────────── ⚛ ─────────────

**In His presence . . . lay down
your pride and obey Him.**

───────────────────────────

THE ABILITY TO CHANGE

*It is no longer I who live, but Christ lives in me. So
I live in this earthly body by trusting in the Son of
God, who loved me and gave himself for me.*

GALATIANS 2:20 NLT

Are you amazed at the sickness of your heart—the way it strays from God's Word, doubts His promises, and wavers during difficult situations? Do your efforts to reform your behavior fail repeatedly, discouraging you again and again?

It may be that though you trust Jesus to save you, you don't really have faith that He can transform your life. And so you work, wrestle, and strive to do it yourself—all in vain.

Friend, the Holy Spirit is both willing and able to produce the character of Christ in you—not through your effort, but through His transformative power. Your job is to abide in Him, which means staying focused on Jesus, submitting to His leadership, and seeing the details of your life as coming from His hand for your instruction.

You cannot change yourself—but God can. And once you learn to let Him transform you, you will have the key to living a truly victorious life.

*Lord, only You can truly change me. Live through
me. Teach me to abide in You always, amen.*

In His presence . . . allow Him to live through you.

DON'T RELINQUISH YOUR PEACE

"Do not let your heart be troubled;
believe in God, believe also in Me."
JOHN 14:1

There is something we all do just about every day—sometimes without even realizing it—and that is relinquish our peace.

To avoid this, we should take time every day to check our hearts—ensuring that sin hasn't blocked our fellowship with the Father. We can pray, believe, and quote His promises, but if we insist on meeting our needs in our own way instead of trusting Him, then we are willfully choosing to rebel against the Lord and separate ourselves from Him.

Likewise, in times of crisis, we may lay down our peace—*allowing* doubts in our heavenly Father's perfect plan to rule us rather than having faith in Him to help us. Yes, friend, it is a choice. We lose our hope because we lay it down.

Today, make the decision to trust the Lord. Confess any rebellion to God and ask Him for help in turning away from your sins. Be purposeful in seeking the Lord and trusting in Him. Because then His peace can flow freely in your life again.

Holy Father, please show me if I've forfeited
Your peace in any way. I choose to believe
You and trust Your plan, amen.

In His presence . . . hold on to His peace.

TIME AND BOUNDARIES

*Be careful how you walk, not as unwise men but
as wise, making the most of your time.*

EPHESIANS 5:15–16

Are you afraid of saying no to people because of what they may think? If so, find freedom in this today: Jesus often set boundaries with others, denying their demands. And because He did, you can and should too.

Why? Because when your life lacks firm boundaries, you become an easy target for the enemy. He fills your life with so many seemingly "good" activities that you're too busy to seek the Lord's will. Eventually you find yourself tired, unfulfilled, and lacking the peace and joy the Father promised you.

This is why it's so essential for you to set wise boundaries and refuse to be drawn off course. Because if you fail to prudently manage the time God has given you, you may become disheartened and weary—missing all He's planned for you.

So today, ask the Lord to reveal His path for you. He will teach you how to walk with wisdom and make the most of the opportunities He has for you.

*Father, bless me with wise boundaries. Show
me Your will so I can always obey You and
say yes to Your opportunities, amen.*

In His presence . . . identify His opportunities.

GOD'S VIEWPOINT

Momentary, light affliction is producing for us an
eternal weight of glory far beyond all comparison.
2 CORINTHIANS 4:17

When hardships arise, we may be tempted to focus on our circumstances, forgetting that God has a completely different vantage point on our lives. But from His view, every event has a purpose that fits perfectly into His plan.

Today's verse reminds us that while we are on this earth, it is not our visible conditions but what the Lord is doing in the unseen that really matters—because what He is achieving is eternal. Our momentary afflictions are producing everlasting glory.

So consider—what "light affliction" is causing you to look away from God? Are discouraging circumstances hindering your joy? Your heavenly Father longs to relieve you of these burdens.

Friend, when you have God's viewpoint, you will be able to face your circumstances with the confidence that He will not just see you through your difficulties, but will bless you immeasurably through them. So trust Him. The Lord will help you soar past your hardships into a victory that you'll certainly not want to trade for the world.

Father, help me face trying circumstances with full
knowledge that You are working in the unseen, amen.

In His presence . . . trust His
perspective and unseen hand.

EXHIBITING GRACE

*Whoever claims to love God yet hates a brother or sister is a
liar. For whoever does not love their brother and sister, whom
they have seen, cannot love God, whom they have not seen.*

1 JOHN 4:20 NIV

There will always be someone in your life who will irritate you in
the most frustrating manner—effectively pushing the buttons that
lead to aggravation, fear, and anger. You will be tempted to despise
that person and, perhaps, even seek revenge. However, today's verse
should serve as a strong warning for you.

Friend, this person is not your foe. Rather, this individual has
been allowed into your life so that God can grow godliness within
you and strengthen your faith.

Whoever is tempting you to anger or frustration is a person in
need of grace. It will take all of your trust in the Father to deal with
that person in a godly manner, but you are called to no less.

Therefore, exercise your faith and ask God to give you the
power to express patience, forgiveness, and love to that person as
He would. Certainly, the Lord will bless your desire to honor Him
with a greater revelation of Himself.

*Father, please give me Your strength to love
and forgive others as You would, amen.*

❈

**In His presence . . . receive His
power to love the unlovable.**

TURNING OVER YOUR DEPENDENCE

We live by faith, not by sight.
2 CORINTHIANS 5:7 NIV

There is a reason you are facing the challenges that are before you today. True, some of it may come from the choices you've made. But the purpose for what you encounter is clear—God is developing your faith (1 Peter 1:6–7). His omnipotent hand has allowed these difficulties to touch you so you will stop counting on your own wisdom or ability and turn your life over to Him.

But you don't understand, you may be thinking. *I need direction today. I'm desperate for help now! I have no idea how to survive this.*

This is exactly where God wants you. You've handled it all for far too long, and now—with your skills and strength failing—you are at the end of yourself. Believe it or not, this is a good place to be.

The Father wants to show you that *He is God—the living Lord of all that exists.* So lay your heart out before Him in prayer. Tell Him you trust Him to help you. And wait on Him to show you who He really is.

Lord, You are truly God! I want to live a life
of faith. Help me depend on You, amen.

In His presence . . . learn to live by faith.

THINK ABOUT HIM

When I look at the night sky and see the work of your
fingers—the moon and the stars you set in place—what
are . . . human beings that you should care for them?
PSALM 8:3–4 NLT

Today, spend time thinking about the Lord God—the unlimited, creative, compassionate Sovereign of all that exists, who has called you into relationship with Him. Consider how He formed the universe—brilliantly conceiving the paths of stars, solar systems, and galaxies, and lovingly naming each one.

He is able to do *anything*—there is absolutely *nothing* impossible with Him. At His command, the earth became the perfect home for you (Genesis 1), the Red Sea parted (Exodus 14), and the sun and moon stood still in the sky (Joshua 10:13). And by His loving sacrifice, your enemies of sin and death were defeated forevermore (1 Corinthians 15:54–57).

Of course, the best news of all is He loves *you*.

Be aware of His presence, friend. Look to Him for everything you face today. Because with Him as your Protector, Provider, and Lord, there is nothing you should fear.

Lord God, truly You are great and greatly to be
praised! Nothing is impossible for You. Thank You for
holding my life in Your omnipotent hand, amen.

In His presence . . . be in awe of your Creator.

Rejecting Self-Condemnation

If our hearts condemn us, we know that
God is greater than our hearts.

1 John 3:20 niv

How often have you heard someone say, "I know God has forgiven me, but I will never be able to forgive myself"? Perhaps you've said it yourself. The issues that cause us shame and guilt are varied, but once you confess your sins, the blood of Jesus completely removes them from you (John 1:9). How, then, can you silence those condemning voices?

Acknowledge: The first step is to recognize that you have not forgiven yourself. Face up to this fact, and begin to deal with the issue.

Repent: Tell the Lord that you realize your self-condemnation is a sin. Then accept and thank Him for His forgiveness.

Believe God: Reaffirm your trust in the truth of Scripture. The Lord says He has removed your transgressions as far as the east is from the west (Psalm 103:12).

Choose forgiveness: By an act of your will and by faith in what Christ did for you on the cross, decide to forgive yourself.

Friend, you can rest fully in what Jesus has accomplished for you. The Lord has given you His Word, so reject all accusing voices and rest on His promise.

Lord, thank You for forgiving me and
giving me true peace, amen.

In His presence . . . receive His grace.

CONSISTENT WITH THE WORD

Your word is a lamp for my feet, a light on my path.
PSALM 119:105 NIV

When we neglect Scripture and don't build it into our everyday lives, we can be all too easily deceived by the enemy. But the better we know God's Word, the more readily we will be able to identify our heavenly Father's voice over the enemy's lies.

Always remember: Satan's goal is to turn you away from the Lord's will and service. He seeks to tempt, discourage, and render you ineffective through his lies. Therefore, he will accuse you in ways that are inconsistent with or distort the Word of God.

For example, if you confess your sins, you're not involved in any disobedience, and you still feel guilty and condemned, you are most likely believing the enemy's lie and living with false guilt though your Savior has cleansed you from all unrighteousness (1 John 1:9). This is why it is so important for you to be firmly grounded in the truth.

Friend, whatever your need—advice on a relationship, help with finances, direction about a job change—the Bible will offer you godly guidance. God will never tell you anything that violates the principles of Scripture.

Father, thank You for Your Word and the light
it provides when my way is dark, amen.

In His presence . . . meditate on His Word.

FUTURE GLORY

*I consider that the sufferings of this present time are not worthy
to be compared with the glory that is to be revealed in us.*

ROMANS 8:18

Many of the souls who have suffered most in this world have become the Lord's greatest witnesses and have borne His glory. Likewise, many of our richest triumphs will come as a result of weathering storms. This is because when we commit ourselves to Jesus regardless of the outcome, God's power is released in us in astounding ways.

For example, the disciples never forgot what it was like to face the gale-force winds of the Sea of Galilee and then witness the result of Christ's simple command, which immediately calmed the squalling waves. It became a part of their personal testimony. And so when the storms of persecution raged against them, they were honored to suffer for God (Acts 5:40–42).

So today, are you facing a tempest that is greater than you can handle? Turn your fear, hurt, and sorrow over to Jesus and allow Him to transform it into a vessel for His glory. And take heart, dear friend because He is with you, there is no need to fear.

*Father, I turn every fear, disappointment, and sorrow
over to You today to use for Your glory, amen.*

**In His presence . . . your adversity
becomes cause for rejoicing.**

VICTORY IN JESUS

Through him everyone who believes is set free from every sin.
ACTS 13:39 NIV

Sin is a big problem. It worms its way into our lives, distorts our viewpoints, and influences our decisions. God knew that none of us could defeat the power of sin on our own, so He sent His Son into the world to conquer it. For those of us who have received Jesus as Lord and Savior, that victory has removed the penalty of sin from our lives.

Unfortunately, though, our acceptance of Christ as Savior does not necessarily stop us from sinning. However, we can find victory over sin by walking with the Savior daily.

How do we do so? We must be honest with Jesus about our sin and invite His cleansing power into the darkest parts of our lives. We agree with the Lord that our behaviors are ungodly; allow Him to transform our thinking; identify—with the Spirit's help—what would please Him; and, in His power, take steps to turn from sin and walk in godliness.

Friend, you can have freedom from sin. Trust Jesus to teach you how to walk away from your old behavior and give you the victory.

Lord, help me turn from my sin and teach
me to walk in Your righteousness, amen.

In His presence . . . find victory over your sin.

INDICATIONS

*Why are you in despair, O my soul? And why have
you become disturbed within me? Hope in God, for I
shall again praise Him for the help of His presence.*

PSALM 42:5

There are times you know something is amiss because of the heaviness or sharp ache you feel. Your emotions rise up quickly, almost uncontrollably. A look, a word, or a combination of circumstances occur and something within you reacts dramatically.

In such instances, you have a choice. You can either give in to your emotions or you can take them as an indication that God is actively drawing you into His presence.

The pain you feel doesn't have to be negative; it doesn't have to destroy you. On the contrary, it can be a bridge to a deeper relationship with the Father if you respond in the right way.

So when you sense those emotions rising up, set your mind to seek Him immediately. Get on your knees in prayer, open His Word, and ask Him what He is teaching you. You will be amazed at all He shows you and how deeply He ministers to your heart.

*Lord, I give You my emotions. Help me
turn to You when they arise and draw me
closer to You through them, amen.*

**In His presence . . . allow Him to
make sense of your emotions.**

BELIEVE THE TRUTH

"You will know the truth, and the truth will make you free."
JOHN 8:32

The enemy will try to convince you that you're not good enough—that you're unloved, inadequate, and unworthy. He knows if he can discourage you, he can prevent you from experiencing the power and freedom the Father created you to enjoy. Do not listen to the accuser.

Instead, allow this truth to set you free: you are a child of the living God—purposefully fashioned by the Father, bought with the precious blood of Jesus, and indwelt with the omnipotent and omniscient Holy Spirit. And because you belong to Him, you're unconditionally loved, abundantly more than capable, and immeasurably valuable.

This is the absolute truth about you—enumerated repeatedly throughout Scripture. And whenever you doubt it, you know the enemy has convinced you of his lies.

Friend, embrace who God says you are. His is the only opinion that really matters because He is the One who created you, saves you, and works through you. You are precious in His sight, so trust His view of you and His awesome plans for your life.

*Father, I know I need to believe who You
say I am. Expose the enemy's lies and teach
me Your wonderful truth, amen.*

In His presence . . . discover who you really are.

LOVING YOUR ENEMIES

"Love your enemies, do good to those who hate you."
LUKE 6:27 NKJV

Have you ever felt as though you were fighting a battle and someone you know seemed to make your efforts that much harder? Not only did that person refuse to help you, but he or she appeared to make the situation even more difficult on purpose. How do you respond to such people?

Jesus commanded His followers to love their enemies. He understood that believers would come in direct contact with people who wanted to oppress them and make their lives impossible. But He also understood that those same persecutors were souls trapped by sin, in need of deliverance.

Whether you are dealing with non-Christians or backslidden believers, the same is true—they need Jesus and they need you to reveal Him to them. Friend, you cannot change them, but you can control your reaction to them (Luke 23:34).

As Christ's representative, you are responsible for how you respond. Therefore, don't give others a reason to criticize you. Rather, obey Him, do good, and show His love. Because by so doing, you show them the way to eternal life.

Lord, help me show Your love and grace to
everyone so others will be drawn to You, amen.

In His presence . . . find the grace to love your enemies.

NOT ABOUT COMFORT

"I am the Lord's servant," Mary answered.
"May your word to me be fulfilled."
LUKE 1:38 NIV

If Jesus asks you to do something and you obey, you can be certain that a blessing will follow. And many times, when you submit to Him, those around you will join in the joy as well.

Consider Mary's response to the angel Gabriel after he announced, "You will conceive in your womb and bear a son, and you shall name Him Jesus" (Luke 1:31). She was a young, single girl whose obedience to God would certainly confound her community. Yet she submitted in humble service and, through her, the Savior changed the world forever.

Mary was not interested in her personal comfort. She realized something much greater was at stake—the kingdom of God. She didn't question the Lord's plan or analyze the situation from a human perspective. She simply obeyed.

This is the challenge for you as well. Questioning, doubting, calculating—none of these build the faith that He wants you to have and exhibit. Rather, it is simple trust like Mary's that exalts Him—and through which He moves in astounding ways.

Lord, help me have the faith and courage
to remain obedient to You, even if it means
setting aside my own comfort, amen.

In His presence . . . have a faithful, willing heart.

THE LIGHT OF YOUR WORLD

*"To you who fear My name the Sun of Righteousness
shall arise with healing in His wings."*
MALACHI 4:2 NKJV

It is in your woundedness that you may feel the deepest darkness, despair, and confusion. After all, you wouldn't hurt yourself or others on purpose—nor would you allow them to injure you. But it's often the hidden places of the heart that drive you in the wrong direction.

Thankfully, at Christmastime, you are reminded of the reason Jesus came—to illuminate the darkness of sin and heal you of it through His provision. And He doesn't merely show you your failings, He is kind enough to reveal what fears, pain, and destructive thought patterns are causing you to commit them.

How does Jesus do so? Through the work of His Holy Spirit and the testimony of His Word, the Savior sheds light on the bondage that is causing your brokenness (Hebrews 4:12).

So this Christmas, invite Jesus to shine His light into the profound recesses of your heart. And thank God for the great, liberating gift of His radiance, which mends your deepest wounds and helps you experience His glorious freedom.

*Jesus, thank You for shining Your healing
light into my heart. I am so grateful for Your
amazing salvation and love, amen.*

In His presence . . . allow Him to heal you.

YOUR GREAT HIGH PRIEST

This High Priest of ours understands our weaknesses, for
he faced all of the same testings we do, yet he did not sin.
HEBREWS 4:15 NLT

Sometimes it's difficult to know who to go to with your troubles. Who can understand your unique challenges, respond with wisdom, and help you in a meaningful way?

In a sense, this was the purpose of the Old Testament priesthood. These godly men were called to represent the people to God and help others understand the Lord's wisdom, character, and direction. However, like all sinful, limited human beings, they often fell short.

But when Jesus came into the world, He became a High Priest unlike any other. He understands your situation perfectly because He knows you better than you know yourself. He is all-knowing, wise, and powerful enough to help you regardless of what you face. But best of all, He not only represents you to God—He *is* God, with every resource in existence at His disposal. He lovingly provides exactly what you need.

Friend, others may fail you, but Jesus never will. So seek Him and be assured you will find wisdom and mercy in abundance at His throne of grace.

Jesus, thank You for being my perfect High
Priest, regardless of the challenge, amen.

❧

In His presence . . . enjoy wise counsel.

GREATER PLANS

When the fullness of the time came, God sent forth His Son.
GALATIANS 4:4

This Christmas, are you waiting for some precious promise to be fulfilled? Do not despair—God always keeps His word. Yet just as the Savior appeared in a way and time that were completely unexpected to anyone—so will the blessings He has for you.

For example, the nation of Israel thought the Messiah would appear during a time of national crisis. But the Lord had better plans. He waited until the message of the gospel could be carried to the ends of the earth so the whole world could embrace the good news.

How Christ came contradicted the Israelites' expectations as well. They imagined a great conqueror who'd build the kingdom of Israel—not a baby in a manger. Yet Jesus had a greater purpose— saving their souls, not just their land.

Therefore, if you're discouraged because God's promise to you is not yet fulfilled—remember, His answer may not appear in the manner or time you suppose. But rest assured, He has greater plans than you can imagine. So continue to trust and obey Him completely, and anticipate the blessings He's promised you with joy.

*Lord, I will trust Your ways and timing. Thank You
for always providing beyond what I imagine, amen.*

❈

In His presence . . . trust His plan.

YOUR PRINCE OF PEACE

Glory to God in the highest heaven, and on earth
peace to those on whom his favor rests.

LUKE 2:14 NIV

Does your heart yearn for peace? The hectic nature of Christmas sometimes inspires more weariness, conflict, loneliness, and feelings of unworthiness than the joy promised by the angels at Christ's birth. The tumult within your spirit and unfulfilled dreams may leave you longing for rest. But be assured, your Savior desires to give you genuine tranquility in the midst of all the pressures of the season (John 14:27).

Friend, you will feel exhausted and overwhelmed when you believe everything depends on you. But Christ calms your soul by taking full responsibility for your needs as you obey Him. You'll find peace when you trust Him, because you're assured that the One who is best able to give you the victory in every situation will never leave or forsake you.

So when you feel overwhelmed, stop and spend time with your Prince of Peace. Then rejoice in the fact that He's got everything under control (Psalm 103:19). Truly, He is always ready, willing, and able to help you (Psalm 46:1).

Jesus, thank You for being my Prince of Peace and giving
me true rest. You are the joy of my soul forever, amen.

In His presence . . . be at peace.

GOD IS WITH YOU

"They shall call His name Immanuel," which
translated means, "God with us."
MATTHEW 1:23

This Christmas, consider this amazing truth: the indescribably awesome, infinite Lord of all that exists took on a form like yours and walked the earth so He could know what it is like to be you (Hebrews 2:17).

Consider the love He exhibited on your behalf as He "emptied Himself, taking the form of a bond-servant, and . . . humbled Himself by becoming obedient to the point of death, even death on a cross" (Philippians 2:7–8). Not only that, but He gave you His own Holy Spirit to counsel and comfort you in every situation you ever encounter.

Friend, you are never, ever alone or helpless. God Himself is with you. Regardless of where you are or what you experience, you are absolutely assured of His wonderful and loving presence.

This is the amazing gift of joy that the Savior gives you—He unfailingly accompanies, empowers, equips, and encourages you through every moment and circumstance of life. So keep your heart set on Him and rejoice in the great gift He's given you!

Jesus, thank You for being with me regardless
of what I face. What a gift You are. To You be
all the glory, honor, and praise! Amen.

In His presence . . . rejoice that He's with you.

DEVELOPING GODLY FRIENDSHIPS

A man who has friends must himself be friendly.
PROVERBS 18:24 NKJV

The Lord desires for you to have an intimate relationship with Him, but He doesn't stop there. He wants you to have enriching fellowship with other people as well. When you are lonely, you are to turn first to the Father. But you can also rely upon the people He has placed in your life.

Friend, God has given you people to love. They may not be the ones you wish you had a relationship with, but the Lord has placed them in your life for a purpose. And your loneliness will be remedied by interaction with them rather than by an escape into fantasy or other addictive behavior.

One of the greatest blessings in life is a godly friend. So don't be reluctant to call upon your loved ones when you experience moments of loneliness, grief, debilitating loss, or profound despair. He has placed other people in your life to love you, spend time with you, and help you break through the wall of separation you feel from the world.

Therefore, don't remain isolated. Reach out to others and thank God for your friendships.

Father, lead me to godly friends who
demonstrate Your love and faithfulness. And
help me be that friend to others, amen.

In His presence . . . turn toward godly friends.

NO WORRIES

"Can all your worries add a single moment to your life?"
LUKE 12:25 NLT

Do you constantly worry about the future? Perhaps you are fearful about your appearance, how others see you, or how to earn enough money to pay your bills. When you are controlled by fear, some of the effects will be increased irritability, inability to make a decision, declining health, errors in judgment, and low productivity, to name a few. Friend, this is no way to live.

The only One who can protect you from worry and fill your mind with peace is God, who provides for all your needs. And the only way you can discover who He is and grow closer to Him is through an intimate, daily relationship with Jesus Christ—who shared in your humanity and understands your fear.

Ultimately, if you will draw close to God and focus on Him—rather than your circumstances—He will enable you to face whatever is happening and come out victorious. You may go through difficulty, hardship, or trials—but as long as you are anchored to Him, you will always have hope.

Jesus, when I feel tossed about by uncertainty, help me focus on You and draw from Your peace, amen.

⚜

**In His presence . . . focus on
God, not your worries.**

Eternally Welcome

*Let us come boldly to the throne of our gracious
God. There we will receive his mercy, and we will
find grace to help us when we need it most.*

HEBREWS 4:16 NLT

God always wants you to go to Him. *Always.* As His child, you are eternally welcome in His holy presence. Any feeling of shame that keeps you from approaching Him originates from you—not from Him (2 Corinthians 7:10–11).

This is one of the reasons the enemy will tempt you to sin or violate the Lord's commands. He knows that if he can get you to rebel against God, you will feel so guilty and embarrassed about it, you will hide from the Father's loving presence (Genesis 3:10). The more the enemy can get you to focus on your unworthiness, the easier it is for him to keep you from the Savior who makes you worthy.

But understand that God wants to forgive you (1 John 1:9) and welcome you into His presence no matter what you've done or how you feel (Psalm 34:18). Go to Him! Pray to Him, turn from sin, and accept His grace. His loving arms faithfully await you.

*Lord, thank You for forgiving my sins. I'm so
grateful I can always count on Your love, amen.*

**In His presence . . . you are fully
forgiven, found worthy, and loved.**

ADVERSE ODDS

*"Arise, for the LORD has given the camp
of Midian into your hands."*

JUDGES 7:15

Do you need special encouragement today because all your sources of security have crumbled around you? Then allow how God delivered Gideon to strengthen your hope.

Gideon faced the challenge of his life when he had to fight the mighty battalions of Midian with an army of only three hundred men. But the Lord provided for Gideon in a manner that he could never have imagined.

As Gideon covertly surveyed the enemy's camp, he overheard two men discussing a dream that, being interpreted, meant God was giving Midian over to the Israelites. The two men were terrified. But upon hearing this, Gideon was overjoyed. He worshiped the Lord, his boldness renewed, because he realized that God had already defeated his enemies.

Allow your confidence to be restored as well—even if all odds appear to be against you. You can know for sure that the Father has not left you to face your foes alone. Rather, His plan to deliver you is already in motion, and He will lead you to victory in a mighty, wonderful way.

*Thank You, Lord, for leading me to victory.
I trust in Your holy name, amen.*

❧

In His presence . . . be confident.

ANTICIPATING HIS WORK

You will make known to me the path of life;
in Your presence is fullness of joy.
PSALM 16:11

As the year draws to a close and you look at the possibilities ahead of you, what is it that seems impossible? What has the Lord called you to do that appears far beyond your ability to achieve? You may not see how it could ever work out, but God does. And He will assume full responsibility for your needs as you obey Him.

So how can you remain in the center of God's will as you anticipate His provision? First, seek the Father's guidance and submit to His direction. Second, keep your focus on the Lord's character rather than your circumstances by recalling His victories. Third, cultivate a godly life by meditating on Scripture. Finally, praise the Lord for His intimate involvement in every detail of your life.

Your heavenly Father wants the very best for you, and He will never lead you astray. So stay in the center of His will—watching for His activity and expecting Him to work on your behalf. Because with Him directing you, nothing will be impossible.

Lord, I know You will fulfill all Your promises to me.
Thank You for leading me in the way I should go, amen.

❖

In His presence . . . expect His
direction and provision.

ALWAYS KING

On His robe and on His thigh He has a name written,
"KING OF KINGS, AND LORD OF LORDS."
REVELATION 19:16

It's amazing how quickly life can change. Perhaps you're looking back today and remembering all that's occurred since the year began. Problems that consumed your heart last January are a distant memory, while blessings and opportunities that didn't seem possible a few months ago have appeared by surprise.

If you focus on the ever-changing nature of life, you may feel insecure and discouraged about the future. But nothing will encourage you more than considering God's absolute faithfulness through it all.

Though this year ends, He remains sovereign over all that exists. Allow this truth to comfort you as you face the unknowns ahead. No problem is too overwhelming for your heavenly Father. He is your perfect Leader, who guides you wisely to triumph no matter what happens. And His love for you never fails.

So as the New Year begins, rejoice that the One who's always King will always be with you. And that's a fact that will never change.

Lord, thank You for always being with me. Help
me know You better in the year ahead, amen.

❦

In His presence . . . welcome the
new year with confidence.

Grow in Your
Understanding of

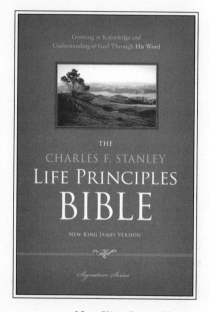

New King James Version
ISBN 9781418550332

Also available in large print!
ISBN 9780718014629

God by Reading His Word Daily

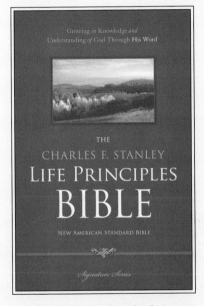

New American Standard Version
ISBN 9781418550325

❧

Visit
Intouch.org